D0146044

LEAVING AMERICA

The New Expatriate Generation

John R. Wennersten

Westport, Connecticut
London

Library of Congress Cataloging-in-Publication Data

Wennersten, John R., 1941-
  Leaving America : the new expatriate generation / John R. Wennersten.
    p. cm.
  Includes bibliographical references and index.
  ISBN 978-0-313-34506-7 (alk. paper)
  1. United States—Emigration and immigration. 2. Expatriation—United States.
  3. Americans—Foreign countries. I. Title.
  JV6435.W46 2008
  304.80973—dc22   2007030222

British Library Cataloguing in Publication Data is available.

Library of Congress Catalog Card Number: 2007030222

ISBN: 978-0-313-34506-7

First published in 2008

Praeger Publishers, 88 Post Road West, Westport, CT 06881
An imprint of Greenwood Publishing Group, Inc.
www.praeger.com

Printed in the United States of America

The paper used in this book complies with the
Permanent Paper Standard issued by the National
Information Standards Organization (Z39.48–1984).

10 9 8 7 6 5 4 3 2 1

For Ruth Ellen, a hard-working, loyal, and loving expatriate wife who was present at the creation of this book.

For my son, Stewart, a Commander who defends America on the high seas.

For my son, Matthew, who is seeking the American Dream in New Zealand.

Contents

Preface

We are a nation descended from expatriates, even if we frown on those who go off to other countries.

John Bainbridge, *The New Yorker*

This book is about leaving America and focuses on the experiences of the modern expatriate generation. It was written principally for two audiences: the general reader interested in international lifestyle trends and for scholars interested in an introductory study of modern American emigration. After five centuries of exploration and encounter, the American, in Western writer Cormac McCarthy's words, has finally "run out of country." The vast American interior of the nineteenth and early twentieth centuries absorbed the petty, the heroic, and the greedy ambitions of restless souls. Huck Finn and Tom Joad had room to roam. And the inner explorations of twentieth-century economic growth and technology for a time contained America's explosive creative energies. The old boundaries, however, no longer hold; and Americans are surging outward in search of new jobs, new identities, and new lifestyles. For today's restive American, abroad is the place to be.

The countries beyond America have no jumping-off place, no center or set destination to mark a goal or an end of a journey. There is no special home place. Abroad is where expatriates roam, wander, circle, and settle and propagate their species. However much Americans have feared different peoples, their fear has not stopped them from crossing cultural boundaries. Today's expatriate is the product of centuries of American exploration, curiosity, and accommodation.

The key to understanding the expatriate rests in his or her boredom with the familiar. It is the tension borne of choosing routes over roots that explains the restlessness of the expatriate. The search is always for a new land, a new experience, and a new country. Without this tension it is doubtful that many people would leave such a bountiful land as the United States. Expatriate Americans of the modern era do not belong to one cultural community, nor do they adhere to a single national heritage or ideology. They are modern Argonauts embarked on a voyage in search of that golden fleece called "lifestyle."

The vast majority of Americans are satisfied with the condition of their lives and the general state of the country. They experience few of the crises and persecutions that in former times set whole populations in motion. Despite our complaints about presidential administrations, the country treats its citizens fairly well; and there is considerable freedom of thought, religion, and movement. Whatever criticism one may have of the country, one cannot deny that for the present, America is comfortable economically and socially. This is what brings the immigrant masses to our shore. Meanwhile the most constant bother that a majority of Americans experience is the problem of being overweight.

More abrasive souls might point out, however, that padded cells in a lunatic asylum are also comfortable and secure. And a perceptive obstinate minority that often comprises the "best and brightest" of the nation senses or fears that America's finest hour may be history. This book admittedly focuses on the restless ones and what their odysseys tell us about the American experience as we explore the twenty-first century.

Global migrations of American people today are as common as the inner migrations across the continent of America in another era. But as Argonauts, expatriates live in a much higher realm of comfort than did their forbearers. Today the literature of travel is a tsunami of information, and Americans have only to go to their computer to find their favorite country explained and dissected on a Web site. Roger Gallo's site, EscapeArtist.com, is a barrier reef of fecund information that would-be expatriates regularly troll. The rate that Americans travel abroad and ingest a seemingly endless number of books on travel and foreign work opportunities speaks to the American fascination with all things pertaining to what writers call "the international lifestyle." In fact, books about living abroad have become an important cottage industry in the publishing world. Given the relentlessly celebratory tone of most of this travel literature, it is a wonder that the whole of America has not decamped to go and live abroad with a fever and fervor equal to any California-bound gold seeker of the 1840s. Look at the words that increasingly crop up in the world of travel and tourism. The word "abroad" is constantly conflated with "exotic," "romantic," "exquisite," "charming," "opulent," "stately," "historic," "quaint," 'majestic," and "awe-inspiring." Missing from the dream of abroad is the vocabulary of alienation, culture shock, pain, and discomfort. Central to all travel writing and all expatriate notions is that it is always better somewhere else than in America. This idea, though often inchoate, is nonetheless deeply felt.

The expatriate life calls forth numerous mental states and feelings that range from contentment to anxiety. Americans who live abroad usually have little difficulty surviving in an economic sense, but they often have difficulty locating themselves on the roadmap of their own identity. The expatriate's landscape is a never-finished mental and moral canvas. And if the canvas of the American dream is to be completed as a work of art, it will have to receive its finishing touches from those Americans who have seen and loved it from afar.

Americans do not deliberately set out to leave the country. It is a process that just happens. Often propelled by a random social or economic event, expatriates usually go abroad with the best intentions of returning to the United States soon. My own experience speaks to this issue. When I was a jobless young would-be professor, I was frustrated by the seemingly endless problem of applying and interviewing for jobs. Late one summer I was offered a position as lecturer in American history at the University of Maryland's European Division in Heidelberg, Germany. That three-year contract opened a world of experience for me as I drifted from military base to military base teaching men and women who turned out to have been some of the best and most motivated students that I have ever had. On weekends my wife and I luxuriated in Paris and Vienna or any number of European centers rich in history and culture. We roamed America's Cold War defense perimeter from bases in Turkey and Ethiopia to Athens and then to Cambridge, England. My wife and I returned to the United States when my contract ended, but more than a few of my colleagues stayed on in Europe as adjunct faculty. In those days the dollar was strong and one could teach part time for an American school overseas and still live quite nicely.

For us, the expatriate experience became like a tropical fever that one never quite recovers from. It returns in full flush from time to time to excite and inflame. Over the years my wife and I left America frequently, often spending one year abroad for every three spent working at an American university. Our children spent a good deal of time in overseas schools in Asia and Cambridge, England. After a while it seemed that my wife, children, and I were spending more time overseas than we were in the United States. Our neighbors in Salisbury, Maryland, began to refer to us as the academic gypsies. Our most recent expatriate experience was a stint in Japan, where I taught American Studies in a Japanese university outside Tokyo.

Expat stories usually begin in bars. This one is no exception. This story began to come together in a tavern called the Drunken Duck in Katsuda, a small commuter town in Japan's Ibaraki Prefecture. Owned by an Australian with a Japanese wife, the Duck was the central drinking and communications center for a disparate crowd of expatriates ranging from Slovenia to Russia and Germany, the United States, and England. Like most *gaijin* bars, the Drunken Duck was a place where foreigners could drink beer in incredible amounts, devour giant hamburgers that astonished their Japanese friends, and swap tales and information on all aspects of living the life of a foreigner in Japan. By profession the expats ranged from scientists and engineers working at the nuclear establishment in nearby Tokai, to ubiquitous English teachers employed by NOVA and other language schools to teach English as a foreign language to countless tongue-tied Japanese students and adult learners. Some were employed as guest professors in several private and public Japanese universities. Others were drifters with dubious enterprises and backpackers who hung out. At the center of the Drunken Duck's expatriate swirl stood a Slovenian named Igor Misic. A burly three-hundred-pound drinker and raconteur, Igor owned an English school in the nearby city of Mito. We all thought this a bit unusual because Igor had no formal training in language teaching and spoke English with a heavy accent. But Igor was undeterred. He always smiled and said, "I can do three things—I can fix toilets, I can build a house, and I can teach English." There certainly was no gainsaying his success in all three.

It was not always fun at the Duck. There were evenings of gloomy departure parties as expats prepared to return to their home countries. There were also sad conversations of lost jobs, hassles with landlords, problems with immigration authorities over work permits, and grand plans and relationships gone awry.

But the Drunken Duck in many respects was an Asian expatriate crossroads, and it was in conversation over mugs of beer with Igor and others that my mind began to shape the story of how expats were a phenomenon that the folks back home were not even aware of. Mention the term "expatriate" in the United States, and people are prone to think of Ernest Hemingway and the "Lost Generation" in Paris in the 1920s. Modern expatriates seemed neither to resonate with Americans nor to exist in their world view.

This book aims to bring into focus expatriate life at the beginning of the twenty-first century and explain what has happened in the United States to propel many of us outward from our native land.

My wife and I returned to the United States after five years in Japan to be traumatized by the events of 9/11 and the Iraq War. The expatriate fever will take hold again, I suspect. Friends who have not seen us in a while always ask, "So where are you off to now?" Like many returned natives, we are uncertain about the future. If we leave again, will we ever come back? At this point we have more questions than answers; but in this global age our most important questions are those shared by many American wanderers: "Who belongs?" and "To what?"

Chapter 1

Explaining Expatriate Motivation

American culture has become a choice between talk shows about high school wrestlers who rape teammates or whether blondes really have more fun.

Lisa Frankenberg, American Editor, *Prague Post*

THE EXPATRIATE DIASPORA

Since the founding of our Republic, social commentators and historians have focused primarily on the people who came to America. They haven't given much notice to those who left. Over the years, however, not everyone has bought the American dream of individualism, democracy, and material success. Even during the celebrated epoch of American immigration (1880–1920), when 17.6 million men and women came to the United States, six million people left America. Between 1900 and 1980, ten million of the thirty million who came to our shore abandoned the country. In that same period, nearly one million native-born Americans chose to live abroad, many never to return. The twentieth century has seen two major waves of American emigration: 1920–1950 and the period since 1976, when once again large numbers of citizens began to leave the country. Since these periods encompassed both fat and lean economic times, other factors may have been at work to propel Americans from their native land.[1]

Today, large numbers of immigrants and natives alike are leaving the United States for safer, more satisfying destinations. Furthermore, among those Americans who are either well educated or earn more than $50,000 a year, reports *Money,* an astonishing one in four reports having serious thoughts about moving to another country. The U.S.

Census Bureau, however, has not bothered to monitor this new and striking population shift. In 1999, when the State Department last assessed the American population resident overseas, it counted around four million. Organizations like Forrester Research, a Cambridge, Massachusetts, marketing research firm, argue that the figure is probably closer to six million. Forrester also projects that by 2015 an additional 3.3 million high-tech and white-collar Americans will be overseas.[2] This is 2 percent of the total American workforce and $136 billion in U.S. wages. Accompanying these jobs overseas is the nagging question of how the U.S. economy can weather the loss of many of its best and brightest.

The prospect of better wages overseas only partly answers why people are leaving America. Another explanation is that American expatriates are a reflection of America's growing globalization and the essential role that U.S. exports of goods, services, and expertise now play in strengthening our economy. It should also be mentioned that as highly visible "ambassadors" of the United States—economically, politically, and culturally—U.S. citizens play a key role in advancing American interests around the world.

The United States does not issue exit visas to those who leave the country lawfully, and in 1957 the Immigration and Naturalization Service discontinued its program for collecting data on American emigration. Ironically, the Internal Revenue Service, which for tax purposes should have a sharp eye on Americans working overseas, has been slow to collect expatriate data. Also, social commentators have been reluctant to focus on those aspects of our history that ideologically contradict the story of America as a chosen Edenic land. As well, because of America's immense landmass, there is a continental insularity to American culture that until recently precluded serious thought about emigration. This may explain why we rarely saw, until recently, stories in the U.S. media about Americans living overseas. Indeed, we have so powerfully internalized the myth of America as the land of affluence and opportunity that we find it difficult to believe that anyone would want to leave the country. After all, the American story is an immigrant story. America has always been a haven in a heartless world, a place that people want to come to rather than escape from. Even now in this age of diminished expectations around eight hundred thousand legal immigrants enter the United States each year along with an estimated three hundred thousand illegal immigrants. With our democracy, equality, and free enterprise system, how could life be better elsewhere?

For many Americans expatriation is a kind of heresy. Expatriates, they argue, shirk the responsibilities of American life; and by leaving they commit some ill-defined crime of betrayal. Also, to leave America raises important questions about what it means to be an American. If the essence of being American is citizen participation in a democratic nation, then what happens when the citizen departs for foreign climes? Centuries ago in democratic Athens the Greeks coined a word for those who shirked the public tasks of citizenship—the word was "idiot." Also in that ancient culture Socrates chose death over comfortable exile in a foreign city-state. For Socrates expatriation was nothing more than a denial of one's existence.

Until recently one of the most popular stories in America was Edward Everett Hale's *The Man Without a Country.* Published in 1863 in *Atlantic Monthly,* the story chronicles the life of Lieutenant Philip Nolan, an army officer caught up in the Aaron Burr conspiracy to form an independent nation in the American Southwest in 1807. In a heated moment during his treason trial Nolan thoughtlessly denounced America. For his punishment Nolan was sentenced to spend the rest of his life on a U.S. naval vessel, forbidden to read, speak, or hear a word about his country. Nolan ended his days on the high seas, a miserable and lonely expatriate. Hale's story of a man without a country was written to inspire patriotism during a dark Civil War winter. What could be worse, sermonized Edward Everett Hale, than to be without one's native land?[3] For America was the story of attachments, a place of sanctuary for the uprooted. Attachment to America was something to be achieved and not taken for granted.

The story went on to become an American classic and helped to define American attitudes toward expatriate life. Surely one could travel abroad for short periods of time. But the purpose of such a lifestyle was to return to the United States better informed about the inequities of other nations and to have one's patriotism whetted by absence. Only for the most immoral and tragic of reasons would one permanently leave the American Eden.

Times have changed, however, and Hale's classic now draws the dust of library neglect. Today people turn their backs on America for a host of selfish reasons that range from tax avoidance to the need for exotic self-indulgence. To some well-connected Americans who hold multinational citizenship, patriotism is just a passport, a useful travel document. Also, many less affluent Americans are routinely investigating the prospects of acquiring a second passport as dual nationals, and others are thinking of forsaking American citizenship altogether for the financial and social advantages of citizenship in what they believe are more attractive countries. The patriotism that motivated Edward Everett Hale's generation seems out of date by today's standards. Americans may in future become interested in acquiring the form of citizenship and passport now available in the European Common Market countries, which allow for the flow of capital and labor across national boundaries.

Canada, Mexico, and many Latin American countries are already likely candidates for such "Common Market citizenship."

Around six million Americans live abroad, with major "Yankee" population centers in excess of two hundred thousand in Canada, Mexico, Germany, the Philippines, and the United Kingdom.[4] This figure does not include U.S. government employees, military as well as nonmilitary, and their dependents. Recently, in an attempt to gain perspective on this phenomenon, the U.S. State Department reported the growth and development of population centers of over seventy thousand Americans in Israel, Italy, and Japan as well as other countries. While the large expatriate population of 158,000 Americans living and working in Israel could at first glance be attributed to religious emigration, most Americans working there are nonreligious, college-educated professionals who have been attracted to career opportunities in high-tech fields and computer software. Currently there are 2.3 times as many Americans in Israel as there are immigrants from Israel in the United States. In addition, Americans have voted with their feet to live and retire in Italy, where over one hundred thousand U.S. nationals enjoy the climate and food of that historic country. Milan, Rome, and Florence have American populations significant enough to populate small towns of twenty to sixty thousand. Similarly, Japan's burgeoning American population of nearly eighty thousand shows how social and economic opportunities in that country outweigh the cultural and language problems of being a stranger in that Asian nation.[5] At any given time demographers can count about one million Americans resident in Mexico, with another seven hundred thousand in Canada. If all these residents were included in an American federal state called "Expatria," it would have a larger population than states like Maryland, West Virginia, Rhode Island, and Montana.

Today, reports the *International Herald Tribune,* international schools in key world cities like Hong Kong, London, Moscow, and Beijing "grapple with staggering demand" as expatriate American families seek to obtain places for their children. Currently China is one of the major expatriate "demand centers" for the creation of more international schools to satisfy the needs of a rapidly increasing overseas business and information services community. School fees are skyrocketing in response to the heavy demand. Tuition at the Hong Kong International School, for example, is 152,000 Hong Kong dollars, or about $19,300. Given the high expatriate demand for school placements, international schools are working almost around the clock to recruit qualified teachers. But many teachers are reluctant to take overseas teaching posts, especially in China and the Middle East, where language, culture, and personal security are pressing issues. Around three thousand international schools have proliferated around the world, educators report.

And according to the European Council of International Schools, in Europe alone there are 245,000 students enrolled in eighty-eight countries. Thus, whether in Laguna in the Philippines, in Shanghai, or in Amsterdam, a growing expatriate population is putting pressure on international schools that until very recently were relatively small institutions.

It's not just the rich and the well-born that are leaving America. It is people with education and talent who are far-thinking and aggressive. The same types of people who used to move to Montana or Alaska to escape are now moving to Mexico, Canada, and beyond. They are even moving to once-shunned countries like Vietnam, China, and Russia. Many of today's college graduates are leaving the United States for Eastern Europe to work for local companies or to teach the English language. In the current atmosphere of cultural flux, downsizing, and diminished opportunities, things seem better in Budapest than in Buffalo. Apparently, not everyone thinks that America is a wonderful place. Although emigrants come from a universe of backgrounds and age groups, the common thread that unites them is that they do not feel they are part of America anymore.

American emigration is part of a global economic shift that is fostering real economic growth in heretofore-neglected areas of the world like Latin America, Eastern Europe, and Southeast Asia. These areas are now experiencing rising incomes, and their state-run industries are being privatized. Capital and trade markets are opening, and these in turn create numerous job opportunities for would-be expatriates. Enterprising Americans are starting a record number of small businesses in these areas of the world. From computer consulting firms in Hong Kong to bagel shops in Budapest, Americans are helping to revitalize or sustain economies that are receptive to Western entrepreneurship. Governments welcoming American expatriates are helpful, and operating costs in these countries are lower than those in the United States. This pattern is part of what demographers refer to as "the globalization of migration," or the tendency of nearly all countries today to be influenced and affected by migratory movements. Also, Americans today may well be part of an entrepreneurial migration chain that may change into other forms in accordance with economic, political, and social changes within the United States and abroad.[6]

Americans don't quit their land with great fanfare. They rarely curse the soil and turn their backs on their families. They just leave and live elsewhere. Convenient international airline schedules facilitate the expatriate life. Through the Internet and satellite television, an expatriate can be as well informed in Madrid as in Manhattan about American life. A subscription to Star TV, CNN, or Direct Television can bring the American lifestyle into living rooms in Beijing or Buenos Aires. Also, data on the Internet, like that supplied by the Central Intelligence Agency as public information, give Americans a tool for researching the quality of life in foreign countries. Every year thousands of Americans retire overseas; as a result, Social Security checks drawn on our national treasury contribute significantly to the economies of Poland, Italy, Greece, and Mexico. Since 1975 the number of retirees living abroad has soared to over four hundred thousand. Most people who relocate overseas adjust to the cold realities of living in a different culture. Generally speaking, expatriates, or "expats," enjoy change and respond well to challenges like developing second-language skills. Although expats come from all age ranks, most are young, in their twenties and thirties. Many marry local citizens.

Unlike tourists, American expatriates know their way around their adopted country. Most are highly individualistic and relocate to countries that have communication, transportation, and public amenities roughly similar to those available in the United States. When asked about their future, these expats register vague plans about moving back to the United States "sometime." For the moment, however, they feel that possibilities seem better *outside* the United States. Today, for example, Japan is a mecca for young talented Americans willing to work there as teachers, translators, and entertainers and as managerial staff in banks with close commercial ties to the United States. As noted earlier, about eighty thousand nonmilitary Americans live and work in Japan. Most seem more interested in a weekend in Tokyo and shopping in the Ginza than in returning to their homeland.

MOTIVES FOR EMIGRATION

All nations are to some extent shaped by the forces of migration. Indeed, the immigration story is older than the Bible itself. It is in the United States of America, however, that the immigration experience has been the central shaping cultural and ethnic force for national development. The great international migration to America's shores in the nineteenth and twentieth centuries has been equaled by a surge of internal migration in the second half of the twentieth century to the Sun Belt region of Florida, California, and the Southwest. Until recently, the great migrations both to and within the United States could be explained by the traditional forces of war, by racial, ethnic, and religious persecution, and by the burning desire for social mobility in a better world. These forces comprise the familiar push and pull of history, and as elements of historical explanation they have been helpful and substantive. These explanations are useful only at the macro level, however, for they tend to break down when we are confronted with new forms of migration that fail to fit the historical paradigm. They are

losing ground is an operative one for white men who rightly or
wrongly see the future as providing fewer opportunities than were
available in the past. Statistics bear out that a disproportionate number
of white males emigrate from America.[15] Many intelligent white males
seem to suffer in America from what the social psychologists term "relative dispossession." What few can dispute, however, is the growing
lack of social mobility in America. Despite impressive American job
growth, most jobs seem to lead to a dead end. Every newspaper in the
United States carries stories about the country's "barbell economy," a
state of affairs that connotes a shrinking middle class, with the poor
and the very rich expanding at either end. The American tax system is
no longer as progressive as it once was, and this damages the faith
upon which capitalism and the country depend. In the United States,
reports the *Washington Post*: "the rhetoric about a shrinking middle class
and giveaways for millionaires? It's accurate."[16] Even conservative
mainstream newspapers like Norfolk's *Virginian-Pilot* have been prone
to comment that "America was once viewed as a land of opportunity in
part because people were relatively free to take a chance." Now numerous forces "make us less free, restrict our choices, and limit our mobility."[17] While this perception can lead to rancor, it can also prompt the
conclusion that leaving the country is the best alternative.

Currently a popular book on college campuses is Tamara Draut's
Strapped: Why America's 20 and 30 Somethings Can't Get Ahead. Draut
argues that more and more young Americans are starting out behind
the financial eight ball—borrowing their way into adulthood and won-
dering whatever happened to the American dream. According to the
Collegiate Employment Research Institute at Michigan State University,
the hiring of Americans for "meaningful jobs" will remain flat well into
the twenty-first century. Currently college graduates are much in
demand with a robust hiring rate at about 14 percent over previous
years; but critics assert that this is just a blip in the long-term employment market, which will see a severe correction from corporate downsizing and the outsourcing of jobs abroad. Also, since 1990 over 1.4
million management employees have lost their jobs. American corporate
culture has become a Darwinian nightmare for those who have staked
their careers on company loyalty and a secure job. In a recent article
in *Nation*, Will Hutton argued that increasingly prosperity in America is
becoming a myth. "America, in the grip of conservative dominance, is
undermining not only the well being of its citizens but its capacity to
create national wealth and economic growth." Hutton and many others
believe the nation has been led into a cul-de-sac.[18] For recent nontechni-
cal college graduates, the job market seems to be a vicious downward
spiral.[19] Too many job descriptions for our youth have "french fries" in
them. Yesterday's $28,000 entry-level job is today's $25,000 no benefits

contractual slot is tomorrow's $15,000 internship. Many expatriate Americans today echo economist Robert Heilbroner's lament: "The country is visibly decaying. I do not know of anyone who sees a bright future for it." Specifically, a "silent depression" in wages is forcing men and women to look for opportunity beyond America's shores. Real wages after inflation are about 20 percent below the level reached in the 1970s. Says Heilbroner, "Our GNP is stagnating and few of us can look forward to a happy and prosperous America."[20]

Few people who leave America understand the complex origins of the economic currents that buffet them. They do, however, understand the realities of daily life. Not since the Great Depression of the 1930s have Americans confronted so many homeless in their midst. In America's great cities the homeless can be seen in front of grocery stores, banks, and fast-food restaurants begging for spare change. Also, there is a Third-World aspect to many American cities, where highway and sewage systems are deteriorating, drug-infested ghettos seethe with violence, and public schools fail to educate. Washington, D.C., the nation's proud capital, has neighborhoods in Anacostia that after nightfall become little more than free-fire zones and crack distribution centers. Even stable midwestern cities like Milwaukee and Minneapolis suffer from drug violence, infrastructure problems, and general disorder. In many urban areas the police state has replaced the welfare state. In California, for example, nearly a million citizens now live in developments behind gates with guards and elaborate electronic monitoring devices. In many of the wealthier areas of that state, public parks are closed on the weekend, reports Peter Schrag, "in an effort to exclude the rabble . . . and other neighboring communities."[21]

Public sector employment, once the safety valve for American economic discontent, has plummeted. A new spatial apartheid of edge cities has intensified metropolitan segregation. Ex-urbanites, mostly affluent and white, fear crime, welfare mothers, immigrants, and other noxious elements of the city. How soon, they worry, will it be before these urban barbarians knock at their gates? According to a recent poll, three out of five Americans say the quality of life in the United States is getting worse, and nearly 58 percent express similar feelings about the economy and job opportunities.[22] As the social scientist Kevin Phillips has noted, discontent is growing in America. Indeed, *Atlantic Monthly*, hardly a radical organ, reported that a "new debate is quickening. It is not over justice and equality. It is over something much more American—the meaning and content of freedom."[23] Whether it is possible to have this debate will determine whether or not the expatriate stream will turn into a flood.

In addition to the trends that Americans find pushing them out of the country are the positive developments pulling them abroad. Today's world has become borderless in many respects. New global economic forces make borders meaningless lines drawn on maps by governments. Nations have very little defense against the information superhighway that blurs their boundaries. To any computer-literate American it is just as easy to locate the home office in Buenos Aires or the Bahamas as in Baton Rouge. Americans at the upper end of the economic spectrum are more closely connected to their peers in Tokyo, Hong Kong, or London than they are to their fellow Americans on the street. With the workplace being virtually "any place," other factors become paramount concerns, among them the environment, a brighter future, intellectual stimulation, scenic beauty, and access to good sporting areas. Expatriates are members of a community with no fixed geographical base and have few communitarian loyalties. Today the prospects of living overseas have never appeared brighter to a generation of cosmopolitan Americans. Inasmuch as job security is disappearing these days, many Americans feel that they ought to be opening up themselves to the world. *Carpe diem* is the operative psychology. There is not much to restrain them when the job itself is no longer the primary tie that binds.[24]

The word "expatriate" derives from the Latin *expatriare*—to leave one's country. But over the years "expatriate" has come to be synonymous with "exile," "banishment," and "renunciation of citizenship." The word, evidently, has a history of negative connotations. Contemporary expatriates, however, mostly define themselves as individuals who choose to live abroad. Americans emigrate for reasons both complex and simple. Some individuals move abroad because they are socially and politically disenchanted with America. Despite the widespread politics of apathy in the United States, a strong core of political dissent exists on both sides of the political spectrum. Critical Americans look to their government and find its policies wanting in every area: from health care to public safety to the income tax.

For those who have chosen to emigrate, the mantra about America's high standard of living is no longer appealing. As one critic of American life put it, "If the standard of living means the number of square feet in your home or the number of channels on your TV, America leads the world. But if you are afraid to go out after dark and worry what your children see on television, then other societies may have more desirable standards of living."[25]

An argument like this resonates in the American expatriate community. Many expats find America boring and are repelled by the uniform sterility of McDonald's-mall culture. Their native country is neither new nor exciting. For some, affluence is the ultimate crime because it drowns the individual in creature comforts. "We become," writes critic Liesl Schillinger, "insulated from life's difficulties and we become bored; and in our boredom we become dissatisfied and dangerous."[26] We have reached the end of newness in America; and some Americans find that only overseas can they chase their dreams. Thus there is a growing feeling of disillusionment reminiscent of the "Lost Generation" of Americans who decamped from the country for Paris in 1918. This feeling intensifies when you add the political ingredient of disillusionment to aggressive conservative politics in contemporary America. After the presidential election of 2004, Americans swamped New Zealand, Canada, and Australia embassies with inquiries about emigrating. The prospect of living in America under the Bush administration, says New Zealand consul Rob Taylor, "is certainly weighing on people's minds."[27]

ENTREPRENEURIAL ADVANCEMENT

Americans have often had to choose between roots and routes. In the past, lighting out for the territories of the great American West was easy. Doing so was risky, but at least Americans could choose to migrate within their own country. Now forces in America restrict mobility and restrict choices, so instead Americans are lighting out for those areas of the world that offer them opportunity and the freedom to take a chance. Members of the new expatriate generation will not be doomed to spend their lives where they began them.[28]

Perhaps the most dramatic development in the American emigration story is the explosion of young Americans' entrepreneurial activity overseas. In places as diverse as Prague, Saigon, Buenos Aires, and Tokyo, Americans are establishing businesses in manufacturing, personal service, consulting, language education, and the media. Some are acquiring fortunes. Others are building new and attractive lives for themselves that make it difficult for them to return to the United States. The key to understanding this wave of entrepreneurial activity is the openness of Eastern Europe and parts of Asia to free enterprise capitalism without the restrictions of age and experience that have traditionally hampered young people in America.

SETTLEMENT AND READAPTATION

As noted, until recently, the American expatriate tended to think of living abroad as an experience of short or limited duration. Few expats tended to think of leaving America altogether and settling in a foreign land for good. In the modern age, however, the unanticipated can become reality, and we are now seeing the development of permanent enclaves of Americans abroad. Many Americans in these enclaves are becoming either citizens of or permanent alien residents in their host countries. Significant numbers of these emigrants were born in their host countries and have now achieved the economic means to realize a successful repatriation, given the advantage of an American passport and a bank account. Others, however, have gone abroad as immigrants to Australia, New Zealand, and Israel with little cultural or national affiliation prior to the actual act of immigration. More than a few emigrants have returned to the United States disillusioned; nonetheless, a large and growing number are settling permanently in their adopted countries. Some expats are part of a retirement diaspora of older Americans who seek cheap and easy living in the "Mediterranean environments" of the world. Others find new jobs and a new sense of identity and purpose in their life in a new country. These individuals often prefer their new life to the one they left behind in America. Settlement of Americans abroad has been facilitated by developments abroad that have allowed U.S. nationals to gain the citizenship of the land of their ancestors. Currently, for example, Ireland will grant a passport to any Irish American who can document proof of an Irish grandparent. According to one recent study, across the world "grandchildren and even great grandchildren of immigrant families are taking advantage of more liberal dual citizenship and right of return laws to get a second passport from the land of their ancestors."[29] Countries like Portugal, the Czech Republic, Greece, and the Netherlands have liberalized their "law of return policies" for grandchildren born abroad. Other countries, like the Dominican Republic, Belize, Dominica, Grenada, and Suriname, offer "economic citizenship programs" whereby an expatriate can obtain a second passport and citizenship in the host country by paying $50,000 to $100,000. Experts, however, advise that for those with little grasp of their new nation's language, history, or culture, such "coming home" can be difficult.

ECONOMIC DISSENT

An increasing number of wealthy and not-so-wealthy Americans are moving overseas and becoming citizens of other countries to avoid the taxes imposed by the U.S. government. Other Americans stay abroad for economic reasons because federal tax legislation exempts the first $84,000 of earned income from tax. In our age of global commerce, expatriate communities are today much larger and play a more significant role in the corporate world abroad than ever before. Given the lifestyle and tax advantages that expatriate Americans enjoy, they are likely to remain exiles for some time to come. Like the younger entrepreneurs who have emigrated solely for business purposes, these expatriates can be engines of social transformation abroad, both good and bad. As American capital increasingly expatriates its managers and directors, as well as their families and those who earn a tertiary living off the expatriate community, we can expect to see an explosion of "Little Americas" overseas.

EXPANDING GENDER DOMAINS

Historically, women have been the unsung participants of the American expatriate saga. They have served principally as spouses to career military, diplomatic, and corporate husbands; and their lives overseas have seldom been easy. Since the early 1970s, however, record numbers of women have been venturing abroad, not as unsung spouses, but as travelers, teachers, business executives, and individuals in search of careers and lifestyles that they could not find in the United States. Women today constitute an important and growing sector of American emigration. Expatriate American women can be found selling tractors in Hanoi, serving as film consultants in Nepal, and establishing newspapers and service enterprises in Eastern Europe. Further, women corporate executives are helping to change business and office practices abroad and are transforming traditional gender roles and expectations of American women overseas. Once abroad, many American women marry foreign nationals; and today significant numbers of American women married to foreign spouses can be found in Germany, Turkey, and Japan. Also, love today has an international scope, and demographers report a major increase in transnational marriages.[30] Americans are just as liable to meet their future mate in Istanbul and Prague as they are in Pittsburgh.

Once the choice of homesick immigrants and disgruntled artists and writers, expatriation has become an important and disturbing phenomenon in our national life. It is a reflection of social and economic conditions in this country that may not bode well for the future. It is not the wretched refuse of our shores that depart for a foreign land but, rather, the best educated, idealistic, and enterprising segments of our population. Already academic researchers have coined a term for this phenomenon. They call it the "Elusive Exodus."[31] There may be no way to reverse this trend, but it is an issue that ought to worry us.

SUMMARY

This chapter has argued that the migration phenomenon of leaving America is as rooted in the history of America as the immigration experience. In addition, this chapter has offered a motivational model that can be used to understand this phenomenon. Population movements overseas have always accompanied demographic growth, technological developments, and cultural and social change. Simply put, one can argue that the expatriate impulse has been strong and lasting in America even though social commentators have, for largely ideological reasons, generally chosen to ignore the impulse because it contradicted the story of America as a haven. In the modern age expatriation seems particularly pertinent to the explanation of how social and economic transformations in this country are making adult Americans rethink their lifestyles and career options. Most Americans give little thought to leaving the United States to live abroad, for their family and economic networks keep them rooted in the country. Yet for those whose horizons are remarkably more flexible because of job skills, education, and cultural orientation, emigration is increasingly becoming an option.

Since the end of the Cold War, Americans have ventured abroad in record numbers. Emigration has been a far smaller development than the current immigration to America, however. Even if the numbers of Americans leaving the country increase significantly, they will remain a small, steady stream against the tidal wave of aliens landing on America's shore in search of the good life. But expatriation in the future will grow and contribute to an ongoing examination in America of what it means to be part of a society. Traditional models of national identity and assimilation may no longer be adequate in explaining what keeps citizens rooted at home. Moreover, current trends in immigration and emigration in America reveal the power of transcultural consciousness and mobility that can only continue to weaken the sense of place in American culture. What we are seeing at work today is the emergence of transnational networks that link societies through emigration and the growth of technological and cultural interchange.

Are expatriates, as some social critics argue, merely seekers on "an idealized and frustrated quest or are they finders of treasures in richer climes than our own?"[32] This question now needs to be seriously addressed as a growing sector of our native-born population severs connections with the United States. For an increasing number of its citizens America has ceased to be the magic city on a hill, a vision that so animated the thought of the early Puritans. Although the United States is still the most popular immigrant destination in the world, for many individuals it is no longer the haven it was once imagined to be. To a degree not seen since the days of Gilded Age tycoons like John D. Rockefeller, J. P. Morgan, and Cornelius Vanderbilt, powerful economic and social forces are dividing America into separate nations, one inhabited by prosperous "winners" and the other by struggling and increasingly embittered "losers." Increased economic inequality is reflected in nearly every significant measure of prosperity in America and is evident in the increasingly lopsided distribution of wealth, employment prospects, and job security. Many American expats no longer want to compete in this Darwinian struggle. For them, the mythic images of America as a golden city on a hill or a refuge have become defunct.

Current expatriate trends also reflect growing disappointment with the quality of American life. The concerns range from personal safety to quality-of-life issues like environmental decay and cultural diversity.

There is as well a general disenchantment with the long-accepted social contract that has come to be referred to as the "Promise of American Democracy." The broad notion of America has never really included everybody. Whereas some individuals were welcome in the Edenic land of America, others were not, even when born here. The use of the term "American" remains ambiguous at best, even though tough debates are taking place in the United States on the meaning of culture and diversity and how these concepts should be taught in the schools. Today, many Americans feel that the only way to escape the enormous political blockages on what it means to be a citizen is through emigration. The greatest irony in modern America may well be that while argument and discord prevail in the edifice of American democracy, the best and most thoughtful citizens have already left the building.

Chapter 2

The Expatriate Archipelago

When talented people think about relocating, they don't consider the job offer;
they weigh whether the place has a community that they can plug in to.

Richard Florida

TRANSNATIONAL AMERICANS

From Paris to Prague, to Moscow and Sydney, an archipelago of expatriate professionals stretches around the globe. Most of these expatriates are plugged into the cyber world of international living and regularly read the *Americans Abroad Digest* that is published monthly on the Internet.[1] In addition to being a link with home, the *Digest* publishes travel information and news that expatriates have to have at their finger tips, providing details about job opportunities, tax information, global danger zones, and problems of dual nationality marriages. Why has there suddenly been a population explosion along this expatriate archipelago? The reasons are as diverse as the people who emigrate: management consultants, students, bankers, writers, and high-tech specialists, all swept into the archipelago by the waves of globalism and interconnectivity that are the hallmark of our age.

The transformation of the economies of Europe, Latin America, and Southeast Asia offer American expatriates unparalleled opportunities in education and business. Also, for many Americans, working abroad appears to be more appealing than remaining in the United States for a life of "McJobs" that have the same dreary pay and career aspects as flipping burgers.[2] No simple "push-pull" analysis, however, adequately explains why Americans decide to leave their homeland. But these

Americans do share some common background features that can explain
why. Most of these Americans seem to be at a crossroads in their life
that severs their personal relationships, employment affiliations, and
family ties. Sociologists refer to this as the dissolving of social bonds in
one's personal life. Often, though, it is easier to explain why American
expatriates stay in a certain place rather than deduce why they came in
the first instance. In many respects, these expatriates are transnational
Americans. That is, their experiences, values, and cultural expectations
transcend national borders. These transnationals identify not so much
with a country as with the world. They are well traveled, easily adapta-
ble to change, and very aware of the professional opportunities that the
world has to offer. Some sociologists, like Professors John and Ruth
Useem of Michigan State University, refer to these transnationals as
being part of a "third culture experience"—high-mobility global nomads
who have gone beyond their own culture to reside in a foreign land and
have thereby combined the national and international into a unique
transnational identity.[3]

While job-hunting is important to them, expatriates also demonstrate
a very high propensity for personal lifestyle enjoyment and the need for
self-fulfillment. Suffice it to say that many of today's globe-trotting
youth are fed up with what Ada Louise Huxtable called "the surrogate
experience and synthetic settings" of America. They want a city or a
country that is "real," not some Disneyland or Frontiertown or Las
Vegas Casino village.[4]

In Europe, especially, the large numbers of Americans resident there
contribute to the major shift in "human capital"—skilled workers and
professionals—employed by multinational companies. Richard Florida
of the University of Toronto is perhaps the most prescient of today's
observers of how the flight of human capital is an accelerating American expatriate phenomenon. Professor Florida asserts that many cities
in Europe and Asia are attracting talented Americans because they have
high "bohemian, gayness, and diversity indexes." By that Florida
means that Americans with marginal lifestyles, such as homosexuals or
those with a preference for tattoos and pierced noses, are attracted
abroad to places that tolerate their lifestyles in exchange for the talent
they bring to creative and intellectual jobs. Florida argues that geography and a sense of place are critical for these people. Cities like Sydney,
Brussels, Dublin, and Vancouver are talent magnets. They attract a variety of talented people—young people who are hip and bright want to
feel energy around them. It fuels their creativity.[5] And today that
energy is lacking in many American cities. Referred to in policy studies
as "new economy workers," these people are not so much interested in
stock options as the job option and the place where it is located. Europe
and Asia are "cool" for this type of human capital because they offer

jobs in interesting spaces where recruits can revel in their access to diversity and cultural electricity. Overseas companies are beginning "to take the guy with tattoos seriously and are liable to hire his boyfriend as well."[6] The expatriation of this type of talent is beginning to be noticeable, says Florida. "High-margin creative industries that used to be the United States' province and a critical source of our prosperity have begun to move overseas. The most advanced cell phones are being made in Salo, Finland, not Chicago. The world's leading airplanes are being designed and built in Toulouse and Hamburg, not Seattle."[7] As countries recruit talented Americans, the United States begins to lose its cutting edge. Florida himself was recruited from his job at George Mason University for a prestigious post at the University of Toronto.

Whereas ten years ago a company like Microsoft or Kraft would have employed local talent for new jobs, today those companies are hiring Americans and posting them overseas despite high costs. A recent survey of multinational companies by William Mercer Inc., a personnel-staffing company, predicts that the number of expatriates in management and professional jobs will increase significantly in the near future as "multinationals position themselves for greater global competition."[8] Currently there are about one million Americans living and working in Europe, a figure that continues to grow despite the nagging problem of unemployment on the continent.[9] Many Americans cannot even speak the language of their host countries, but they have what is known in the trade as the "Golden Fleece," an MBA from a good American university.

Also, as Valerie Belz, an American journalist based in Munich, has written, American young people's "flexibility and adaptability to take root and flourish in foreign soil also make them prime specimens for transplantation." Furthermore, American expatriates know that all jobs are not necessarily that interesting. A dull job in your hometown is a dull job. The same position in Munich or Paris, however, is an opportunity to become multilingual and marketable to foreign firms and to establish a launching pad for an international career. Adds Valerie Belz: "Even everyday tasks performed in foreign places confer a sense of mastery. Who hasn't taken some small degree of pride in having figured out the washing machine or bus route?" A large number of young expatriates who have flocked to Europe from America are college-educated women like Kimberly Kiefer, who went to study in Munich as a Humboldt Scholar. Once she developed a working familiarity with German, she recognized that she would be able to capitalize on her college education and professional skills to make her globally employable.[10]

Although Americans have always gone abroad to live the good life, most of these new international Americans are well-trained individuals who are cashing in on career opportunities in Europe, the Soviet Union, Israel, and Australia. They are young professionals like John Lynch and

Ann Malin, who went to Poland in 1991 to teach English and stayed to capitalize on their MBA training and the business opportunities that have become available there. Living on $700-a-month combined income at first, they put together $100,000 of their own and borrowed money to open a shirt factory in Warsaw. From shirts they branched into printing and now own several small factories in Poland and are well on their way to joining Poland's class of new rich.[11]

In 1992 Robert Brooker and Adam Haven-Weiss were burned out with their law school studies at Columbia University and dreamed of starting their own business. Through friends they learned that business opportunities were good in Hungary, and the two law students hopped a plane to Budapest to check it out. After doing some serious research and scouting out possibilities, they pooled $20,000 apiece and launched Hungary's first New York Bagel Store in June 1993. New York bagels were an immediate success in Budapest, and Brooker and Haven-Weiss plan to open a number of bagel stores in the country. Says Haven-Weiss: "The opportunities here are endless. Entrepreneurs always need a country their own age, and economically Hungary is very young."[12] Of course, the business climate in Eastern Europe is far different from that of the United States. The business infrastructure is badly managed, and just getting a telephone can try the patience of Job. Often, getting building permits and other public licenses requires a considerable amount of discreet bribery.

Sara Roe found Hungary to be a lively and enterprising place when she landed a job in Budapest working for the *Central European Business Weekly* after writing to over twenty-five different English-language newspapers around the world. The job was cash-poor but opportunity-rich, and soon Roe was filing stories in her newspaper that more than justified the chance that the Hungarian editor had taken on her. Roe spoke to everyone in Hungary who spoke English, and she soon learned that she could mingle with enough English-speaking Hungarians to avoid the "expat bubble" of Americans. According to Roe, her job gave her "considerable freedom. One of its best features was that I could send articles from different areas of Hungary." Thus Roe, like many Americans in Eastern Europe, has been able to gain the kind of professional experience unavailable to her in America. This expatriate scenario is being played over and over again throughout Europe and Asia.[13]

Americans who study or work in Russia often experience severe culture shock because living conditions there are more trying than those the typical expat working in Europe might expect. In Russia there are shortages in almost every commodity necessary for the good life—from meat to toilet paper. Language problems constitute a major inconvenience, and cramped, expensive living conditions in Russian cities like

St. Petersburg quickly discourage even the most tenacious expatriate. Moscow, for example, is one of the most expensive cities in the world for apartment rentals. There, a simple apartment can cost upward of $2,500 a month, with utilities averaging an additional $250 a month. These are the economic facts of life in a country that was supposed to be an inexpensive worker's paradise. Plumbing and electrical problems occasionally drive expatriate Americans to despair, and major repair problems can be solved only with generous amounts of American cash. What Americans take for granted in their own country, they have to live without in the former Soviet Union. Telephones, both public and private, are unreliable, and finding everyday necessities in local stores is difficult. Convenience shops like 7-Eleven that are a mainstay of everyday American life just don't exist in Russia. Staples and meat are often scarce, so American expatriates find that shopping for variety is not advantageous; one buys what is available. Most of the time expats have to queue in long lines to shop for necessities. According to relocation expert Marthe Haubert, the operating rule of expat life in Russia is simple: "If you see something you need or might need, buy it."[14] Expats also have to pay cash for everything, since credit cards and checks are largely foreign to everyday Russian commercial life. Russia's computer network is an American cyber nerd's worst nightmare, and so the safest way of communicating is through the fax machine.

Barbara Duvoisin was drawn to Russia while still a university student. At university she had studied Russian history, Soviet economics, and international finance. After graduation Duvoisin worked a number of jobs in the financial sector. When a multinational corporation offered her a job running its Moscow office, she jumped at the opportunity. Working in Russia seemed much more fascinating and challenging than working a corporate job in America. Like many expatriates who wind up in Europe, Duvoisin was prompted by reasons both personal and professional. She wanted to make a good salary and at the same time benefit from the experience to be derived from working closely with the momentous changes taking place in post-Soviet Russia. For Duvoisin, nothing rivals the excitement of working in contemporary Russia. "There is no doubt in any 35-to-45 year old's mind that in Russia you are given more responsibility and more exposure within your organization than anyplace else in the world," she says. Barbara Duvoisin has lived in Russia for many years and does not plan to return to America in the near future. She has a Russian husband and two young sons, who could keep her in Russia for some time to come. Duvoisin admits, however, that Russia has more than its share of negative aspects. The family had two cars stolen at gunpoint, and Duvoisin's husband regularly confronts the Russian Mafia in his business dealings. Duvoisin also admits that she misses American television and asks friends to send her videos of popular programs like *CSI: Miami* and Shark. But on the whole, Duvoisin is happy with her decision to go to Russia. "It's a question of which quality of life we want, how much that costs, and what we have to do to make that money," she says. That calculation for Duvoisin factors out in Russia.[15]

There are significant American communities abroad in places one would not expect to find them. Egypt is a case in point. Currently over ten thousand Americans reside in Cairo and Alexandria. Some are Americans who have married Egyptian nationals and converted to Islam. Mandy Bush is one of these Islamic spouses. She owns a bookstore in Cairo called The Book Spot and Café, a small English-language bookstore in Maadi, one of the ritziest parts of Cairo. The primary goal of opening the bookstore was to have fun, says Bush. Basically, she wanted "to show people who many not know many Muslims that we choose to be in this religion and still be our fun, funky selves." But Muslim converts are just part of the American expat surface strata. There are also English teachers, businesspeople, college backpackers, and dropouts of various sorts who can take advantage of the country's relatively relaxed visa policies and live well in Egypt on the American dollar. The biggest danger facing American expatriate men is the courting by Egyptian families seeking husbands for their daughters.[16]

Many expatriates get their start in business overseas by serving Americans working for multinational corporations who have a ravenous need for personal services like messenger delivery, apartment searching, and translation. Whitney Brown, for example, left Aspen, Colorado, and moved to Prague in 1991. Today her company, Affordable Luxuries, provides expat Americans and other international business people with everything from apartment rentals to dry cleaning and babysitting. Labor costs are cheaper in Eastern Europe, where entrepreneurs can launch businesses with far less capital than it would take in the United States.

Americans these days continue to follow the expatriate writer tradition in Europe, and the capitals of Europe contain more than a few budding writers in addition to well-established ones like Paul Theroux, who has long lived in London, and Gore Vidal, one of America's most famous writers and polemicists, who makes his home in Rome. Jonathan Carroll, for example, is a successful American novelist who could live anywhere but has chosen Vienna as his home. One of the best literary fantasy writers in the field, he uses his knowledge of Europe's folklore to write what one critic, Michael Field, called "eerie, sexy, and addictive novels."

As the son of the famous screenwriter Sidney Carroll, who wrote *The Hustler* starring Paul Newman, Jonathan Carroll may have chosen Europe to get out from under the shadow of his father's fame as much as to find a quiet place to write. When Carroll and his wife arrived in Vienna twenty years ago, they were fresh out of the University of Virginia, unknown and unemployed. Both were lucky in that they soon secured teaching jobs at the American School in Vienna. With a stable economic base, Carroll was able to write; but his early novels, which were published in the United States, sank with hardly a trace. A German publisher, however, read Carroll's work and encouraged him to publish in Europe. His novel *The House of Laughs* was a sensation in Europe, and in 1987 Carroll was awarded the French Prix Apollo for fantasy literature. His subsequent novels, like *Outside the Dog Museum*, were also hits, and Carroll currently has a large cult following in Germany, Sweden, and Japan. Carroll believes that his success in Europe has mainly been because booksellers on the continent tend to read the books they sell and become advocates for them. In America, he says, booksellers sell books without reading them. Carroll recognizes that living in Austria has had its disadvantages. "I know that if I'd stayed in America all these years and had been talking to the right people and going to the right parties, etc., my career would be a lot further than it is. But I have had 20 years in Vienna and most writers can't claim such a quality of life. Books are an enormous part of my life, but they aren't the only thing."[17]

Until recently Americans were content to turn their backs on the outside world and focus their interests primarily on what was happening in their hometown or state. Despite international wars and a host of revolutionary developments in the media and in telecommunications, most of our citizens pursued an "America First" approach to the problems of daily living. That insularity began to dissolve in the 1970s when Americans in record numbers began to go abroad as students, tourists, and employees of multinational corporations and the federal government. Today Americans are more at home abroad than ever before. Consider these social indicators: more Americans are studying foreign languages than a decade ago; more Americans are working or living abroad; more are enrolling in international studies programs.

Finally, the Peace Corps, long a haven for idealists, is being recognized for what it is, a ticket to foreign adventure and a life abroad. Since 1961 over 145,000 Americans have served in the Peace Corps in countries ranging from Afghanistan to Zimbabwe. Its programs have been especially successful in education, agriculture, and public health programs for Third World countries. As an instrument of American idealism, the Peace Corps has served as an outlet for those young Americans who have sought creative alternatives for their energies overseas as well as for those for whom American life has no longer seemed sufficiently interesting or meaningful. Most who have gone abroad had never been overseas before, and for them the Peace Corps has opened a new international universe of awareness and cultural insight.[18] According to Brendan Daly, a public spokesman for the Peace Corps, the number of inquiries about this overseas program soared from 100,000 inquiries in 1994 to 150,000 in 1997. "People understand that this is a global world," he said, "and you can get a leg up on your career" by joining the Peace Corps. Thus the Peace Corps today has its own selfish uses that its founders never intended.[19] Though probably the best-known agency, the Peace Corps is just one of numerous over- seas service organizations that are sending Americans abroad today. These organizations run the full spectrum of relief and development and rely on the skills and commitment of ordinary Americans. World Teach, out of Harvard University, for example, sends American teach- ers to schools in Latin America. Americans working for Habitat for Humanity International are building houses in Tibet, and Volunteers in Overseas Cooperative Assistance sends Americans to Europe and Asia to work as grassroots volunteers on agricultural and environmental projects. International volunteering is popular in America now, and over forty organizations routinely send Americans overseas. Lonely Planet Books now publishes an extensive guide to volunteer opportuni- ties abroad.

Expatriate trends are currently being fueled by a record amount of American overseas travel. In 1986, for example, twelve million Ameri- cans traveled abroad, excluding Mexico and Canada. There are now fifty-five million U.S. passports in circulation, and with the ending of the Cold War many barriers to foreign travel have been removed; this has intensified American interest in travel abroad. Overseas phone calls have soared from 411 million in 1985 to 2.8 billion in 1997, according to the Federal Communications Commission. The net effect of travel and communication has been a bold and dramatic restructuring of Ameri- cans' views of lands beyond their shores and a re-altering of lifestyles to include expatriate careers.[20] The number of Americans living abroad has more than quadrupled in the last thirty years to around 3.3 million according to conservative State Department estimates. Overseas groups like Americans Abroad Inc. say, however, that many expatriates go uncounted and that the number of Americans living beyond our shores may be as high as five million. A sea change in sentiment has taken place in American perceptions of the world. In the old "America First" days, our citizens could laugh at a cartoon where a husband on vaca- tion with his wife in Paris turns to her and says, "Did you ever see so many foreigners in your life?" Today globalization has rendered such parochial humor obsolete. The number of colleges and universities offering international studies programs has mushroomed, and each year five thousand to six thousand graduate students undertake studies abroad, often in international business programs. Similarly, the number of Americans who study abroad for credit increased from 89,242 a year in 1996 to 200,000 in 2006.[21] Study abroad was once thought to be an elitist undertaking; but now students see it as a necessary part of their university experience. Also, students are aware that internships abroad with foreign companies often result in employment with multinational firms after graduation.

The Internet sector has grown just as fast. The Internet, experts say, is itself a new culture that spans multiple cultures. The Internet has become the new "Pidgin" language of convenience, a medium through which dozens of countries and cultures interact daily. One day in the future, a whole generation brought up on the Internet will perceive it not as a Pidgin or Creole language but as the medium of global communication. Currently dozens of Web sites in cyberspace are oriented toward overseas life, international study, and work-abroad programs. The University of Michigan, for example, has a Web site about working abroad that tells students everything from how to apply for a passport to how to find a summer job harvesting grapes in France.

To cater to this increased interest in working abroad, the number of telecom providers in Europe and Asia with English-language Web sites has increased exponentially. For example, the city of Vienna, with a population of only 1.7 million, hosts twenty-three telecom providers that offer information on every aspect of living and working in Austria. The explosion in Web use is the result of drastic reductions in telecommunications costs, and today's computer-literate Americans can search for a job as easily in Vienna or Tel Aviv as they can in their own hometown.[22]

Austria and other countries in Europe have now become home to people whom employment consultants refer to as "Creatives." These people live exclusively in computer worlds of commerce and information and are dedicated to learning, knowledge, and technology. These American Creatives are giving a new global dimension to information resource use in Europe, and their numbers are continuing to grow as countries, especially in Eastern Europe, find themselves starved for computer-literate talent. Also, through expat involvement, these new Web sites in Europe will help to standardize consumer behavior around the world, and consumers will become more similar than different, especially in their use of computers and other media. What expatriates are doing in Europe is to hasten the organization of work as a modemed, cell-phoned, and electronically banked system.

Until the 1920s, immigration to America was fueled by a few simple facts: the country was rich in resources and industry, and it was significantly under-populated. That situation no longer prevails, and America has to struggle with the problems of burgeoning population growth even while immigration continues to soar. There are countries in our modern era, though, that are experiencing the same problems of under-population that the United States experienced in earlier times. These countries tend to be modern, affluent nation-states with literate populations and a high standard of living. What they lack are young people to provide a workforce commensurate with national growth. Singapore and Japan, for example, suffer from birth dearth and under-population.

Currently both Singapore and Japan are trying to solve their workforce problems by relying on means other than immigration. Singapore is famous for the pressure it places on young college graduates to marry and have children, whereas Japan looks to its own expanding female workforce as an alternative to large-scale immigration that may disrupt the country's ethnic and cultural life. Canada, Israel, Australia, and New Zealand are different stories, however. These four countries combined now have over 971,000 Americans living in their midst, and in the future they will continue to attract a growing stream of American immigrants.[23]

EXPATS IN FRANCE AND ENGLAND

Americans and Frenchmen have had a long and occasionally tempestuous relationship that antedates the famous exploits of Lafayette in the American Revolution. Americans, even those long resident in France, tend to find the French mysterious, while the French find American honesty and forthrightness both charming and a bit weird. Americans determined to experience the "Frenchness" of the culture as expatriates often have visions of Hemingway at a Paris café in the novel *The Sun Also Rises*. But often what passes for real French culture is a kind of stony Gallic placidness that eludes American understanding. On the surface at least, what is important to the American expatriate is friendliness; what matters to a Frenchmen is good manners and a decent respect for the power of ideas.

Many Americans come to France as exchange or university students and end up staying, even though the French immigration bureaucracy can be cumbersome and frequently maddening. The easiest way to live an expatriate life in France is to marry a French national. Many American women have followed this route. In her delightful novels *Le Mariage* and *Le Divorce*, Diane Johnson chronicles the life, marriage, and divorce of an American woman who has married into and exists within a French family. In these delightful comedies of manners, Johnson describes the intense preoccupation of French families with tradition and material wealth and the Americans with their breezy lifestyle and democratic ideals.

Most expatriates who stay on share Diane Johnson's view that France is endlessly fascinating—from food and culture to history and city life. According to Diane Johnson, "One thing that is fun for me about living in France is that there are social norms here. They are much harder to perceive in America. But France is a smaller country, it's more stable, it has less social fluidity, so it has social norms."

Many American expatriates quickly realize that as soon as they land in Paris they have to start from scratch in understanding the French. When it comes to France, there are no fixed common reference points that make it easy for the expat to make a transition into the culture. Most have little or no knowledge of French history. Thus for the new American resident in France, the culture may be as bewildering as that of Japan or India.

Currently, over one hundred thousand Americans are resident in France. Most are expatriate birds of passage. There are, however long-standing communities of American expatriates in Paris, Marseilles, and Strasbourg. These expatriates are usually well-off financially, support local charities and their Protestant church, and speak good French. The churches contain notice boards of the activities of these older or settled American communities. Though they seem to blend into their various neighborhoods, the French always know where Americans reside as well as their drinking and marital problems.

Young Americans usually get "expat jobs" like translating or picking grapes in vineyards. Without a Common Market passport or sponsor-ship by a company, job hunting is a fierce grind. Many young Ameri-cans often work without documents in the underground service economy of restaurants and cafes. Today in France, the easiest path to sure employment is to have a resume with computer expertise or engi-neering training in it. In the 21st century, the French business commu-nity is eager to become competitive in the global market. Words like "analogue" "interface" and "web master" are the Open Sesame for a work permit in France.

Americans in Great Britain find themselves living in a country where language is a problem. Expatriates complain that Americans and Brits are heirs to the English language; but they are as often as separated by it in terms of common understanding as they are united by it. What especially infuriates British subjects is that Americans breezily refer to all of Great Britain as "England." The Scots are particularly touchy on that subject. As in France and other Common Market countries, Ameri-cans scale a wall of difficulty in securing work permits. With the recent influx of thousands of Polish nationals armed with new Common Mar-ket passports into the country, the market for casual or unskilled labor, once a mainstay for backpackers and university students is beginning to dry up. At the other end of the employment spectrum, however, Ameri-cans are enjoying high wages in financial and technical fields that ena-ble them to survive the astronomic costs of daily life in London. They are usually recruited from the United States through interviews and teleconferences. Investment banks and news organizations still remain the best sources of high-end employment for expatriates in Great Britain Also, notes expatriate journalist Jill Gordon, "the process of expatriating and settling here is full of confusing and sometimes even ridiculous requirements that will acquaint you with Britain's backward—if still loveable—idiosyncrasies before you ever leave home."

Recently, the British government has become supportive of Americans who wish to establish businesses as independent entrepreneurs. Sensing that American success with business development in Eastern Europe may be salutary for their own country, the British government supports with work permits the development of small computer and engineering firms in London, Oxford, and Cambridge. Of late, many talented Americans have been gravitating towards Cambridge. In addition to having one of the most prestigious universities in the world, Cambridge is emerging as the Silicon Valley of the United Kingdom. In the past ten years, there has been an explosion of high-tech firms on the outskirts of Cambridge; with its good connection by rail, Cambridge has become the high-tech suburban adjunct to London, currently the world's premier financial metropolis.

For American expats in Great Britain, where you live determines to a great extent your notions of time and place. Certain geographic areas in Yorkshire, for example seem much farther removed in time, perhaps closer to the 1940s than to the 21st century. London pulses with transnational exuberance and an ethic mix that challenges the perception that London is an English city. Like many areas in the United States, London is sprawling outward, bringing the force of urbanization and changes to areas that just yesterday were small villages with quaint pubs. Meanwhile in the north of Great Britain, many areas are still pastoral. Those steeped in history can still hear the battle cries of distant history and sense the tragedies of Macbeth and Lear.

France and England are curious islands in the expatriate archipelago. Perhaps defined symbolically by their paté and sausages or croissants and Cornish pasties, these countries offer numerous and satisfying challenges to expats who are eager to make a departure from the worlds of shopping malls and Las Vegas and Disney.

OIL PLATFORM EXPATS

The expatriate archipelago is not just an island chain of companies, entrepreneurs, teachers, and students. It includes a hardy breed of businessperson, housewife, and engineer that follows the pipelines of oil from Houston to Venezuela to Scotland to Stavenger, Norway, to Kuwait, Saudi Arabia, Lebanon, and the Persian Gulf emirates and Africa.

If you are in the oil business or one of its collateral industries, inevitably you end up in the Middle East. Living conditions are dictated by the requirements of Muslim culture, which frowns upon many features of the American lifestyle, from drinking, Western dress, and manners to political discussions. Expats who work in countries like Saudi Arabia often embark on freewheeling, hard-drinking, hard-loving holidays in Europe. An ascetic, tightly controlled, drab desert society awaits their return.

Venezuela is where all oil riggers would prefer to live because of its oil reserves, the beauty of its cities, the power of the American dollar, and the country's general ambience. The left-wing regime of Hugo Chavez has nationalized the country's oil reserves and sent the major oil-drilling companies far afield in search of newer and more profitable oil reserves.

Angola is the world's hottest oil territory right now, and oil riggers and expatriates have flocked to this former Portuguese colony to make quick money out of the projected flow of 740,000 barrels of oil a day being pumped out of the country. Oil experts hope that Angola's reserves will produce as much as Nigeria's two million barrels a day. When not out on the oil rigs, most expatriates can be found in Cabinda City, a town of sleazy bars, dirt roads, and shacks that serves as the country's informal oil capital. To protect against violence and banditry in Cabinda, oil companies like Chevron have constructed a secure police-protected living compound where workers can rest and relax. Holidays in Luanda, Angola's capital, are filled with parties, available women, and fine liquor; and the rough-and-ready atmosphere of the country makes Angola far more exciting than the "bolted-down social atmosphere" of some of the Middle Eastern oil countries.

Unlike most expatriates, the oil workers in Angola are global commuters. American employees like Larry Jostes, a Chevron project manager, work twelve-hour days for twenty-eight days straight, then jet back to their homes in the United States or England for twenty-eight days of rest. Jostes commutes regularly between San Francisco and Angola. Most of the oil workers have left their families back home, and a majority of their spouses do not even know where Angola is. But the prospect of large six-figure salaries draws Americans to Angola. In 1990 only a few international aid workers could be found in this civil war–wracked country. Today the American population has soared to over one thousand. According to one oil field technologist, Don Nicholson, it is a very exciting time for an American to be in Angola. Nicholson is a long way from his native Utah but enjoys working out on the sea at the oil platform rigs. "We are at the cutting edge of the business," he exclaims enthusiastically. The magnitude of Angola's oil resources make it certain that in the future more Americans will be drawn to its oil fields, regardless of the country's social and economic instability. Money and politics are the two guideposts for expatriates along the oil field trail.[24]

SUMMARY

With the globalization of the economy we are seeing a new kind of "citizen," a growing class of people whose ties to communities in which they live become ever more attenuated. Place has a different meaning now, and the emerging network of Creatives is less susceptible to the controls of geography. For the first time in our history we may be seeing a generation of internationalized Americans that is connected to no geographical region or place. These will be the kind of Americans who will have little interest in their nation's social, political, and racial problems. If they are interested at all, they will watch their homeland as a kind of spectator sport. It is doubtful that a new sense of place and a new civic life will emerge to cope with the Internet and the global economy. As political analyst Richard Sennett has succinctly warned, the global economy "does not grow personal skills, durable purposes, social trust, loyalty, or commitment."[25]

Chapter 3

Dissenters, Tax Fugitives, and Utopians

You've been abroad for thirty-five years? Then you're no longer an American.

Ballot Clerk, Jackson County, Illinois, 2000

A BACKGROUND ON DISSENT

Since the founding of this country many Americans have become expatriates either through their own will or through exile. Thomas Danforth, for example, a wealthy Massachusetts lawyer, was a Tory during the American Revolution. After independence the 40-year-old attorney was banished from the United States "under a pain of death" to London, England, where he had no friends or social connections. Massachusetts solicitor general Jonathan Sewall suffered a similar fate. Sewell fled to St. John, New Brunswick, Canada, where he was appointed admiralty judge for Nova Scotia and New Brunswick. Neither he nor any of his family returned to Boston after the Revolution. Nearly seventy thousand Loyalists like Danforth and Sewell left the new nation. They represented one of the earliest and largest groups of Americans to live outside their homeland as expatriates or exiles. Most, like John Randolph, the attorney general of Virginia who went into exile, had wealth and were able to transition into a new life in England. Others, like merchant Joshua Hardcastle, were short of money and of middling social rank and had to struggle to establish themselves in England. Hardcastle is remembered for his paid advertisement in the September 9, 1775, issue of the *Williamsburg Gazette*, in which he proudly stared down the democratic rabble of the community and said, "I intend to leave the country."[1] And he did so forthwith! This was indeed a significant exodus because the country at the time numbered only 2.5 million in population.[2] Unlike expatriates of the 1920s or those of today, they had their homes and material possessions confiscated by the U.S. government, and many expats faced death if they returned. They had to relocate to what in many instances were unwelcoming places. Many of these loyalist expatriates were former slaves who had fought in the British army for their freedom. While most settled as expatriates or exiles in Canada, a fair number settled in England. But as members of a lost cause, they remained outside the land of their birth and strangers in their new homeland.

Black emigration grew out of the slavery issue and serves as a good example of the kind of socially forced expatriation common to many countries at this time. The American Colonization Society, formed in the United States in 1816, was a white-sponsored movement to colonize ex-slaves in Africa. A few thousand slaves moved to Liberia, a country created by the U.S. government; but many black leaders in the United States, like Frederick Douglass, opposed black immigration to Africa.

The second wave of expatriate dissenters to leave the country occurred at the end of the American Civil War when leaders, planters, and slaveholders of the Confederacy chose to leave their homeland rather than accept the new order of emancipation and "Yankee domination." With the end of the Civil War, Union authorities were not inclined to be magnanimous and branded over three million Southerners as traitors. Unsurprisingly, many Southerners concluded that it was impossible to remain in America and looked to emigrate. Judah P. Benjamin, the Confederate secretary of state, moved to England and enjoyed a second career as a successful lawyer. He was but one of several hundred Southern men and women who settled in England after the war because they could not bear to live in what to their eyes had become a conquered province.

William Hesseltine and Hazel Wolf, in a remarkable book, *Blue and Gray on the Nile,* tell the story of Confederate and Union officers who left the United States to take up arms as military advisers to foreign heads of state. The bulk of the Confederate officers went to Egypt to work for the Ottoman khedive Ismail, who at that time was expanding his empire southward into the Sudan and building the Suez Canal. The ex-Confederates accepted commissions in the Egyptian army and established military schools to train officers and enlisted men. Many of these expats had been trained before the war as engineers. Southerners like Charles Chaille-Long undertook perilous journeys to map the Nile and discover its source. Others explored the desert regions of Darfur and Kordofan. Two Confederate generals, William Wing Loring and Henry Hopkins Sibley, did important work as advisers to the khedive on the matter of military defenses for the Suez Canal and the city of Alexandria. Both were hot-tempered officers, and their views infected their subordinates. A notorious shooting incident occurred in Alexandria between three Southern officers and the nephew of General Benjamin "the Beast" Butler. The officers sought to settle the score stemming from General Butler's infamous military occupation of New Orleans when he had declared that every Confederate woman in the city be treated as a prostitute. Confederate blood ran hot in the South and on the Nile. Fortunately, the only wounds on the Nile were to expatriate dignity.[3] Meanwhile other Confederate officers roamed the globe as soldiers of fortune in the late nineteenth century. General Jubal Early went to Canada; others went to take military postings in Japan and Australia.

Most Southern expatriates, however, moved to Latin America. General Joel Selby took his troops with him and removed to Mexico. So many ex-planters and their families relocated to Mexico that the Mexican government appointed the ex-Confederate admiral William Fontaine Maury as commissioner of immigration. Maury helped some two thousand ex-Confederates settle in Mexico in the American settlements of Carlota and Cordova between Mexico City and Veracruz. Others settled in Honduras, Jamaica, and Cuba. While slavery was outlawed in the United States in the aftermath of the Civil War, it was still legal in Brazil. At this time the Brazilian government sent immigration agents into the Southern states to offer cheap land to planters who would settle in Brazil. Dom Pedro II, the emperor of Brazil, had sided with the Confederacy during the war and wasted no time in welcoming the defeated "confederados" to Brazil. Much of Brazil was still frontier jungle and land was cheap. Many confederados took advantage of land grants and settled in the southern Brazilian provinces of São Paulo and Paraná. In these provinces Confederate expats developed the towns of Americana and New Texas, which today remain enclaves of the descendants of these rebel expatriates. Many resident families retain their Anglo-Saxon names of Stonewall, Jackson, and Butler. In the town of Americana, present-day descendants still make pecan pies, hold debutante balls, and sing Southern hymns in their Protestant church.[4] Although Brazilian culture was far different from that of the lost Southern world of the confederados in terms of racial attitude, religion, and language, the Southerners did eventually assimilate. While many of the three thousand Dixie planters returned to the United States in the 1870s, some six hundred ex-Confederates remained. They established coffee plantations and cattle ranches. Brazil is still home to the descendants of these Confederates. These early expatriates in Brazil built happy, successful lives in culturally diverse Brazil. President Jimmy Carter visited this community during his presidency in the 1970s.[5]

Later in the nineteenth century, wealthy and talented Americans distanced themselves from America and established residence in England,

France, and Italy. Among these were the artists James McNeill Whistler, John Singer Sargent, and Mary Cassatt. Novelists like Henry James and Edith Wharton also put down roots in Europe. These artists and writers left America to immerse themselves in the advanced cultural currents of Europe. They sought a wider cosmopolitan culture, for America was just too provincial for them. Also, cultural expatriates like Henry James and Edith Wharton were sufficiently affluent to live where they chose. They also moved to Europe, like John Singer Sargent, to make money through art commissions as well as to become part of Europe's emerging modernist culture. Thus by World War I there was an established tradition of American expatriation to Latin America and Europe that would condition future American attitudes toward living abroad.

In the 1920s hundreds of Americans settled in Europe and became known as the "Lost Generation," writers and journalists who had returned home from the Great War to find a philistine business culture triumphant in their native land. In contrast, the café society of Paris, the coffeehouses of Berlin, and the salons of London were infinitely more attractive to them. Writers like Ernest Hemingway, John Dos Passos, and Dashiell Hammett became a who's who of Americans that could be found at the bullfights of Pamplona and in the crowds of heavy drinkers on Paris's Left Bank. Theirs was a religion of living for art; and for a brief period before the Great Depression of the 1930s and the rise of Hitlerism they were able to lead an idyllic existence. News dispatches to American and Canadian newspapers gave them a small income that went far in the cheap restaurants and neighborhoods of Europe. The Russian Revolution intrigued many Americans also at this time. Left-wing Americans nurtured in a Marxist tradition flocked to Russia to participate in the building of a postrevolutionary Soviet Union. They saw Soviet Russia as a testing ground for their working-class theories. During the height of Russia's popularity with the liberal left of America, some two thousand Americans settled in the Soviet Union.

After World War II another generation of Americans descended on Europe. This time the expatriates had a more pragmatic bent. As veterans of the war, they could stretch their GI Bill benefits much farther in European universities than in American ones. J. P. Donleavy took his GI Bill money to Dublin, where he lived the hilarious life of a dissipated student, which is amply chronicled in his novel *The Ginger Man*. The money that he earned as a novelist allowed him to acquire a large estate and a beautiful Irish wife and a life far better than he had ever known in New York City. The popular humorist Art Buchwald got his start in postwar Paris as a student and as a columnist for the *International Herald Tribune*. These men were part of a flood of Americans who came to Europe to live a lifestyle like that of the famous reporter and expatriate

Martha Gellhorn or their great cultural icon Ernest Hemingway. As U.S. military bases became a permanent fixture of 1950s Cold War Europe, they also offered numerous employment opportunities to ex-GIs who wanted to remain in Europe after their GI Bill benefits ran out. More opportunists than dissenters, this generation kept the expatriate dream alive for future Americans who would become increasingly estranged from America in the 1960s.

During the Vietnam War, twenty-five hundred to three thousand war resisters fled the United States to avoid the military draft. Most sought asylum in Toronto, Canada, married Canadian women, and busily got on with their lives. The high point in the war exile movement occurred in the late 1960s, when record numbers of American soldiers were sent to Vietnam to fight. In the 1970s U.S. troops were withdrawn from Vietnam and the hated draft ended. President Jimmy Carter pardoned many of the exiled war resisters, but these exiles never returned in large numbers. By the time President Carter pardoned them, in January 1977, they had already established themselves in their new land. For them, the United States was now a nice place to visit, but not many wanted to live there. In comparison, more Vietnam War resisters who fled to Sweden have returned. But this may have more to do with the vagaries of the long Scandinavian winter than the welcoming climate of America. Military deserters were not pardoned and still face criminal prosecution if they return to the United States.

American dissenters and exiles, then, are part of the historical American landscape. They have sought sanctuary in foreign lands for a variety of reasons—political, cultural, and social. Although many of these expats have struggled with their estrangement, their rate of citizenship repudiation has been quite low, a testimony to their desire to remain Americans. They just don't want to be Americans in America. There is a close historical continuum of past and present when it comes to the Vietnam War. There are fifteen thousand Americans living in Prague at the moment, and many young expatriates there believe that freedom triumphed in Vietnam when America's Vietnamese allies were vanquished. Prague remains a center of American agitation over issues involving the global environmental future, feminism, and the role of the United States in the global AIDS epidemic. "Anti-Americanism is very popular among these Americans," says Michael Semin of Prague's Civic Institute.[6]

ANGRY EXPAT VOTERS

The complex issues confronting American dissenters living abroad came to a head during the American presidential election of 2004. Many American dissenters, who left the United States in the 1960s over

Vietnam and other social issues like racism and the country's attitude toward homosexuality, had never bothered to vote. But they were stirred to action by a partisan sense of urgency over the war in Iraq that surpassed anything veteran U.S. political activists in many countries say they have ever witnessed. Republican and Democratic organizations abroad were also surprised by the upsurge because most absentee voters abroad tend to be politically conservative. Party preference abroad during the election of 2004 was as razor sharp as it was at home. But for left-wing expatriates the focus was more on issues of foreign policy and the United States' standing in the world. Expatriate voter registration overburdened an already unwieldy absentee ballot system and showed the problems of absentee voting abroad. Many dissenting Americans abroad chose absentee ballots because they were alarmed and feared the policies of the Bush administration would make them targets of anti-American attacks. Writer Laura Carlson noted that expatriates feared that as global hostility grew, they would all be painted with the same brush.[7] Eric Napoli, an American lawyer resident in Madrid, noted during the election that the foreign cultures in which they are immersed could exert enormous peer pressure on Americans. "In Spain there is a generalized anti-Bush opinion in the media. Spaniards think it's unthinkable to be pro Bush."[8] In Canada, one hundred thousand dissenters who fled to exile there rather than condone the Vietnam War constantly speak out against the American invasion of Iraq, which some say is turning into a quagmire reminiscent of the Vietnam War.

Ann Brandt, a sixty-six-year-old writer living in Mexico, last cast a ballot in 1960, when she voted for John F. Kennedy. Driven by anger over the war in Iraq, she voted for John Kerry using an absentee ballot in Florida's election. Others were not as fortunate. Their applications for absentee ballots were either lost in the mail or refused by county election boards who through either nativist prejudice or ignorance refused to service expatriates from their home district. Many ballots went out with insufficient postage, and at least eighteen states failed to mail absentee ballots to Americans abroad before September 19, a deadline considered necessary so the ballots could be returned on time.

One example of expatriate problems with absentee voting is instructive. Joffre de La Fontaine, a seventy-two-year-old Air Force veteran living in Mexico, reported that his request for an absentee ballot went unanswered until he called a clerk in Jackson County, Illinois, the last place he voted. "You've been abroad for thirty-five years? Then you're no longer an American," he said the ballot clerk told him. But La Fontaine persisted and finally received his ballot. Others who were intensely committed to voting against Bush in this election simply bought a plane ticket and flew home in time to vote against President

Bush and the war. Also, in voting in the 2004 election many dissenters took risks with the state tax collector, especially since many had not voted in decades and had quietly avoided paying taxes to their home states as well. Meanwhile the presidential election of 2004 pitted dissenters against conservative Republican supporters of President Bush in battleground states. But this time those battleground states were in the expatriate communities of Italy, Mexico, Canada, Spain, and France. In 2004 in Israel forty thousand Americans asked for ballots, whereas only fourteen thousand Americans cast absentee ballots from Israel in 2000.

According to the Zogby poll that surveyed overseas Americans with passports, expatriates supported Kerry over Bush, 58 percent to 35 percent. Thus in the future absentee ballots cast by dissenting Americans abroad may play a crucial role in the determination of presidential elections. With six million Americans living abroad, the expatriate vote, if administered fairly, could tip elections in Florida, Washington, Michigan, Pennsylvania, and Ohio. These states each have in excess of nearly two hundred thousand absentee voters living abroad. Currently there are around 680,000 Americans living in Canada. Thus expatriates in Canada can probably make a crucial difference in any future election, and this explains why the Republican and Democratic parties both court them so assiduously. These expats can also influence Canadian elections because many of them have dual citizenship, something that Canada and the United States allow.[9]

Many Americans abroad view the Bush administration and its war in Iraq as representative of an ugly resurgence of American bullying and hubris. During the presidential election of 2004, the Kerry campaign swept through Spain. Diana Kerry, the Democratic candidate's multilingual sister, made appearances in Barcelona and Madrid, home to many of Spain's two hundred thousand American expatriates. The Republicans sent George P. Bush, the Spanish-speaking son of Florida governor Jeb Bush. Thus the political contest of 2004 in the United States galvanized the overseas American electorate as never before. Expats in Germany and Austria turned out to hear Arnold Schwarzenegger campaign for George Bush; and Jim Brenner, executive director of Americans Overseas for Kerry, campaigned for the Democratic candidate in every major expatriate center in Europe.[10]

EXPATRIATES, TAXES, AND CITIZENSHIP

Although living abroad has its share of hardships, many Americans find it immensely rewarding financially. Companies often provide expats with living allowances, hardship pay, additional vacation leave, and other financial perks. Multinational corporations traditionally have given their American expatriate employees a wage premium of 20 percent for living overseas.[11] Also, in 2004 the U.S. Tax Code was revised to allow ample tax breaks for American expatriates. The new provisions eliminate expatriate double taxation under the alternative minimum income tax provision (AMT). Previously, expatriates could count only 90 percent of their foreign-paid income against their AMT liability. The new law increased that amount to 100 percent, eliminating the chance of double taxation. Also, the U.S. Tax Code allows citizens who live abroad to exclude up to $84,000 of their foreign wages from American tax. Expatriates do pay taxes to their host countries; indeed, countries like England, Belgium, and Finland are far more vexatious in collecting taxes than is their American counterpart.

Tax matters often force overseas Americans to consider whether it is to their personal and financial interest to renounce their citizenship. For those who are wealthy, like the Dorrance family, heirs to the Campbell Soup fortune, the loss of citizenship is not terribly bothersome. Many countries, ranging from the Bahamas to Costa Rica to Ireland, are eager to recruit wealthy citizens. Currently, however, it is not as easy to renounce citizenship as it used to be; and renunciation of American citizenship to avoid paying tax is now violation of federal law.[12] For the wealthy American elite, though, citizenship is just one more commodity that can be bought on the market. In an age of high federal inheritance and income taxes, expatriation has become the ultimate tax-planning tool. Often citizenship in a reliable foreign country like Ireland can be had for a modest investment in local real estate or business. Also, countries like Barbados and St. Lucia in the Caribbean offer exemption from local taxes and no capital gains for overseas investors seeking to combine citizenship with a tax haven. The New York law firm Cadwalader, Wickersham and Taft, for example, advises wealthy private clients on matters of citizenship and capital expatriation. The firm advertises that it represents "U.S. citizens and residents and foreign nationals on a global basis and imaginatively responds to their needs, often by crafting estate plans using structures and entities such as domestic and foreign limited partnerships, corporations, limited liability companies, private trust companies, and private and charitable trusts, either alone or in combination." Such tactics do have their rewards. Just ask John Templeton, the famous mutual fund director who moved to the Bahamas in 1962 and gave up his citizenship. As a result, he saved over $100 million in taxes from the sale of his investment management company while continuing to invest in American companies. John Dorrance III, the Campbell Soup heir, saved his family from U.S. taxes on his fortune of $1 billion by taking citizenship in Ireland. Whereas Dorrance has to pay tax on dividends that he receives from America, his heirs will only have to pay 2 percent Irish probate tax on the family fortune after his death, which is a considerable savings. The list of wealthy Americans who have given up their citizenship includes Mark Mobius, the mutual fund guru; Kenneth Dart, the billionaire shipper; and Michael Dingman, chairman of Abex Corporation. These individuals show that there are financial limits to the costs Americans are willing to carry with American citizenship.[13] Since *Forbes* first wrote about this expatriate trend in 1994, a total of 4,415 wealthy Americans have turned in their citizenship, among them Tara Getty, the grandson of J. Paul Getty, and Joseph Bogdanovich, Jr., heir of the Star-Kist Company tuna fortune. Congress has tried to stop the flow of tax fugitives by imposing a ten-year tax on expatriated Americans. It has also forbidden tax-avoiding expatriates to visit the United States again. Neither directive has worked. Meanwhile tax fugitives who have given up their American citizenship rest comfortably on their yachts at Lyford Cay, Bahamas. Most men and women of wealth in the United States, however, do have patriotic and practical reasons for keeping American citizenship, one of which is that once given up, one's American citizenship is very difficult to regain.

Most expatriate Americans have other concerns. They campaign against impediments to their children becoming American citizens through naturalization if a spouse is foreign born and the couple continues to reside abroad. Expats also complain constantly about the undercounting of Americans abroad in the decennial census, which has great impact on congressional apportionment in their home states. This diminishes their leverage as overseas voters. American Citizens Abroad, an expatriate organization based in Switzerland, currently works to register voters overseas for U.S. elections and is dedicated to getting an accurate U.S. Census count of Americans living abroad.[14] Summarizing the group's position on the census issue, Gloria Otto wrote, "The psychological and political impact of including Americans abroad in the national censuses cannot be over-estimated. How can Americans abroad be recognized as a valuable national asset (economic, political, and cultural) when it is not even known how many there are?" If the federal government can tax Americans abroad, Otto argued, it should be able to count them.[15]

The only Americans abroad that the U.S. Census Bureau tracks are those who are "federally affiliated"—around 567,000 employees and dependents of government agencies and the U.S. military. In its attempt at running a test sample questionnaire of Americans living abroad for Census 2000, the U.S. Census Bureau was able to obtain only fifty-three hundred completed questionnaires from the test sites of France, Kuwait, and Mexico. These questionnaires proved to be quite expensive— around $1,450 per response against $56 per domestic household in the United States. Currently the U.S. Census Bureau has gone on record as stating that counting Americans overseas in the upcoming 2010 census "would not be cost effective."[16] Further, the U.S. Census Bureau argued that it had discretion under the Constitution and federal statutes to decide whether to count Americans residing overseas. Article 1, section 2, clause 3 of the Constitution and section 2 of the Fourteenth Amendment refer to the enumeration of "the whole number of persons in each state" as a basis for apportionment of the House of Representatives. It says nothing about counting Americans abroad. The U.S. Census Bureau has currently taken the position that data collection is too difficult for a census overseas and "the universe of overseas Americans is unknown so participation rates cannot be determined." Kenneth Prewitt, who served as director of the 2000 census, cites the many bureaucratic obstacles to counting Americans abroad. "I would never say it (an overseas census) could never happen, but there are a lot of problems," Prewitt said. Without additional census legislation passed by Congress, there will be no accurate estimate of the total number of Americans living abroad.[17]

Critics of the census, however, point out that much is at stake in counting Americans abroad. Perhaps the most celebrated case has involved Mormons. In January 2001 the state of Utah sued the U.S. Census Bureau's parent agency, the Department of Commerce, claiming that it lost a congressional seat because Census 2000 excluded the state's eleven thousand Mormon missionaries and other citizens abroad. Had they been counted, Utah would have gained another congressional seat. Utah lost the suit in federal court.[18] Meanwhile overseas groups like American Citizens Abroad continue to agitate for an overseas census of Americans because of its immense political implications for such matters as apportionment of the Congress and federal benefits programs like Medicare and Social Security. Currently, even if one accepts the low estimate of three million Americans living abroad, this group of expats has a higher population than at least twenty states.

Sooner or later, life overseas also raises the question about the desirability of dual nationality. Citizenship in a Common Market country like Ireland, for example, permits an individual the right to obtain and hold employment anywhere in western Europe. Also, because many expatriates have foreign spouses, it may be to their personal and political interest to acquire dual citizenship. At present the U.S. Constitution does not forbid dual citizenship. In its 1967 ruling in *Afroyim v. Rusk*, the Supreme Court used an argument derived from the Fourteenth Amendment to the Constitution to affirm a right to dual citizenship. Children who are born abroad to American citizens but who have never lived in the United States, however, are not U.S. citizens. This rule was designed to prevent the proliferation of endless generations of foreign-born and foreign-raised Americans. Current law states that any child born outside the United States with at least one parent who is a natural-born citizen of the United States is an American citizen. If both parents are natural-ized citizens, certain residency requirements in America as part of nat-uralization may have to be fulfilled. Such a ruling prompts some expatriates to return to the United States to live with their children for a least one year prior to their child's twenty-first birthday. This is not necessarily a harsh requirement, but it rankles expats who believe that citizenship overseas should be treated the same way as citizenship at home.[19]

Until recently the U.S. State Department was quite combative in its handling of dual nationality claims and citizenship of Americans born abroad. But now it has changed how it handles these matters. The situa-tion is less clear, however, for individuals who become American citi-zens and still wish to take advantage of their old foreign citizenship. People who go through U.S. naturalization are required to state under oath that they are renouncing their former citizenship, and conduct inconsistent with this pledge could theoretically lead to the loss of American citizenship. The State Department is no longer pursuing cases of this nature, however. Since the collapse of the Soviet empire and the end of the Cold War, citizenship questions in the United States have lost some of their emotional and ideological volatility. It is too soon to ascer-tain whether or not controversies involving illegal immigration in the United States will reignite the issue of who and what is an American.

"I NEVER PROMISED YOU A ROSE GARDEN"

Although the adventures of American expats are intriguing and appeal to our romantic sensibility, there is a counterpoint to the expatri-ate game that often does not find its way into travel magazines and life-style sections of the American press. Living abroad is not without its difficulties. Even fairly welcoming countries like Canada, France, and Japan can test the patience and resolve of the expatriate.

Nora Jacobson is an American medical sociologist living in Toronto. She moved to take a lucrative job after the 2000 presidential election. She was interested in the challenges of a new job and was happy to leave the United States, given that Republican George Bush had won the election. Jacobson reflected at that time, "I wanted to live in a country that was not a superpower; a country I believe to have made the right choices about fairness, human rights, and the social compact."

Yet despite the satisfying nature of her work, Nora Jacobson has become uncomfortable in Canada and tells friends, "If you are thinking of coming to Canada, let me give you some advice: Don't." What Jacob-son discovered is that a powerful and not very subtle anti-Americanism pervades Canadian life. In numerous conversations and intellectual exchanges, the subject of the United States invariably arises. Canadians make comparisons between their country and the United States that mix a kind of smug contempt with a wariness that "alternates between the paranoid and the absurd." Specifically, Canadians believe that their relationship with the United States has to be colored by distrust and fear because of the overwhelming economic and military might of their neighbor to the south. With a population under thirty million and a three-thousand-mile border, worried Canadians complain about the dilemma of sleeping with an elephant. If the elephant rolls over, they are liable to get crushed. But at the heart of Canadian anti-Americanism lies a cultural bitterness that takes an American expatriate unawares. Canadians fear the American media's influence on their culture and talk critically about how Americans are exporting a culture of violence in its television programming and movies. After the initial shock of the 9/11 attack on New York's World Trade Center wore off, Jacobson was appalled to hear Canadians say that the Americans had finally gotten what they deserved. Also, said Jacobson, Canadians were relentless in their comments that the U.S.–Canadian border is the "longest one-way mirror in the world." Canadians always gaze southward, trying to make sense of their American neighbors, whereas "the United States sees only its own reflection."

What Jacobson found to be so irksome about Canadians was their constant definition of Canada as a negative: "We're not the United States." By looking at American problems and refusing to examine their own social issues, Jacobson believes, Canadians trumpet their moral superiority. Thus in multicultural Canada, a land practicing political correctness long before the United States, the only acceptable prejudice is to be an anti-American xenophobe.

Perhaps it was Jacobson's own naïveté that made her so surprised by Canadian anti-Americanism. The experience has been constructive because it forced her to confront her own beliefs and values about the United States. In fact, Canada's eccentricities and contradictions made her more willing to understand those of her own country. Meanwhile, says, Jacobson, "as long as there is more homelessness, racism, and income inequality to the south, Canadians can continue to rest easy in their moral superiority."[20]

Sometimes the difficulties of expatriate life are more basic than dealing with local xenophobia. Sometimes the difficulties boil down to a simple ongoing problem like finding an apartment. The wealth of affordable housing and livable habitats does not necessarily extend beyond America's borders. In America, everything is big—big people, big houses, big rooms, and big closets. Abroad, you learn what the opposite of big is—unless, of course, you are an affluent expatriate with rent subsidized by a corporation. Most often, daily life is a small cramped apartment with antiquated electricity and antediluvian plumbing. It is life lived on a small scale. In countries like Japan, for example, an apartment may consist of a six-tatami-mat room scarcely larger than a broom closet. Cramped and often cold quarters can induce culture shock in Americans whose ideas about personal space and comfort are as broad as the prairies. Also, in the expatriate habitat there are never enough elevators, and it always seems that the lucky-to-find comfortable apartment is a fifth-floor walk-up.

After the honeymoon period, when the expatriate celebrates and enjoys his or her new culture, problems arise. A different, often difficult, language, bureaucratic tyrannies, and strange social customs can drive the expat to exasperation. Family life can be problematic, for the traditional safety net of relatives and friends that exists in the United States has to be constructed with foreign friends and well-meaning professionals. As one expatriate remarked, "It is a bit different when your husband is away and your child gets sick in Kinshasa than it is in Kansas City." Adds journalist Barbara Rosen, "This expat stuff can be hard enough when you don't have kids. When you do and they're in trouble, it's for the birds."[21] Early on in their new lives abroad, expatriates can experience an emotional crisis brought about by the lack of an American context. Some recover from the shock and get on with their lives. Others seek refuge in English-speaking ghettos. The defeated return to America embittered by their experience, often recalling to friends their despair when they could not buy a turkey for Thanksgiving in Singapore when a universe of delectable food surrounded them.

Although expatriates tend to be disdainful of tourists, there is an interesting symbiosis between the two. In countries like Mexico and Thailand, expatriates live off tourists by serving as eco-adventure guides, selling souvenirs, or purveying food in "American" restaurants. Furthermore, expatriates were once tourists themselves and to a certain extent retain many of the tourist's attributes. Both tourist and expat embrace their new culture as would-be lovers and indulge their fascination for things foreign, but both the tourist and the expat are held at arm's length by the host society.

Americans abroad have a variety of temperaments and come from diverse backgrounds. Thus, it should come as no surprise that Americans occasionally get into trouble with the law overseas. Sometimes Americans land in jail because they have been drunk and disorderly. At other times they may face serious charges for alien political activity in a particular nation. The most burdensome problem for American embassies abroad, however, stems from drugs. Plainly put, overseas officials don't take the drug war lightly. In prisons that range from Pakistan to Singapore to Mexico and the Bahamas, more than twenty-two hundred Americans are confined on drug charges. A surprising number of those confined on drug charges are women. Prison terms for illegal drug activity in many foreign countries often range from eight years to life. In 1994 Stephen Royce, for example, a Los Angeles movie producer, was arrested in Bangkok with seven pounds of heroin hidden in his luggage. He claimed he was researching a script. The Thai courts thought otherwise and sentenced him to life imprisonment.[22] A life in prison is not exactly what Americans have in mind when it comes to living abroad.

EMIGRATION AND UTOPIA

The *sine qua non* of all expatriate experience is the quest for that perfect land where one can enjoy surcease from the problems of the world. Since the colonial period Americans have sought some space, some community that would go beyond the boundaries of ordinary experience and give dynamic release to the American moral and intellectual imagination. Such a quest brought the Mormons to the Utah desert and the Mennonites to the Nebraska plains. The communal experience of the 1960s with experimental lifestyles was part of this quest. In our modern age the idea of finding or creating a perfect community remains vibrant. In the future there may come a time when expatriates create a brand-new country out of abandoned or unwanted real estate somewhere in the world. This is precisely what John Ham is currently undertaking. He is carving a utopian community in the foothills of the Andes in southern Ecuador. Settlements like Ham's are part utopian and part business venture. In the words of a recent television news report, Ham's mission was "to pick up where the American dream left off." Ham and those like him say their reasons for leaving America were fairly simple: "expensive housing, scarcity of prime farm land, and especially the emphasis on material things." After a hard day of working a twenty-four-hundred-acre bean, corn, and sugarcane farm that he bought for less than $10,000, Ham has little interest in returning. "You give up a lot to live in the United States and I knew I couldn't do that," Ham explained. Since he started, Ham has been joined by several families, and they live kibbutz-style on the farm. While America is offering fewer and fewer opportunities, the Ecuadorian government has an open immigration policy that welcomes foreigners who invest in the land. Says Hernán Holguín, consul general of Ecuador: "It is cheap to live here, our communities are welcoming, and we will soon have a bright economic future that the United States will help make possible."[23]

A foreshadowing of these approaches to utopian communities overseas occurred when a group of expatriate investors and warm-weather idealists sought to erect a new nation on an abandoned atoll in the South Pacific. In 1972 an adventurer named Mike Oliver sought to erect the Republic of Minerva on a set of reefs four hundred miles south of Fiji. The uninhabited reefs were considered a hazard to navigation, yet Oliver and his compatriots envisioned the creation of a city-state of approximately thirty thousand inhabitants on an engineered lagoon. Unfortunately for the Republic of Minerva, the government of Tonga was only 260 miles away and took vigorous exception to the lagoon nation. Tonga dispatched a military force and drove off the would-be nation builders.

One suspects that in the future such developments will occur with greater frequency and may meet with success. There are many countries with secessionist tendencies that would welcome large expatriate populations. As well, engineering advances in the construction of drilling rigs far out in the ocean can offer the technical wherewithal to construct a platform republic on the high seas. Erwin S. Strauss, an international consultant, has written a how-to book on the subject entitled *How to Start Your Own Country*. Planning and creating a new country is a complex, delicate process, he says. "The most important thing is to have a firm grasp of the costs and risks one is willing to accept in pursuit of the venture and the benefits one is seeking."[24]

Perhaps the most intriguing of these new-country proposals are found in "The Principality of New Utopia" and "Oceania," libertarian republics to be constructed on drilling rigs in the Caribbean with a "wide open free enterprise system" that would ensure the development of tourism, encourage residential development, and offer a tax haven for expatriates seeking a retreat from the U.S. government that would be cheaper than residence in the Cayman Islands.

Using three-hundred-by-three-hundred-foot platforms in shallow international waters off the coast of Yucatan, Mexico, "The Principality of New Utopia" would be a kind of Caribbean Monaco with affordable residences, convenient banking, floating parks, and a luxury spa.[25] The architect of this new expatriate community, Lazarus Long, proposes to finance this new expatriate haven through the construction of 642 apartments and condos averaging fourteen hundred square feet each at a cost of $70,000 per unit, a $15 million shopping mall, a $20 million hotel for sea lovers and scuba divers, and a rentable warehouse complex at a cost of $3 million. Says Lazarus Long: "All construction is anticipated to be of preformed reinforced concrete, prefabricated on land and installed in place on the platforms." The cost of police and social services in the new country, Long adds, would be paid out of a 20 percent duty on imported consumable goods. He envisions that New Utopia's medical center, which will offer "the best anti-aging and rejuvenation treatments available anywhere in the world," will attract large numbers of expatriates. Here on platforms in the Caribbean the "American dream" will be reborn in accordance with the libertarian principles of

Adam Smith and Ayn Rand and serve as a haven from taxation and American "entitlement" bureaucracy.

Similarly, free enterprise investors are proposing construction of the community of "Oceania" fifty miles off the coast of Panama. Envisioned by Eric Klein, an affluent Nevada businessman, Oceania will be a "floating city" on "hexagonal modular units [each about 1.6 acres] in accordance with the principles of Adam Smith, Ludwig von Mises, Frederick Hayek and Ayn Rand." Klein envisions that the major industries of Oceania will be private banking, tourism, and fishing. And when the country is firmly established, "life extension technology can be pursued" at Oceania's medical research center. Since Oceania is strictly an individualistic, free-enterprise society, drug use would be legal under the philosophy of "My body, my business." Currently the Oceania project is headquartered in Las Vegas, and Klein reports that since 1995 his Oceania Web site has received 244,336 accesses a week from curious Americans and would-be expatriates. Oceania's plans call for a republic of ten thousand to thirty thousand inhabitants that would cost roughly $1 billion to construct.[26]

Many people believe that attempts to establish micronations like Minerva, the New Utopia, and Oceania are so much libertarian nonsense. The projects continue to generate financial interest, however. Attempts to establish these micronations in supposedly "international waters" will continue. As one expert has pointed out, "Creating artificial land mass is not new technology. Roughly one third of the Netherlands is below sea level, and is kept habitable via a complex system of dikes." Oil platforms, military structures, and docks are all examples of "freestanding structures in marine environments."[27] As long as the organizers of these floating utopias can raise money, they will not lack an audience of potential citizens. New ideas come to the forefront every day with projects that range from oil-derrick-structure cities in international waters to superships that would have all the benefits of permanent self-governing communities.

Advocates of such ocean utopias call the process of colonizing the ocean "seasteading." Many challenges await these developing projects. For example, will people be able to live on these platforms in harmony when many of the conveniences of modern life might be foregone? Also, insofar as the current projects for "microtopias" are geared around libertarian ideologies, many people may find life in such communities unappealing. How will these microtopias protect their platforms from invasion by armed thugs? How will they sustain themselves through the production of food energy and exportable goods? Will existing governments view such new nations in nearby waters as threats or nuisances and destroy them, as did Tonga in the case of the Republic of Minerva? The best to be said for these microtopias is that they offer a base of thinking for community designs from the ground up. Although it is unlikely that these communities will become independent nations, their existence in the future as semi-autonomous communities is possible.

At this point, however, Lazarus Long's and Eric Klein's plans for building new nations in the Caribbean are long on vision and short on financing. They nonetheless reveal a strong utopian streak in contemporary American expatriate thinking. Just as expatriate founding fathers created colonial America out of the wilderness and made it a political and religious haven, so too do Lazarus Long and Eric Klein believe that the principles of the American faith will be reborn on engineered platforms in the Caribbean and other locations at sea far from the grasp of tax collectors and intrusive government. In an age of global asset flight and rampant real estate development, one can only remark that far wackier dreams have come true for Americans who have migrated. Already plans are afoot to build floating resorts or "sovereign, self-sufficient floating platforms," thus creating new territory on the oceans. Some of these floating platforms would cater to the "sin industries of drugs, prostitution and gambling."[28] Seasteaders also envision underwater resorts catering to affluent scuba divers who want to enjoy their own private reefs.

For new-country analyst James Lee, microtopias "seem to project our own dreams and inner landscapes." They also, he concludes, "represent a need to create idealized worlds of our own."[29] An age that now routinely contemplates space colonization can certainly entertain the idea of new self-created nations emerging on platforms on the high seas. At one time, every country was a "new" country; a new era of nation formation may be just around the corner. Certainly such projects reveal expatriates as seekers on an idealized quest whose natures are more adventurous than the homebound remaining in their society of origin. Whether these utopians will lose one country to gain another of their own creation will remain an interesting speculation. But should this come to pass, these new countries will need the expertise, money, and leadership of a new kind of international man—the modern American expatriate.

SUMMARY

There has always been a ragged edge to the American expatriate experience that is at variance with romantic notions of life abroad. From the colonial period onward America has sent its dissidents and grumbling malcontents outward either as exiles or as sojourners. While few go to great lengths to announce their departure, they leave nonetheless and become "confederados" in some area of the world that will welcome them. Dissenters often leave because they can no longer stand American culture and want to swim in a more advanced cultural stream. Then, too, there is always the money angle—wealthy Americans wanting to hide their fortunes from the U.S. tax collector by repudiating their citizenship.

Until recently the expatriate voter was taken for granted as a some-time absentee voter of little consequence. The presidential election of 2004 showed otherwise, and expatriate voters will be an important part of the national political equation in the future. Finally, the American expatriate experience has always had a utopian dimension that ranges from building communities in Latin America to creating new countries on oil rig platforms. If the dissenters, tax fugitives, and utopians have anything in common, it is this: They may very well change the concept of citizenship as we know it into something more universal but in the end less protective.

Chapter 4

The Expatriate Countries: Canada, Israel, Australia, and New Zealand

We finally captured the American Dream. It's just a shame that we had to come to New Zealand to do it.

John Roosen

CANADA: THE OTHER SIDE OF THE MIRROR

Until the 1920s immigration to the United States was fueled by a few simple facts: America was rich in resources and industry but the country was significantly underpopulated. That situation no longer prevails as America struggles with the problem of burgeoning population growth even while immigration continues to soar. There are countries in our modern era, though, that are experiencing the same problem of under-population that the United States experienced in earlier times. These countries tend to be modern, affluent nation-states with literate popula-tions and a high standard of living. What they lack are young people to provide a workforce commensurate with national growth. Singapore and Japan, for example, suffer from birth dearth and underpopulation.

Currently both countries are trying to address their workforce prob-lems by relying on means other than immigration. Singapore is famous for the pressure that it places on young college graduates to marry and have children; and Japan looks to its own expanding female workforce as an alternative to large-scale immigration, which may disrupt the country's ethnic and cultural life. Canada, Israel, Australia, and New Zealand are different stories, however. These four countries combined now have over 971,000 Americans living in their midst, and they will continue to attract a growing stream of American immigrants.

Canada is a relatively sparsely populated country whose neighbor to the south is an aggressive, well-populated social and economic colossus. Canadians believe they must increase their population to escape American cultural and economic engulfment. Since the end of World War II, Canadian immigration agents have scoured the planet in search of people who want to make their home in Canada, and today the country boasts significant population increases largely attributable to immigration. Ironically, from the standpoint of Canada's concerns for its cultural identity, one of the largest groups of immigrants to settle there have been the Americans, some 570,000 strong at last count. Also, major numbers from Eastern Europe have flocked to Canadian cities like Montreal and Toronto; and overnight Vancouver has become a north Asian city with a significant Chinese population. While some American expats resent the xenophobic smugness of Canadians, others are quite happy to live north of the border. Thus Americans as well as Chinese and Europeans have greatly added to the cultural and social diversity of the Canadian national landscape.

Canada has always been a haven for American dissenters and political refugees, of course. After the American Revolution, one hundred thousand British loyalists resettled from the United States to Canada. In the antebellum period, runaway slaves followed the North Star to freedom on the Underground Railroad that led to a new life in Canada. To this day many black communities in Ontario can trace their roots to the struggle over racial slavery and the flight from the plantations of the American South. Mennonites and other pacifists who were persecuted in the United States established farm communities in Canada's western provinces. Similarly, in the Vietnam War era draft resisters fled the United States and took refuge in Canada rather than serve in the U.S. military forces.

Recent immigration to Canada has fluctuated from six to ten thousand Americans per year. A critical aspect of American expatriation to Canada that should be mentioned, however, entails a state of mind. Most Americans who go to Canada do not perceive themselves as going to a "foreign" country, as do expatriates who move to Japan or Israel, for example. Since the troubled times of the Vietnam War, most Americans have moved to Canada for nonpolitical reasons such as job opportunities and quality of life. Today many Americans are crossing the northern border because Canada offers a safer and more tranquil life than does the United States. A relatively open country, Canada is receptive to young people with new ideas who want to help the country grow. Canada's immigration office maintains a point system based on age, education, personal skills, and professional occupation and uses this point system to award visas to worthwhile aspiring immigrants. Each year 250,000 people are allowed to immigrate to Canada. Under legislation presently in force in Canada, an American expatriate wishing to move to Canada must obtain a minimum of 70 points out of a total 107 points. The Canadian government actively recruits those who have the best educations and skills.[1] Schoolteachers in Canada, for example, are in oversupply, whereas chefs and cooks and machinists are actively sought, as are computer and systems analysts.

When Dennis Raphael left his native Brooklyn, New York, more than twenty years ago to attend graduate school in Toronto, he was pleased to find an efficient metropolis with friendly people. Raphael decided to stay and ultimately became a Canadian citizen. Although he came to Canada when many draft resisters were fleeing northward, he had a medical deferral and was under no pressure. Yet Canada held a mystique for him. He liked the Canadians' easygoing ways and their lack of social and racial pressures. After completing his doctorate, he took a job at the University of Toronto, married a Canadian, and settled in. He decided to become a citizen when names like Saskatchewan and Alberta started sounding more normal to him than the names New York and California. What made the ultimate difference to Raphael is that he doesn't have to be constantly looking over his shoulder in fear for his personal safety. According to Raphael, "Canadians are concerned with peace, order, and good government." Even if he lost his job, he declared, he would not return to the United States. "To me it's inconceivable moving back to the States. I came up here because I wanted to be up here. This is a great country, I'm staying."[2]

A JEWISH SILICON VALLEY

Americans were in Israel long before it became a state in 1948. Many of these early American expatriates were Protestant missionaries who had come to Jerusalem with the specific mission of converting Jews to Christianity. As early as 1919 there were about 220 Americans living in Israel. Since then the number has soared to 158,000, with most Americans resident in the cities of Tel Aviv and Jerusalem.[3] In the 1960s, when the Israeli government began to keep statistics on American immigration, about two thousand Americans annually came to settle in Israel. Most came as religious immigrants making *aliyah,* or return to the Holy Land. American expatriate numbers jumped sharply during the 1970s, when an average of about six thousand Americans annually settled in Israel. Unlike their earlier counterparts, many of these Americans came to Israel to find jobs. Though these immigrants were mostly Jewish, economic considerations often explained their expatriation better than religious ones. In the past ten years the American population in Israel, which long remained stable at about 78,000, has doubled.[4]

Most Americans who arrive in Israel are usually married, a statistic that differs markedly from American expatriate trends in other countries. But like other expatriates, Americans electing to move to Israel have done so out of a sense of frustration and dissatisfaction with American Jewish life in particular and American social life in general.[5] They believe that through immigration they can enhance their personal lives, a belief not altogether different from the values expressed by American expatriates in Asia and Europe. Like most expatriates, Americans in Israel are willing to accept a deterioration in their standard of living in exchange for an increase in the quality of personal and community life. Significantly, less than 10 percent of modern American immigrants to Israel list religious reasons as their motive for expatriation.[6]

Such reasons are best summed up in a recent interview with an ophthalmic surgeon who gave up a million-dollar practice to work in a hospital in Israel: "I came because when I treat somebody here, I'm treating family. I mean it really makes a difference to me that these people are mine and that I can identify with them. I have had many more interesting cases back in the States, and there's nothing to talk about as far as money goes, but ... here I'm helping a man or woman or child who I really care about because together we make up this place."[7]

Israel forces Americans to make crucial and at times painful adjustments. Most Americans are thrown into the Israeli universe of expensive, cramped apartments and experience the innumerable delays of red tape and bureaucratic confusion. To make anything happen in Israel, you have to know someone who can pull strings for you. Says Benjamin Phillips, an American immigrant: "No wonder that the first Hebrew word that an American expat learns in Israel is *savlanut* [patience]."[8] This is especially difficult for any American who is trying to build a business in Israel. In addition to the normal problems of entrepreneurship, the expat must deal with inefficiency and a generally lackadaisical attitude toward work standards.

Also, says Benjamin Phillips, an American who worked for General Motors in the United States before moving to Israel, the lack of any long-range planning and the constant improvisation quite bother American immigrants. Americans are accustomed to a more settled and predictable lifestyle; hence, of all the migrants to Israel, Americans have one of the poorest rates of successful absorption. Only about 60 percent of American expatriates in Israel stay more than three years. Finally, American Jews confront in Israel the same problem that black Americans experience in Africa. American Jews believe that they have come "home" to Israel and are shocked and annoyed when they are treated as foreigners. To help these immigrants, the Israeli Ministry of Absorption runs a series of public seminars on culture shock for weary Americans who find Israel not to be the Promised Land they hoped it would be. Americans in Israel tend to seek out each other and often do not mix well with the natives after work. Currently numerous organizations in Israel help Americans adjust to their new life; of these agencies, the most important from a social standpoint is the Association of Americans and Canadians in Israel. This volunteer organization based in Jerusalem helps the North American *olim* (settlers) make Israel their home.

The surprising news today is that Israel is short of engineers and scientists and is recruiting Americans with an ardor that has to be seen to be understood. Why does a country with a superabundance of skilled personnel now want to recruit Americans? The answer is simple: in Israel there are six thousand unfilled technical jobs for which there is no local talent. Despite conflict in the Middle East, there has been an economic explosion in Israel that may in future make this country look more like Silicon Valley than a land of kibbutzim. In fact, many of the once-rural areas of Israel are being plowed under to make way for burgeoning suburbs and high-tech industrial parks. For American expat Lisa Avigdor, the many changes to the beautiful Israeli landscape have been disconcerting. Job postings routinely appear on the Internet for high-tech positions in Israel and are the fodder for a global industry that hungers for talented men and women.

A country rich in historical and religious tradition, Israel has a vibrant social and cultural life. Given the population's intellectual level and diversity, it is difficult to be bored in Israel. Also, professional salaries are now 75 to 80 percent of U.S. levels. Elmer Winter, cofounder of Manpower Inc., believes that Israel's need for trained personnel is the beginning of a new economic *aliyah,* or immigration. Today agencies like Manpower have offices all over Israel and report that recently the demand for engineers and financial personnel has climbed by 50 percent. Americans who have been downsized out of jobs in the United States are now finding work in Israel.[9] Skills are important in the new, technical Israel, and one does not necessarily have to be Jewish to immigrate there.

Americans like Avi Moskowitz discover new careers in Israel. When he first came to Jerusalem, getting e-mail for nonacademic use was next to impossible and required filling out a ten-page government form. But in addition to being a religious Zionist, Moskowitz was also an accomplished computer hacker. Within two years of his arrival, Moskowitz took advantage of the Internet to launch Virtual Jerusalem, the world's largest Web site for Israeli and Jewish-related material. Once a country of farmers and socialist pioneers, Israel has become a haven for embryonic high-tech companies. With so many Americans seeking work abroad, Moskowitz effortlessly put together an English-speaking staff of computer programmers in Jerusalem. Outside their office is Israel. Inside the office at Virtual Jerusalem the atmosphere is more like San Francisco.[10]

With a $17,000-a-year per capita income, Israel has a standard of living close to England's. And since most of the new wealth generated in Israel today is not in agriculture but in high technology, immigrants like Moskowitz are extremely important to the country. As Israel continues to develop its knowledge economy, skilled immigrants will come to work at Israeli computer companies like Mirabilis, a ten-year-old communications company that develops programs to enable users to exchange computer files while online. Recently Mirabilis's Russian immigrant owners sold the company to America Online Inc. for $278 million. Mirabilis is currently recruiting American and Russian immigrants and is having little difficulty finding qualified applicants. Currently Israel has about four thousand high-tech firms, seventy of which trade on Wall Street with a combined capitalization of $22 billion, according to the Israeli Export Institute. High-tech exports, adds the Israeli Export Institute, amount to over $6 billion annually, or over a third of all exports.[11] For the first time in Israel's fifty-year history, a significant portion of its population of six million—perhaps 10 percent or more—is neither Arab nor Jewish. Much of this reflects the influx of Americans and Russians. Furthermore, Israel's high-tech investments are in people, not factories, and cannot easily be destroyed in the event of a war in the Middle East. Japan and the United States are now the largest investors in Israel's computer industry because Israel has what Japan and the United States need—information technologies.

But Israel attracts more than scientists. People from all walks of life immigrate there too. They are like Norma Schneider, who gave up a secure life as a magazine editor in New York City for a new life in Jerusalem. Israel gives her a sense of belonging that she had never had before. Despite initial problems of resettlement and learning the language, Schneider was able to find an editorial position with the Hebrew National University Press. She now works as an independent freelance editor on book projects. An inveterate traveler, Schneider keeps two passports, one American, one Israeli, to avoid any problems when traveling in the eastern Mediterranean. In sum, despite high unemployment rates in Israel, the American influx there continues. Most Americans wind up in Tel Aviv, where—after the predictable year of language and settlement difficulties—they usually find jobs.

THE LAND OF OZ

Currently Australia boasts a rather significant population of "Yank" expatriates. Although some form of social alienation pushed a minority of these expats to leave the United States, most came to Australia because of their fascination with the country's sheer rugged beauty and the pull of the country's "laid-back charm." Today you can find

Americans teaching in Australian public schools and working in companies as large as Coca-Cola Australia or in small computer consulting firms.

In 1971 a Gallup Poll asked a sampling of Americans: "If you were free to do so, would you like to go and settle in another country? Which country?" One out of eight answered yes, and Australia was their most popular choice. Today Australia is home to over fifty-seven thousand American expatriates, many of whom have little thought of ever returning to the United States. Although historically the numbers of American immigrants has been dwarfed by countries like the United Kingdom and Greece, a flood of nearly thirty-two thousand Americans entered Australia in the 1970s, and their numbers and visibility prompted significant attention in the Australian media.

Harry Gordon, an American reporter based in Sydney, wrote that the reason for the American exodus to Australia was prompted by a desire to avoid the social upheavals caused by the Vietnam War and racial conflicts and to find a country that still had the values of the old West. Gordon made these reflections in his essay "Emigrating to Australia: In Search of the USA."[12] Since the troubled 1970s, American immigration to Australia has tapered off somewhat. The Australian government's tighter controls on immigration and the country's economic recessions dampened American enthusiasm for life Down Under. Since its high point of six thousand in 1972, immigration has hovered at fifteen hundred a year.

Most people immigrating to Australia today fall into two categories: "The Endless Summer Boys and Girls" and "The Supereducated." The beaches of Australia and the Great Barrier Reef draw thousands of Americans to Australia for a temporary life in the surf and sun. Many expats end up working on luxury boats as crew and hostesses or in surf and dive shops in Queensland's Port Douglas and Cairns. Many American college students come to Cairns to vacation on the Great Barrier Reef and stay on. They can enjoy the life of diving on the Great Barrier Reef and find work at the resort hotels or on luxury yachts.

"The Supereducated" concentrate in Melbourne and Sydney, where many work as financial and business consultants with Australian companies that are getting ready for the storms of global economic competition that are just beginning to crash on Australia's shores. Matthew Wennersten, my son, is an interesting case in point. After graduation from Cambridge University in England and extensive travel in Europe and Asia, Matt took a job in Washington, D.C., working as a computer software troubleshooter for transportation companies. When his firm, Roadshow Inc., had an opening in Melbourne, he applied for it and in a short time was on the road in Australia working as a consultant for a Malaysian Chinese-owned consulting company. If Matt knew anything, he knew a lot about trucks and distance, and to companies in Australia he was quite useful, helping them figure out transportation and distribution problems that were continental in scope. Matthew regularly commuted by air between Sydney, Melbourne, and Auckland, New Zealand. Although the work demands were punishing, Matt found time to join a rowing club on Melbourne's Yarra River and go motorcycling in the outback. "Getting a visa and work permit was not all that difficult," he says. "If a company wants you, they will hire you regardless of nationality." While working in Melbourne, Matt was approached on the Internet by a subsidiary of Roadshow in Johannesburg, South Africa, and offered a job. "By that time," he reflects, "I was getting a little too burned out to relocate to South Africa. This kind of thing shows you what opportunities are out there, though."[13]

THE LAST GREAT PLACE

For Americans the real frontier is New Zealand. To counteract a fall in population in the 1990s, New Zealand has launched an international advertising campaign to attract new migrants, especially college graduates and professionals. According to Max Branford, New Zealand's minister for immigration, the government pulled out all stops to promote the country abroad as a migration destination. Jobs, Bradford stresses, are plentiful for university graduates and professionals. "We have vacancies in most areas. In 1997, for example, eight hundred teachers successfully made the move. We also have jobs in information technology, skilled trades and the medical profession." He said 30 percent of people are not required to have a job offer before applying for immigration. Added Minister Bradford: "We are a small country and our population is falling, but with this new drive we will hopefully make people realize that you can move to New Zealand quite easily."[14] Like Canada, New Zealand operates a migration scheme based on a points system and a pass mark, with most points awarded for occupations, skills, and age. New Zealand's drive for immigrants constitutes a moment of happy convergence for many American would-be expatriates. The type of migrant New Zealand wants happens to be the kind of individual that is leaving America in large numbers. Not surprisingly, in western states like California, with large numbers of disenchanted college-educated professionals, Kiwi immigration offices are busy.

Since 1970 some thirteen thousand Americans have settled in New Zealand to enjoy the good life in the South Pacific. To the first-time visitor to New Zealand, the country seems to combine the qualities of the United States and Great Britain of the 1950s. There is a slowness to the culture, and New Zealand is relatively unaffected by the hectic tempo of modern change. It is a country of great scenic beauty where sheep still outnumber the human population. But it is a safe and decent society, and its national priorities in terms of environment and social policy offer a high quality of life to the citizenry. John Roosen and his wife, Susan Rogers, discovered this when they visited New Zealand in 1992. They were awed by the country's fantastic scenery and impressed with public schools that offered everything to students from forestry to Japanese. The schools, especially, were at the heart of their decision to leave their native California and emigrate. "In the U.S., we open too many prisons and close too many schools," says Susan Rogers. They left because all around them in California they saw the forces of social decay. The school that their children attended was decrepit, and the textbooks they used were out of date and in short supply. The decision to emigrate took great courage and faith. Roosen and Rogers had a thirty-eight-hundred-square-foot home north of San Francisco and a $150,000 annual income. But they decided that the quality of their life was more important than affluence. The family emigrated in 1994, and in New Zealand both parents found jobs and a better life. Their children were enrolled in a school that had ample supplies and challenging teachers. Says John Roosen, now employed as an environmental engineer near Auckland: "America has to understand that if it can't provide citizens with what they need, it will lose more and more of them. We finally captured the American dream. It's just a shame that we had to come to New Zealand to do it."[15]

SUMMARY

Many of today's globe-trotting Americans seem to have gone abroad as a result of reaching an important personal or professional crossroads in their life. It is easier to explain why expatriates remain in a certain country, however, than it is to figure out why they emigrated in the first place. Most of these expatriates who move to Canada, Israel, Australia, or New Zealand are well-trained American professionals who move abroad for economic reasons. Most are repelled by a decline in the wholesale quality of life in the United States and seek a better, safer, and more enjoyable haven overseas. They sense that America has gone too far in the wrong direction in terms of crime, the economy, taxes, and the environment; consequently, they have moved elsewhere. Mostly these Americans are eager to gain experiences from overseas living that are not easily available to them back in the United States. With respect to Australia and New Zealand, many expats are trying to find a lifestyle that seems to have disappeared long ago in the United States.

Chapter 5

Black Exiles and Sojourners

America is a huge fraud, clad in narcissistic conceit and satisfied with itself, feeling itself unneedful of any self-examination nor responsibility to right past wrongs, of which it notices none. It's the kind of fraud that simply wears you out.

Randall Robinson, *Quitting America*

"ANY PLACE BUT HERE": THE CONTEXT OF BLACK EXPATRIATION

African Americans have not, for the most part, been predisposed to leave the country. They have fought and died for America and have endured centuries of slavery and racial oppression to become a major force in the nation's moral and civic life. In the last forty years, the enormity of black achievement in American life cannot be overstated, says Harvard sociologist Orlando Patterson. "A mere 13 percent of the population, they dominate the nation's popular culture." Black achievement, he writes, is today evident in the arts, civic life, and the military; in government as well as in popular and elite literature. Today the black middle class in America is well entrenched, and its offspring will be the leaders of tomorrow's economic transformation. Compared to the mass illiteracy that characterized the American black population fifty years ago, there has been great relative progress.[1]

Such progress, however, is not without its negative aspects. Despite black economic and cultural achievement, nearly a third of all black families are mired in poverty. In most cities the disintegration of black working-class families has led to social pathologies and anarchy that are the despair of the American Republic. Thus, while the upper two-thirds of the black community move upward, the predicament of the bottom third remains nearly insoluble without a major redistribution of wealth in America. When whites and blacks lived apart, there was little opportunity for conflict. Now that they are coming together in an increasingly desegregated society, they have more opportunity to criticize and judge each other.

Today, argues Professor Patterson, there is a "strange tendency to more loudly lament the black predicament the better it gets." This is the "paradox of desegregation."[2] Despite the general improvement of black life in this country, residual economic and racial discrimination has produced a cultural despair and spiritual alienation among many blacks that leads them to question whether they really have a future as citizens in this country. Today blacks have few political channels to voice their discontent, and many are suspicious of the American ethos of assimilation and reform. Therefore, despite the growing prosperity of the black community, many blacks are seeking answers in alternative survivalist solutions based on either cultural or physical separation of the races. Louis Farrakhan's Million Man March in 1995 spoke to these feelings of racial pride and cultural despair.[3] Even a black columnist as conservative as Carl T. Rowan sounded the tocsin of racial alarm about the fate of blacks in the United States. In Rowan's words: "We are sliding headlong into terrible racial conflict that will dwarf the Los Angeles riots precisely because the baby boomers have not grown up devoted to racial equality the way we thought or hoped they would. In fact, white youngsters—the children of the baby boomers—have swallowed more of the stereotypes that engender fear and hatred in recent years than at any time I have known."[4]

The paradox of expatriate blacks is that they are the most-rooted Americans in terms of their background and history, yet their sense of alienation is the strongest of recent emigrants. They have bred and bled in America. Often black Americans have something that they wish to leave behind: a humiliating experience, the tensions and problems of life in America, a sense of depression that they can't shake, or a feeling that life has to be better elsewhere. Sometimes blacks leave the country to find their identity as Americans rather than remain categorized as "black Americans." Finally, that black expatriates may be alienated does not necessarily mean they are unhappy. Expatriates generally tend to be a far happier group than anyone imagines. The miserable ones usually go home.

To despair of America is certainly not a new idea in the black cultural and political domain. It is as old as the African American experience itself and has most often taken the form of black nationalism, expatriation, or both. Early in the history of the Republic blacks realized that perhaps America was not the Promised Land. The first blacks to leave America in significant numbers where loyalist African Americans who supported the British cause during the American Revolution. Many came from Virginia, where the British commander Lord Dunmore had promised freedom to any black who joined his army. These blacks later settled in Halifax, Nova Scotia. In slavery days large numbers of former slaves and mulatto offspring of southern planters left America and made their way to England and France, where they carved out new lives for themselves. In France, especially, these multiracial offspring had money and education and circulated with the local elites of Paris as part of a "Creole aristocracy" much in the way that a mulatto elite thrived in New Orleans at this time. African Americans were the settlers and leaders of the new nation of Liberia, the home of many free Negroes from the southern states. Until the Civil War many escaping slaves followed the North Star to Canada, where they established significant black communities in Ontario. Black expatriates settled in the Soviet Union during the 1930s, when their skills were more valued under communism than in their homeland. During the civil rights revolution of the 1960s many blacks left the United States for Ghana, Guinea, and Tanzania. In 1960 the idea of resettlement was not new.

Hoping to create a sovereign nation-state and to formulate an ideological basis for a national culture, early black nationalists like Paul Cuffe (1759–1817) sought the return of the Afro-American population to Africa. Paul Cuffe was a wealthy black merchant and sea captain who had been raised in Massachusetts by a former slave father and an Indian mother. Cuffe's interest in Africa stemmed partly from his father's having been born there. During his life he earned a fortune in the whaling trade with ships manned entirely by blacks, but his wealth was no shield against the racism of his day. By 1815 Cuffe was convinced that the future of American blacks lay in the colonization and regeneration of Africa. Using the business principles that he had learned from his Quaker allies in New Bedford, Massachusetts, Cuffe accepted support where he could find it. This tactic won him the aid of the American Colonization Society, a racist organization determined to rid America of free blacks. It also earned him the condemnation of his own black countrymen and women. Like his white contemporary Thomas Jefferson, Cuffe found it self-evident that black and white populations, especially where many of the former were enslaved or penniless, could not intermingle on an equal basis or merge to form one happy society. From Paul Cuffe through James Forten and other black capitalists, to Robert Allen Young's "Ethiopian Manifesto," to Marcus Garvey and Louis Farrakhan in this century, blacks have dreamed of living away from whites, preferably in another country. Marcus Garvey, especially, captured the hearts and minds of millions of African Americans in the 1920s by championing black cultural independence and a back-to-Africa scheme. And today, despite the great successes of the American civil rights movement and breakthroughs in employment and educational opportunity, the expatriate ghost of Marcus Garvey haunts many blacks. "Any place but here" has often been the operative sentiment of black expatriates who have sought to define themselves outside the context of American racist culture.

From the eighteenth century onward the African American has been part of what one might call "a double diaspora." The larger diaspora has been the scattering of African blacks to the four corners of the planet as a result of the commercial revolution and the slave trade. The smaller or other half has been the dispersion of African Americans to Europe, Asia, and back to Africa. This chapter concentrates on blacks who have left America and examines how black perceptions of America have helped develop an exceptionally strong ethos of expatriation, even though black expatriate numbers have not been large. In particular, this chapter looks at a variety of black expatriates—from writers and musicians to businesspeople and sojourners.

If anything unites African American expatriates of another era with our own, it is that at some point in their lives blacks decided to leave America and reside in another land. Most of them still retained their American nationality when possible. But they found life beyond our shores more fulfilling. In candid moments black expatriates point out that most writing about racial progress in America comes from white authors.

AT HOME IN EUROPE

Ironically, Europe, the birthplace of the slave trade, has historically been more attractive to African Americans than Africa. In part this is because until recently much of Africa was under the control of imperialist white nation-states that were not much interested in black repatriation. Also, it was difficult and expensive to get to Africa in the postcolonial period, nor did skin color automatically guarantee the status of the black expatriate in African societies. Besides, Europe has historically been the traditional refuge of American exiles of all colors.

Through two world wars and the Cold War that followed, African Americans discovered Europe while on military service and stayed to enjoy the splendor of Rome, the racial tolerance and warmth of France, and the clipped civility of everyday life in England. Afro-Americans discovered Scandinavia, where people were predisposed to like African Americans simply because they were black! And today Stockholm has a small but flourishing black expatriate community. This is not to say that

Afro-Americans have not had bad racial encounters in Europe. Racial prejudice is not limited to the United States, and black expatriates living in Europe are sometimes surprised by its virulence. The context of hatred, slavery, and segregation that gave American racism such a raw and devastating edge, however, never flourished in Europe. Many times blacks in Europe never knew whether they were discriminated against because they were black or because they were American or both. But they did know in some inchoate way that life in Europe was easier and better for them than life in the United States. Some, like James Baldwin, the writer and novelist who soared to fame in the 1960s, found that "only through expatriation could they feel themselves free of the omnipresent, insidious, coercive myth of the 'American Negro' and recover their individual humanity and accept their racial heritage in a true perspective."[5]

Black expatriates have held a variety of views on America and had myriad reasons for leaving their native land. Some had been deeply alienated and wanted nothing more to do with their homeland; others had merely opted for a comfortable situation. Some went abroad to discover their blackness and create a new positive self-identity, whereas others went to a new land and discovered how "American" they really were after all. Some expatriates even discovered that as artists and writers they could flourish in totalitarian societies like East Germany, where their work was found useful.

I'LL TAKE PARIS

More than anything else, it was the American preoccupation with race that drove Josephine Baker, the well-known singer and entertainer, into exile and a new home in France. In the 1920s the United States entered one of its more violent stages of antiblack hysteria. The Ku Klux Klan marched down Pennsylvania Avenue in Washington, D.C., and lynch law prevailed in the segregated South. Although black American soldiers had distinguished themselves for bravery on the battlefront during World War I, their lives in postwar America were as violence-ridden and problematic as ever. Many soldiers took their mustering-out pay and returned to France, where they were well received. France remembered their bravery! And Josephine Baker found a ready audience of blacks and whites in the theaters and cabarets of Paris. Baker performed in the Folies Bergere in the 1926–1927 season and soared to fame with her "banana dance." Paris afforded her more acceptance than she had had in the United States when she played on Broadway as a "star" in the 1924 production of *Chocolate Dandies*. Baker's popularity in France never diminished, and during World War II she served in both the Red Cross and the French resistance movement. She was awarded the Croix de Guerre and Medal of the Resistance in 1946. A pioneer in French race relations, Josephine Baker refused to sing in clubs that would not permit an integrated audience. Her performances usually included songs in a number of languages and were an extension of her cosmopolitan view of racial harmony.

Like Josephine Baker, many blacks who ventured to Paris ended up staying there for significant periods of their lives. Paris was a magnet, a tolerant city where black entertainers, writers, sojourners, and ex-soldiers could enjoy a cup of coffee or a glass of wine in a café without being discriminated against because of their color. In Paris, African Americans found new meaning in their existence as black Americans. Although in Paris their expectations of Europe as a color-free society were never fulfilled completely, they found that Afro-Americans were more respected here than in their own society.

Nonetheless, expatriate blacks, especially those who came to Paris, faced many problems. They lost touch with their home community, and through intermarriage with French women they faced a continual crisis of national and ethnic identity. Who were these women that they had married? How could they relate to their own native American experiences? Could the children they were begetting fit into the American mold?

Living abroad in Paris did, however, offer blacks a chance to think critically and examine the direction that they had taken as Americans. It also gave them an opportunity to reflect on the direction that America was taking. On the more mundane level, Paris tested their ability to survive economically. They had to master another language and compete with the native French for daily sustenance. Some expatriates, like Richard Wright, did more than survive. In the words of one critic, the Afro-American artists, writers, musicians, and sojourners who settled in Paris "became legends in their own time, influencing both European and American society and shaping world culture."[6]

The black American's expatriate story in Europe is to a great extent an inversion of the American success story, as historian Tyler Stovall has noted. A group had to *leave* the United States in order to make good.[7] A brief sketch of the careers of three well-known black American expatriates, Richard Wright, William Gardner Smith, and James Baldwin, will explain this inverted success story.

Richard Wright

If Paris in the years following World War II had a "First American" in its African American expatriate community, it had to be the distinguished novelist Richard Wright. As a writer, Richard Wright shared an anger as deep as the waters that his ancestors had crossed from the shores of Africa. As a humanist, Wright felt an idealism reflecting the hopes of a race that defied oppression. As an American, he sought and achieved an identity that was unchained by the pressures of race, conformity, and politics. Simply put, Richard Wright was very much his own man. He had gone into exile in France during the period right after the war when thousands of Afro-American soldiers discovered a racial egalitarianism in France they had never experienced at home. Ironically, it was Gertrude Stein, a white American expatriate, who discovered Wright and introduced him to the intellectual community of Paris. At that time, Wright was on a lecture tour as a guest of the French government. Paris had a much better racial climate at that time than New York City, and inasmuch as Wright was married to a white woman with an interracial child, he found it relatively easy to lay down his burden as an American black man and rediscover himself as an artist. In fact, friends like Ollie Harrington, a black expatriate cartoonist, remarked that in Paris Wright lived a conventional middle-class existence.

Wright and his wife, Julia, became permanent expatriates in Paris in 1947. The financial and intellectual success of his book *Black Boy* gave him the means to live a life he had only dreamed of as a sharecropper's son in Mississippi, and the cultural life of Paris was rich enough to fulfill his interests in the large questions of authority, power, and freedom in the rapidly unfolding postcolonial world. Subsequent visits to Ghana and Southeast Asia convinced Wright that American attitudes towards Africa and Asia were based on false assumptions based on the continued oppression of people of color. In America Wright was tortured by the same racial identity that had driven Bigger Thomas to murder in *Native Son*. In Paris, Wright conjured up in *The Outsider* a new existentialist vision of justice transcending cultural and racial problems. In Europe he managed to write seven books that paid well despite indifferent reviews. He was well known in the city, where his picture regularly appeared in Parisian newspapers.[8]

In the 1950s a series of journalistic assignments took Wright all over the world, and so he was able to see the emergence of the new nations of the Third World. Wright's problem as an expatriate was his continuing rage against America. It would be the task of other blacks to enjoy the refinements of Europe and add to the rich cultural mosaic of the black expatriate community unfolding in France at this time.[9]

William Gardner Smith

William Gardner Smith, a black expatriate journalist from Philadelphia, had a much more difficult time in Paris than his more famous acquaintance, Richard Wright. He had difficulty selling his stories, and although his novels were published, they promptly sank out of sight.

His wife lost patience with his Left Bank life and returned to the United States. Smith seemed condemned to hang out at the Café de Tournon and cadge drinks and small loans from his friends.

The Café de Tournon was a favorite café of black expats like Richard Wright, Chester Himes, and William Gardner Smith. Every day they and native French would gather to drink beer or coffee and to play checkers and chess. On raw winter days in the 1950s, the Café de Tournon served as the unofficial headquarters of black expatriates. Even though the café was dirty with hideous paintings of the Luxemburg Gardens on its walls, it was unofficial home to Richard Wright, James Baldwin, the black cartoonist Ollie Harrington, actor Gordon Heath, and jazz musician Art Simons. Chester Himes wrote the better part of *If He Hollers Let Him Go* from notes scribbled over coffee at the Tournon. In those days it was easy to meet European women, and with the exception of Richard Wright most black expats had white mistresses. The women were usually well educated and connected with the French or German Marxist left.

Throughout the 1950s and well into the 1960s Paris had a relatively small black population of roughly twenty thousand from Africa, the Caribbean, and the United States. In those days there were no "Negro" neighborhoods in Paris; nor were there such places as Negro cafés, restaurants, or barbershops. Black expats enjoyed the freedom of the city. Racial segregation in Paris would come later, starting in the 1970s, and when more recently a deluge of legal and illegal immigrants from Algeria and other developing nations poured into France.

Although blacks like Wright, Himes, and Smith enjoyed the freedom of Paris, they were constantly harassed by the U.S. State Department, which worried about the political implications of having significant numbers of black American intellectuals with Trotskyite or Communist Party connections residing overseas, where they could be part of the Soviet Union's propaganda war against the United States. The U.S. Passport Office thus kept black expatriates on a short leash, renewing their passports for only two years at a time and requiring them to visit the U.S. embassy to swear an anti-Communist oath of allegiance to the United States. When they left Paris, federal agents from the FBI kept tabs on them. Meanwhile, the possibilities of Wright's returning to the United States grew increasingly remote because of his affiliation with the Communist Party and the risk of a subpoena by the House Un-American Affairs Committee. (The Communist Party had been the only group to take a deep interest in Wright's life and had at one time offered to teach him how to write Marxist analysis.) Even in France, Wright and other black intellectuals were under the surveillance of American security organizations, a fact that sometimes prompted Wright to believe that the U.S. government was engaged in a plot to destroy him. Perhaps more than anything else, it was Wright's ability to write about the human condition in the twentieth century, particularly as it applied to the African American, that made him seem so dangerous to American authorities. When Wright died in Paris in 1952, many American blacks in the expatriate community of the Left Bank were convinced that U.S. agents had poisoned him.[10]

Equally harassed by American agents was William Gardner Smith, whose novels about racial apocalypse and the inevitability of socialism did not endear him to J. Edgar Hoover and the FBI. In 1957, under protest, Smith signed an affidavit to the effect that he was not nor ever had been a member of the American Communist Party. But Smith suspected that his real crime was to have been a writer, a journalist, and a member of the Philadelphia branch of the National Association for the Advancement of Colored People.[11] Such experiences pointed out why many American blacks had come to France. Speaking at a conference entitled American Artists and Writers in Paris: Then and Now, Smith said whites came to Paris for the cheap life and artistic stimulation. "I think *we* came for negative reasons. We came because we were pushed out." When Smith was discharged from the army in the postwar period after having been stationed in Germany, there were few jobs in America for black intellectuals. "When I got back to the United States I had the feeling of stifling. The two negative things were politics and race. McCarthy was around; I don't get along very well in that kind of atmosphere."[12] Smith had originally planned to come to Paris for just a year. He ended up remaining twelve years and then taking a residence in Africa before returning to the United States for a short visit. Life was different in Africa, where the visible signs of black sovereignty swiftly struck Smith: black ministers of state, black heads of corporations, black managers of big department stores, and a socialism that "took the context of Africa into account."

Smith's financial problems ended when he secured an English-language editing job at Agence France-Presse, the national news network. A short time later he was offered the position of assistant editor-in-chief for television programs in Accra, Ghana, a position that he accepted with alacrity because by 1963 Africa seemed to be the cutting edge of the freedom movement for colonial peoples. But Smith's honeymoon with the Third World was short lived. He was arrested in Accra and threatened with deportation for his political views. Apparently, airing a radical American black on Ghana television had resulted in American pressure being put on the Ghanian government. Smith feared that the U.S. State Department would confiscate his passport if he returned to the United States, so he returned to Paris and got his old job back at Agence France-Presse and rented a comfortable apartment on the Left Bank. To a great extent, William Gardner Smith's career as an expatriate

Afro-American explains why blacks left America. For twenty-five years Smith remained abroad, where he enjoyed a creative life. Ironically, in the 1960s the Agence France-Presse sent him to the United States to cover stories on the American civil rights movement, accounts that showed the injustice and violence with which American blacks had to contend.

The black American flight to Europe represented a flight away from American society, where many Afro-American intellectuals felt absurd and without an identity. In Europe they came to a certain self-realization. Thus black expatriates could use their American experience to help them to define their culture and their racial heritage without ever intending to become Europeans themselves. American society in much of the twentieth century did a thorough job of alienating black artists and writers, and Europe was much more respectful to blacks in general. Although they did not find a racial haven, Paris was far less racist than America and accepted black expats for what they were. Nevertheless, black expatriates in Europe faced significant problems.

James Baldwin

James Baldwin's career as a writer and an expatriate black intellectual is singularly instructive. Unlike many expatriates, Baldwin devoted a tremendous amount of time and creative energy toward answering the questions "Who am I?" and "Who am I not." For Baldwin, coming of age in New York City during the Depression and World War II, all that a black man in America could become was a "freak or a corpse." People who were holding power over him determined Baldwin's perception of the world and himself. As long as whites had the power, blacks were taught to despise themselves.[13]

Growing up poor and "frog-eyed" in New York City, Baldwin was a talented student who haunted libraries and worked on high school literary projects. At DeWitt Clinton High School in the Bronx, which he attended, there were few blacks and the student body was composed mainly of ambitious and highly articulate Jews who gave Baldwin the intellectual companionship he did not have in his own Harlem neighborhood. Throughout his life, Baldwin's family always criticized him for having white friends; but in high school and later in Greenwich Village, his friends helped him to nurture the great talent that would earn him international acclaim. As he worked at a series of dead-end jobs by day and continued to write at night, Baldwin had increasing difficulty communicating with other blacks. He didn't seem to have a place. France would give Baldwin that place he so yearned for. Even though Baldwin frequently commuted between France and the United States, after 1948 France would be the place that nourished his art and his spirit.

When James Baldwin arrived in Paris in November 1948, he had $40 in his pocket and a restless urge to write. His money quickly ran out, though, and in Paris the unknown and poor writer often hung out in dirty cafés with similarly dispossessed expatriates from Algeria. In Paris Baldwin could get a good meal for seventy-five cents at a café and a hotel room with dirty sheets for a dollar a night. His money didn't last long, however, especially since he spent a fair amount of time hanging out at the trendy Deux Magots, a café in the Latin Quarter. Financial desperation and sickness set in, forcing Baldwin to sell his typewriter and his clothes. An intellectual quarrel with fellow black expat Richard Wright left him cut off from his more financially stable colleagues on the Left Bank who did not wish to offend Wright. At critical times a young actor named Marlon Brando lent Baldwin small sums of money to tide him over when he became desperate. But Baldwin's money problems haunted him. And since his hotel room had no heat, he spent most of his time loitering in Algerian cafés. The French ignored him, and so he had to come to terms with himself alone.

Baldwin did find friendship and love in Paris in the form of Lucien Happersberger, a Swiss painter determined to make it in Paris after running away from his comfortable bourgeois family life. During their early friendship Baldwin suffered a nervous breakdown. Who was he? Who was he not? The questions that had plagued him in Harlem nearly ended his life in Paris. Happersberger took Baldwin back to Switzerland to recuperate; and after that, the old identity nightmare receded into a mental file cabinet where Baldwin could deal with it intellectually rather than emotionally. Also, it was during this time that Baldwin realized that he had to come to terms with himself.[14] He could not reject his past. Rather, it was that past that had to nurture his growth as an artist; this was the path to survival. Baldwin soon enjoyed great success with the 1956 publication of *Giovanni's Room*, a novel about European homosexual life. After the publication of this book, recognition would follow. Baldwin would never again have to sit in a miserable café, fearful that the French police would arrest him for some petty crime, as they had the time he had been falsely accused of stealing a hotel bed sheet. He returned to the United States for a few years to eke out a freelancer's existence as a journalist and public speaker and to get actively involved in the civil rights movement in the South. Sitting on a comfortable patio in Corsica while writing his book *Another Country* did not make sense to him when the country of his birth and his people faced mob violence. "Everybody was paying their dues," he later wrote, and it was time I went home and paid mine."[15] In America Baldwin quickly became a spokesman on race, and it was then that his fame as a writer and speaker skyrocketed.

Yet Baldwin realized that he could not write in the United States. For that, he had to return to Paris. Baldwin the protester and orator returned to fight the good fight of the civil rights movement. Baldwin the writer never returned to the United States. During this time, also, in 1962, Baldwin went to Africa. Although too much an American to have any sense of homecoming, he shrewdly observed that anticolonialism and the struggle for civil rights in Mississippi were part of a worldwide struggle. At the time of President Kennedy's assassination, in November 1963, Baldwin circulated in the highest intellectual circles in France and the United States. Later, his villa at Saint-Paul de Vence overlooking Nice and the Mediterranean would be an important salon for writers and artists of all colors. With increasing black estrangement and escalating protests over the war in Vietnam, Baldwin began to question his own ability to lead in a society that was breaking down. "Everybody in this country is desperate and crazy," he wrote at this time. "Everybody in this country is strung out ... and their whole ambition is to make you part of it." To Baldwin, America at the time of the Kent State Massacre seemed to be going crazy. There was no air for him to breathe as a writer, he felt, and he returned to France, where he always felt happier and more creative.[16]

What mattered most to Baldwin when he lived in France was that there he was always treated as an "American," not as a black man. Even when harassed in a Swiss village by children who had never seen a black man, Baldwin felt that he could be comfortable in Europe. At least no one in Europe was trying to kill him. There were no nightriders in Swiss villages. To live in America was, for Baldwin, to be "trapped in history." In Europe, where he had no history, he was free to reconstruct himself.[17] In his important essay "The Negro at Home and Abroad," Baldwin wrote that racial prejudice in Europe "is not news." One did not have to look very far to find the Europeans' unconscious assumption of racial superiority. At least, according to Baldwin, Europeans deal with the black man in terms of who he is, rather than what he is. Basically, Baldwin argued, in Paris even a black man is still a man, whereas in America a black man is a problem, a freak that no one wishes to deal with.[18]

Also, America, Baldwin believed, has always had difficulty dealing with men and women of education and strong conscience. America is "distrustful of the independent mind," Baldwin wrote. Further, this distrust becomes profoundly menacing when it comes to dealing with educated and principled blacks. Blacks are either freaks or corpses in the United States, Baldwin argued, and a black person with an independent mind ultimately ends up dead. Baldwin resolved to leave America because he was convinced that he would die if he remained. Either whites would take out their animosity on him, or he would avenge himself for four hundred years of hatred and oppression. His death would result either way.

Unlike William Gardner Smith and Richard Wright, however, Baldwin did not hate America. The United States was the place of his roots, the place of his people, a people that meant more than just race or color. Of America and his own expatriate experience, Baldwin once wrote, "It is not necessary to hate this country to have a good time somewhere else. In fact, the people who hate their country never manage, except physically, to leave it and have a wretched life wherever they go."[19] Once Americans got over the myths that their native land was peopled not by heroic ancestors but by people who were as rapacious, intolerant, and as optimistic as any in history, then a real understanding of the meaning of freedom could commence. For Baldwin, this meant that history, particularly America's brutal racial past, was something to be understood and transcended. Heritage does not liberate, and all the myths of heroes seeking freedom cannot save the American. "A person's freedom can only be judged in terms of his flexibility, his openness to life; it is not his situation which makes him free, but himself."[20] In Europe, at a particular time in the history of the United States, James Baldwin found himself.

Black Americans who have come to Paris have really set down roots, says John Williams, a black novelist who visited Paris nearly every year in the 1990s. "It is a very cosmopolitan and beautiful city and it does exude a sense of an entirely different kind of freedom than one finds in the States." Williams cautions, though, that one does have to be aware of France's Third World colonial past and the problems of ethnicity and immigration that occasionally plague Parisian life.

The Black Expat Business Community

But not every black man and woman who comes to Paris is a writer, artist, or musician. Many are business people who work hard in the city and deal with the daily stresses of life in a foreign country. When Patricia Laplante Collins arrived in Paris to enroll in classes at the Sorbonne, she had romantic visions of Josephine Baker's Paris. The boulevard life, the shops, and the local arts scene were intoxicating. Collins believed that somehow Paris would open up new avenues of freedom and spiritual growth. Reality proved different, however. Just as James Baldwin and other blacks found that Paris can be a tough place when you are broke and down on your luck, so too did Patricia Collins find that the real Paris was not exactly romantic. "Any place you live stops being glamorous when you're confronted with day-to-day life," she reflects. Collins was able to capitalize on her previous job in corporate communications in Atlanta to obtain a part-time media consulting position and working papers. She met and married a Frenchman and took out citizenship. She now works as a consultant in establishing networks of opportunity in business and the arts for black Americans in Paris. It takes talent and hard work to succeed in Paris, says Collins, and any expatriate, black or white, who expects to have an easy time in Paris is deluded.

Pamela Grant-Fronval fell in love with a Frenchman while working in the Peace Corps in Dakar, Senegal. That assignment was her first overseas experience, but the diversity of French and African cultures opened up avenues of experience that she had heretofore not known. Returning to Paris with her lover, she married and became a French citizen. Grant-Fronval has been particularly successful as a cofounder of Sisters, an organization that promotes African American culture in France and serves as a support group for black expatriate women. Sisters allows black American women an opportunity to meet and discuss issues that affect their lives in Paris, issues that range from racism to interracial marriages to adapting to the workforce. The number of black Americans living and working in Paris has reached a sufficient critical mass to make it profitable for Grant-Frontval to publish *Black Paris*, a guidebook for American and Caribbean blacks who are new to France. Furthermore, the Sorbonne has a Center for Afro-American Studies that annually sponsors a conference on the impact of African American artists and musicians on contemporary Europe. Thus Paris may be well on its way to becoming one of the most important Afro-American centers outside the United States.

Currently black expatriates in Paris work in most of the city's professions—from restaurant managers to cabaret singers to computer programmers and corporate executives. The one factor that unites these expatriate blacks is their feeling that, for them, life is better in France than it is in the United States. With its extraordinary sense of style, Paris is liberating. African Americans are respected because they are considered as primarily American. Says black entertainer Ammon Moore, who fled rural Georgia: France may not be better than America, "but black Americans feel more comfortable and are respected in this society."[21]

Many Afro-American expatriates immigrate to France to escape the racial labeling that has become so prevalent in American life. A large number of these expats are not black but multiracial Americans, individuals claimed by many groups yet belonging wholly to none in a society that forces them to choose an identity or imposes one. For them, it is easier to live abroad, where the only identity that matters is that of being an American. Alison Perry, a well-educated multiracial professional woman, whose father was black and mother Italian American, finds that mixed-race Americans function more easily abroad than at home. No one knows how many Americans consider themselves multiracial, but the U.S. Census of 1990 identified two million children younger than eighteen whose parents are of different races. It is safe to assume that more than a few of these mixed-race Americans will one day find their way to Paris and a new life in the City of Light.[22]

BUSINESS PEOPLE, JAZZ EXILES, AND SOJOURNERS

The Lure of Africa

After years of coping with American racial prejudices, African Americans are occasionally happy to enter a foreign country where people are predisposed to like them *because* they are black. Also, many blacks leave America simply because, like their white counterparts, they want to see something of the rest of the world. They get jobs, marry, and never return. Tom Feelings, a magazine illustrator, left the United States because he could not find enough work. He immigrated to Ghana, where he found employment on a national magazine. Though far from well paid, Feelings has found steady work and enjoys an openness with people in Ghana that he did not have at home. But his life is different. Standards of morality and behavior are not the same as in America, and an Afro-American must sometimes practice circumspection. But, says Feelings, "Ghana is one of the few places that I know where the racial thing is absent . . . and that's something marvelous." Whites and blacks work together in Ghana. "If Americans want to see integration really working, they should come to Ghana."[23] In recent times a number of politically outspoken black radicals like W. E. B. Du Bois, Stokely Carmichael, and Robert Williams have chosen exile in Africa or Cuba.

Not all black experiences in Africa are happy ones, though. Sometimes they lead to surprise and disappointment in areas of the world where black Americans least expect to find hostility. Today, black American businesspeople are finding a chilly reception in post-apartheid South Africa, where, they find, the differences that separate them from their black South African colleagues are much more profound than the black skin they share.

Johannesburg is currently the showpiece of the new booming South Africa, a South Africa that the new African regime is anxious to showcase to the world as a multiracial model of economic development and black progress. Though there are no accurate statistics, most experts estimate that about five thousand black Americans are presently working in South Africa. Many have come as representatives of the three hundred American corporations that have secured footholds there. But others have come to work for nonprofit agencies or to establish independent businesses. For many, the experience is also a way to escape the difficulties of being black in America. Many American blacks have long been interested in South Africa and its fate; and since the days of the freedom struggle against apartheid, blacks have been emigrating from the United States in the hope of building a prosperous black nation.

Junette Pinkney, a former producer for the *Phil Donahue Show,* came to South Africa to do freelance media work in 1997. She says that being in a country where most people are black has been wonderful for her mental outlook. "There is an enormous psychic relief," Pinkney said. "The American dream never got to be real for me and I'm one of the successful ones. Here, I feel there's the possibility of being truly part of this society, of being at home in a way that America will never be home." Many blacks do have positive experiences, and in many cases their color is an asset. Black South Africans tell journalists that despite their anger toward America, they would rather do business with black Americans than American whites.

The bond that many black Americans feel with Africa is a source of tension, however. Black Americans are not perceived as being part of South Africa because they were not born there and have no family living there. Black South Africans often chide black Americans who insist that they have come "home." South Africa, say natives, is home to South Africans and not to American blacks. Clearly, all the talk of emotional bonds and skin color cannot ignore that American blacks are culturally Americans.

One especially sensitive point of contention is just how much influence the American black community had in ending apartheid. Americans like to take credit for prominent black Americans like Reverend Leon Sullivan, who in 1977 devised a set of principles for American companies doing business in South Africa. In 1978 Sullivan and his political allies in Washington called for corporate withdrawal and disinvestment. South Africans, however, prefer to point to Nelson Mandela and their own freedom fighters in the streets of Soweto who helped destroy apartheid.

American blacks can also be very patronizing, and complaints about this fact regularly surface in the press and on South African television. Peter L. Nyshona, a black South African executive with Iscor, a major steel producer, remarked at a journalist's panel recently that many black Americans come to South Africa with an offensive attitude. "There is always a sense of paternalism, a sense that we can show you the way." Too often American blacks talk about the personal and financial sacrifices that they have made to come to what they refer to as a developing country. Yet, says Nyshona, when black American expatriate businesspeople come to South Africa, they install themselves in the fanciest white neighborhoods with swimming pools and maids.

On a practical, day-to-day level, American black expatriates have to deal with economic realities they were unaware of before they arrived.

Many of the promises that bring them to Capetown or Johannesburg fail to materialize. Loans for business capitalization, for example, are difficult to get. Educated black workers, especially those who are computer literate, are hard to find. Black corporate executives often confront a cultural void in trying to implement business strategies in a country where until recently a black businessperson was a rarity. Also, South Africans often criticize black American expatriates in multinational companies for taking jobs that should be reserved for South Africans. In response to this growing chill toward black Americans in the country, some U.S. companies have decided not to send over any more black executives.

Finally, black expatriates do not have color immunity from the growing crime wave in Johannesburg and other parts of South Africa. Black Americans routinely have their cars stolen just as do white South Africans. They also have to worry about whether they will be held up at gunpoint, in broad daylight, in front of their downtown Johannesburg bank. Small wonder, then, that black American business executives house their families in well-protected white compounds in the suburbs.

Yet, some American blacks are flourishing, particularly those like Charles Moses, an American businessman who served as Governor Mario Cuomo of New York's adviser for black affairs. Moses has a good business consulting practice and valuable skills to offer a country that since 1994 has suffered a huge brain drain caused by fleeing whites. He currently helps American businesses relocate in South Africa. Julia Wilson, another black American, has set up a successful marketing business in South Africa and has lived in Johannesburg since 1994. She says that newcomers have to be willing to listen and learn. One of the services that Wilson's company offers is an intensive professional seminar on how American companies ought to behave if they want to succeed in South Africa. But all too often, reports Wilson, black Americans leave the country in frustration. They have difficulty with local black discrimination and have problems crossing cultures. One friend, Wilson said, was cutting short a two-year contract after only nine months in South Africa and was "practically in tears." He said, "If a black man cannot be accepted here, where can he go?"[24]

All That Jazz

Like American writers of the 1920s who went to Europe and became part of Gertrude Stein's "Lost Generation," American black musicians have been an important part of the black expatriate scene since the time after World War I when musicians like Sidney Becket, Alberta Hunter, Coleman Hawkins, and Louis Armstrong found steady employment in the nightclubs of Paris. Currently many of America's prominent black musicians live and work almost exclusively in Europe, and the program of any European jazz festival reads like a jazz honor roll of black America. Black jazzmen can be found in France, Sweden, Germany, and Eastern Europe and increasingly are finding appreciative audiences, good incomes, and homes in Japan. Jazz greats like Phil Woods, Dexter Gordon, and Bud Freeman reached their mature jazz styles while working overseas.[25]

One of the first lessons that drummer Donald Bailey learned when he arrived in Japan was that Afro-American jazz musicians were liked and respected. "If they want you for a gig, it's not just a phone call," says Bailey. "They invite you out to dinner, like they do with other businesses.... It puts things on a different level. It's all first class." Bailey notes that jazz musicians are paid extremely well in Japan because "they hope you'll come back." Bailey not only went back to Japan several times, he ended up staying. Originally, Donald Bailey was Peggy Lee's drummer; but after he listened to offers from Japanese record producers, he took up residence in Tokyo. "It took me time to get adjusted," Bailey says. "I was kind of angry about being an American. It was something in me, but after that I developed."

Unlike in Paris or Stockholm or Copenhagen, there was no colony of black Americans to keep in touch with in Tokyo. "I was the only black face," he recalled, in his first gigs in the club scene at Ropongi. "There are certain things that you need to be whole. Japan was the first place I went I didn't feel like I was black.... I was treated very well with a lot of respect." In the 1960s and 1970s, jazz was just becoming popular in Japan; today the black jazz scene in major Japanese cities like Tokyo and Osaka is a major cultural fact of life. Japanese fans have branched out to appreciate a variety of new music acts in the clubs of Tokyo. Although Bailey recently returned to the United States, the lessons of his jazz career in Japan remain strongly felt. "When I came back to this country, I could see that there was a big change in me. I learned to deal with people, tolerate different styles, the way they feel their music." Bailey would have stayed longer, but he had immigration and personal problems that could not be worked out. "I would rather be over there and live as a human being and be appreciated as a jazz musician," he reflected in a 1992 interview. "I had more friends over there than I ever had in my life.... In this country, it'll be a long while before we get there."[26] Black jazz continues to thrive in Japan. So much so that Michael Coleman, a black expatriate and music fan, writes a regular column on Japan's African American arts scene, called "Tokyosoul," for the *Japan Times*.

In an upscale suburb of Brussels, black jazz pianist Mal Waldron knows what "getting there" is all about. Unlike those he once knew in the United States who were interested primarily in money and material comfort, Waldron is interested in experience. He has lived and played jazz in Europe since 1958. Waldron emigrated from his homeland to live and work in Europe, though he had no steady job lined up, and he never looked back. He moved there for the quality of life. For Waldron, the important thing was to escape the alienation-induced drug scene. Drugs were the medium of introduction and employment in American jazz at that time, Waldron recalls. "If you didn't shoot up heroin in the afternoon, you would probably not play on the record date that night. The whole set up in America was very bad.... Eventually I over-dosed.... I needed shock treatments and a spinal tap to bring me back. So I just got out of there." Waldron started out in Europe as an accompanist to John Coltrane, Billie Holiday, and other jazz singers. He then found a niche of his own and for more than twenty years played in the jazz clubs of Munich, where he became a popular music idol. Later Waldron settled in Japan, married a Japanese woman, and amassed a sizable holding in apartment real estate. The rents tide him over during lean periods. At age seventy Waldron embarked on an important three-week jazz tour of Japan with his wife, ex-wife, children, and grandchildren. While in Hiroshima on the anniversary of the atomic bombing of the city, he performed "White Road, Black Rain"—his piece for voice, flute, and piano—which was a protest against nuclear weapons. As a child learning classical piano, Waldron concluded that he had to break the rules if he was to become a good musician. When he grew older, he realized that jazz enabled him to make his own rules. Yet he never learned how to survive in America, where the racial rules of his time seemed to suffocate him. But America is part of the past, Waldron reflects. He now is very much alive in Europe. At age seventy-three Waldron has his music to interest him and seven-year-old twin sons to keep him physically active. In residence abroad, Mal Waldron has found what he calls "an affirmation of life."[27]

Sojourners and Searchers

Such dilemmas as faced by Mal Waldron raise anew the question that James Baldwin posed when he first came to France: Who am I? Who am I not? Clearly, the race conundrum that haunts black Americans does not cease when they cross the borders of their native land. Rather, it takes a variety of shapes and raises angles of vision that are at once both liberating and depressing. "K.B.," an affluent black college student, found his own answer to the question while studying abroad in 1996. While attending school in India, as the only black person among a group of American students he asked the Indian students, "What matters most, the color of my skin or my nationality?" Wherever he traveled on the subcontinent, he says, "It was my nationality that mattered most to them. To them I was an American and my being black really did not matter to them. It was the first time I had ever felt like a real American. I had to see myself through someone else's eyes to understand what it meant to be an American."[28]

In the 1960s black artists began to migrate from the United States to what were welcoming centers in Scandinavia. For example, singer Mattiwilda Dobbs established an operatic career in Stockholm. Dobbs, who married a Swedish journalist, found Stockholm to be the perfect combination of "the progressiveness and efficiency of America combined with the fine old qualities of Europe." As a ballet instructor in Helsinki, Diane Gray established a comfortable life and devoted her spare time to reading Afro-American writers so that she did not forget who she was. Both Gray and Dobbs found what has been consistently true over the years. It was easy for an Afro-American expatriate to live in Finland and Sweden.[29]

Expatriate racial epiphanies can take a variety of forms. When Vicki Radden, a black American, followed her white boyfriend from college in San Francisco to his homeland of New Zealand, she believed that she had found love and a bit of heaven in her new country. Radden had long dreamed of New Zealand's green rolling hills, lush pastures, sheep, and fjords, and was not disappointed. What she did not expect to find, however, were strong antagonisms between the indigenous Maori Polynesians and the whites of New Zealand. Although New Zealand was far safer than the United States and considerably more serene than most Western nations, racial tensions and problems worsened during her stay. People, she wrote, "reacted first to my being an American, and then to the fact that I was black. This was a new but not altogether refreshing experience, as white New Zealanders would often complain to me about the Maori, using the same racist terminology I'd heard about black Americans back home." One day she told a farmer who had been speaking abusively about the Maoris: "Look at the color of my skin. Whose side do you think I'm going to be on?" Radden ultimately broke off her relationship with her boyfriend and took a job working in a Maori rape crisis center, where she gained firsthand knowledge of the deplorable living and working conditions of the Maoris. Radden ended up loving the food and the pristine, unpolluted scenery of New Zealand. Yet, apart from the Maoris, she did not have much enthusiasm for New Zealanders.

Ultimately Vicki Radden, too, had to answer Baldwin's question. Who was she? She concluded that she was the sum of what she valued and believed in, and those values could be sketched in neither black nor white. This sadder but more experienced black American decided to immigrate to Japan and made a home there as a journalist, teacher, and novelist.[30]

Recently one of the most prominent African Americans in the United States quit the country and moved to St. Kitts in the Caribbean. For years Randall Robinson was well known in the United States and abroad as president of Trans Africa, a human rights organization that focused on improving American foreign policy toward Africa and the Caribbean. Articulate and well connected, Robinson flourished in the highest circles of Washington policy-makers. He helped craft policy toward South Africa that ultimately contributed to ending apartheid. But after 2000 Robinson grew restless in America, and his decision to immigrate to his wife's family home in St. Kitts in the Caribbean was an indictment of white attitudes toward blacks in America. After decades of struggling against racism in his homeland, Randall Robinson simply had had enough.[31] In his book *Quitting America*, Robinson writes that the "erosion of those ideals of equity and compassion which are the written tenets of any democracy" disillusions him. Whereas he was once optimistic about America, now he sees only "unregulated greed."

Robinson has gone to St. Kitts to build a house and live on land that his wife has owned since she was sixteen. On St. Kitts he will not have to worry about entertaining and influencing white people. He will not have to worry about the fact that in the United States whites "control the instrumentalities of national, if not global information." He will not have to worry about soaring black unemployment or about white wealth, which is ten times that of African American wealth. Although Robinson retains his American citizenship, he recognizes the crucial difference between the country of his recorded birth and the country of his heart. He wishes that the two could be the same. He writes, "I have only left America, and not the country that I love—the country of Africans in America where my mother lives."

For most of his life Randall Robinson fought for Africans' civil rights in the United States and abroad. He fought the good fight. His accomplishments in the struggle for human rights are amply documented. But he has stopped trying to love America and has embraced the nation of St. Kitts as his new homeland. For Robinson, being a black expatriate has become "a measure of unexpected contentment."[32]

SUMMARY

Blacks have always had a strong sense of identity; what they have not had is the feeling that they can be comfortably incorporated into American culture. The answer to why blacks have left America is embedded in the country's racist experience and has been echoed by black expatriates since the time of the American Revolution, when first black loyalists left Virginia for Nova Scotia. On personal and intellectual levels, from jazz artists to novelists and business people, many blacks have been profoundly alienated by America. They are torn and estranged, often involved in self-doubt and a search for a heritage that has been withheld from them. What black expatriates have found is that a life abroad is hardly utopia. Black expatriates have had their share of difficulties overseas. They have experienced racial discrimination, been hounded by their own government, and often been in danger of losing touch with the sustaining forces of the black community back in the United States. But they have done more than survive. Their experience has allowed them to leave the American scene and look at American society from the outside. For many, expatriate life has been much more comfortable than the life they had experienced in the United States. Even now, at a time in the United States when the material and political conditions of the black population are improving at exponential rates, many African Americans, as Randall Robinson has noted, are finding that the struggle to remain a native son is no longer worth the effort because racism is so firmly embedded in the entire structure of national life. The Afro-American experience abroad, Ernest Dunbar wrote, allows blacks "a chance to live an existence beyond race, beyond nationalisms, beyond ideologies."[33] For black Americans, the more practical aspect of earning a living while abroad has seldom been as significant as finding a country or a people where a black American's quest for a better lifestyle could bear fruit. The moral embrace of racial integration in America seems neither plausible nor desirable. Thus, African Americans are keeping the dream of a racial liberation alive through emigration. Abroad there is at least the chance for a dialogue of survival between whites and blacks. At home there is only the dialogue of the deaf.

Chapter 6

Women Expatriates

*I am called an expatriate. As if I have scrawled an X on my patria, my father-
land, and moved on.*

Janet McDonald

NEW ROUTES TO SUCCESS

One of the most important developments on the expatriate archipelago
has been the increase in the number of women who are leaving their
native land for life abroad as writers, businesswomen, teachers, and
entrepreneurs. They are expanding professional opportunities for themselves as well as for women of their host countries; and their lives across
cultures are simultaneously rewarding, challenging, and difficult. Women
as expatriates offer a new dimension to the story of expanding gender
spheres because they are internationalizing the American feminine experience. It would be wrong, however, to give the impression that male and
female expatriate experiences are totally different. The differences may be
more of degree than kind. Expatriate women tend to be just as well educated and upwardly mobile as their male counterparts. But the experiences they encounter tend to be more problematic and are resolved in more
novel or creative ways. Also, women have demonstrated a strength and
resiliency overseas that stems from their struggle against discrimination
in the workplace and their having known downward mobility sometime
in their lives. They have a strong instinct for surviving tough times.

Today women are climbing the ladder of power and responsibility
within American corporations by accepting highly visible overseas
assignments. As Ronald Inglehart and Pippa Norris have pointed out,

the move from industrial to postindustrial societies has generated substantial gains for gender equality in the public sphere and work-place. In turn, cultural changes lay the basis for support for public poli-cies that reinforce and accelerate the process of gender equality and mobility.[1] Today, writes Janet McDonald from Paris, "the expatriate life is a voyage that has taken me home, a place whose locus is not geo-graphic but visceral." It is abroad that many women now find "an inner experience of liberation and joy."[2]

Women, like men, also occasionally fail. Lifestyle choices can turn sour, and empowerment and responsibility take their toll. Marital status rather than gender is often the greatest problem for expatriate women insofar as many societies in Europe, Asia, and Latin America treat being single as a liability. Often foreign businesspeople do not know how to comfortably fit a single person into their social lives.

EXPATRIATE WOMEN IN HISTORICAL PERSPECTIVE

Until recently, the role of American women in the expatriate story was largely ignored. In part this was because the common vision of the American expatriate as the disenchanted Hemingwayesque writer filled the cultural canvas. Other than Gertrude Stein and Alice B. Toklas, women expatriates were mentioned only in passing as spouses and drinking buddies of writers and party boys like F. Scott Fitzgerald and Harry Crosby. According to the prevailing stereotype, American women expatriates had nothing inherently interesting to add to an ongoing dialogue of lifestyle change, exile, and political and cultural dissent. Often women abroad were portrayed as nothing more than "spoiled spouses."

Once ignored, women expatriates are now being rediscovered. Their careers show a diversity and liveliness that more than equals that of their male counterparts. Both then and now, women abroad have con-stituted an exceptionally diverse segment that has ranged from sexual and cultural rebels, to missionaries and idealists, to hard-driving busi-ness executives. Europe and Asia have been social laboratories where women were free either to lose or remake themselves. In turn, women have made a distinct contribution to the special alchemy and ambience of expatriate life.

The first women American expatriates fell into one of three major cat-egories in the nineteenth century, when the economic growth of the United States enabled American families to broaden their horizons beyond the American shore. Aside from the usual spousal role as the wife of a diplomat or businessman, American women ventured abroad in search of a social climate more in tune with their personal and cultural needs. After 1880 the first major wave of American women appeared in the capitals of Europe as trophy wives. Like the wealthy Jenny Jerome, who married Randolph Churchill and sired a world leader, or the Vanderbilt family, whose daughters married into the British aristocracy, these women provided the fortunes to uplift an aristocracy that was high in prestige but financially distressed. Europe had what the industrial barons of the United States so desperately needed for their families, the aura of power, privilege, and respect that money alone could not buy. But American women of wealth and education also came to Europe in a search of love and art that had the sharp edge of sexual rebellion to it. Harriet Hosmer, the American sculptor, Djuna Barnes, writer and journalist, and Sylvia Beach, Paris bookseller and publisher of *Ulysses*, were unapologetic lesbians at a time when such conduct was taboo in America.

Edith Wharton, cool-headed observer of society's ironies, flung herself into a dalliance with English journalist Morton Fullerton, who at the time was engaged to his first cousin, while Wharton neglected her own clinically depressed husband. In the 1920s, flapper Caresse Crosby shared the opium highs and sexual excesses of her poet husband, Harry Crosby, and then managed their Black Sun Press after his suicide.

In late nineteenth-century Asia, American women played an important role as Protestant missionaries. In China at this time 60 percent of all missionary volunteers were American women. They encountered numerous obstacles in the profession of their faith, the most notable being the fear and hostility of Chinese men, who were repelled by feminine white skin that to them had a ghost-like quality. Most of these missionaries worked as teachers, nurses, and church administrators. Women missionaries worked among lepers and fought a constant battle against the filth of the countryside and the grim fatalism of the peasant population. According to a recent study, these American missionaries wrote that they encountered diseases and social situations that they thought had existed heretofore only in the Bible.[3]

Pearl S. Buck grew up in this missionary-teacher milieu. She was raised in China and learned to speak Chinese before English. As the daughter of missionaries, Buck remained in China for nearly thirty years and taught English at the University of Nanking. When war and civil strife broke out in China in the 1930s, Buck returned to the United States to write *The Good Earth* and other memorable novels of daily life in China. In 1938 she became the first woman writer to be awarded the Nobel Prize.

Pearl S. Buck was one of many American women writers abroad who worked to change cultural perceptions and broaden the sphere of inquiry on the nature of the human condition. They "pushed the envelope" of experience for challenges and opportunities that allowed them to transcend the limits imposed on them by culture and gender. In many ways they resembled Martha Gellhorn, the third wife of Ernest Hemingway.

Martha Gellhorn was a hard-drinking, tough journalist for *Collier's* magazine in the 1930s who had published a novel and several short stories. She had a strong desire to fight against General Franco and the fascists in Spain and was daring in her reporting. Starting in 1937, when she arrived in Madrid with nothing but a knapsack, $50, and an assignment from *Collier's*, Gellhorn brought the horrors of the Spanish Civil War into the homes and public reading rooms of America. She was also stunningly beautiful, and Ernest Hemingway fell for her when the two met in Key West, Florida. A tempestuous affair ensued; and in 1940, at the end of the Spanish Civil War, Hemingway divorced his wife Pauline and married Gellhorn. The union, however, proved to be one of the shortest and least understandable of Hemingway's four marriages. Gellhorn was a fiercely independent, stormy woman. In a matter of months she left Hemingway in Cuba and went off to Europe to cover the war against Hitler. Despite Hemingway's supposed reputation for courage, it was his wife who got into the war first. Later Hemingway came to Europe as a foreign correspondent for American magazines on his own terms and at his own time. While in the confines of British pubs and French cabarets, Hemingway boasted about hunting, bullfighting, and wars, Martha Gellhorn slogged along with the GIs on the battlefront.

To her annoyance, Gellhorn discovered that the only wound that her husband received during World War II was a head injury in a civilian car accident. Martha returned from the front to see him, and instead of comforting the banged-up Hemingway, she simply laughed at his pathetic state as he lay in the hospital. That was the end of Martha as far as Hemingway was concerned.

Martha moved on with the battlefront. After their divorce Martha Gellhorn was always the reporter who covered civil wars in Europe and Asia and walked in the path of danger. She wrote the big stories about the Nazi concentration camps and was with the Allies when the troops liberated Dachau. In 1989, at the age of eighty-one she was still an intrepid foreign correspondent and left her home in Wales to be out on the front reporting the U.S. invasion of Panama.[4]

As writers, American women continue to thrive in Europe. The *roman à clef* novels of Diane Johnson, like *L'Affaire* and *Le Divorce* (Penguin Books), reveal a Paris-based writer's intense American fascination with the French and their culture. The mystery novels of the late Patricia Highsmith captivated American audiences even though this dark and brooding London-based novelist did not care much for her readership. Highsmith's novels like *The Talented Mr. Ripley* and *Ripley Underground* (Everyman's Library) continue to gather appreciative audiences on both sides of the Atlantic. Today the mystery writer Donna Leon is growing in international popularity. She bases her mysteries in Venice around the detective Commissario Guido Brunetti, a food-loving Italian with a rich professorial wife. Inspector Brunetti seeks to understand modern Italy by reading Cicero for moral direction, and it is with Inspector Brunetti that Leon takes her readers on brilliant historical and sociological odysseys. Her novels are punctuated with dark observations about corruption in Italian politics and society. In *Death in a Strange Country* she also seems to have little regard for American tourists or the military commanders who run the U.S. Armed Forces bases in Italy. Her recent book *Through a Glass Darkly* (Grove Press), her fifteenth novel, examines Italian crime through the prism of the Murano glassworks of Venice. Like Jonathan Carroll, she became popular as a writer and best-selling novelist in Europe long before she achieved recognition in the United States. Leon moved to Europe to teach English on military bases in Italy for the University of Maryland and never returned. She writes of a Venice that is sadly sinking in a sea of tourism, with the waters of the Adriatic rising every year.

EXPATRIATE WOMEN AND ADVENTURE

In recent times it has been relatively easy to find adventurous American women. During the Vietnam War, for example, hundreds of American nurses risked their lives to give medical assistance and comfort to soldiers who had been wounded in the rice paddies.[5] Such adventurous American women are regularly seen in the media as television correspondents from the war zone of Iraq, and in International Red Cross relief and rescue programs. They work in harm's way in the danger zones of Africa and the Middle East. Many women join the Peace Corps for unique opportunities in underdeveloped countries.

Daphne Topouzis is part of that tradition. She left the comparative safety of life in New York City to work as a journalist in Senegal. Originally, she ventured to Senegal to research how French colonial rule had affected black politics in Africa in the 1930s and 1940s. She found in Dakar a life far different from anything she had experienced in American middle class life. Despite bouts of malaria, fears for her personal safety, and frequent troubles with the Senegalese government, Topouzis stayed on to found *Africa Report*, an American bimonthly magazine of African affairs. She never knew whether her dispatches would get her deported or thrown in jail. In addition to adjusting to different foods and a different language, Topouzis had to get used to a different social construct—polygamy. The Senegalese found the fact that she was unmarried and without children to be a source of amazement. Topouzis was also forced to deal with a near total lack of privacy and, as she explains, "their unshakable belief that, being white, I had an inexhaustible supply of money."[6] Topouzis went on to earn a PhD in sustainable development and worked for years for the United Nations on issues such as women's poverty and AIDS in Africa. After several years of development work in Kenya, Topouzis settled in Rome, where she serves as a consultant to the United Nations.

Often women expatriates, like their male counterparts, choose to take the difficult path. Adrienne Su, an American of Chinese descent, for example, could have taken advantage of her citizenship and her money to lead a privileged life in China. Instead, she followed a more arduous route, living in China like an average citizen. She slept on planks on Chinese trains rather than take the "soft sleeper" train reserved for foreigners. She was often ignored, put last in line, and even pushed around. But she had a chance, in the 1990s, to see China as few Americans ever would. Even more difficult than the attitudes of the Chinese toward her were the attitudes of her fellow Americans. "When I came across other white Westerners on the road," she writes, "their attitude towards me was high-flown and condescending until I spoke English. It wasn't entirely their fault: the environment had deluded them into seeing the Chinese as less than people." The one thing that Adrienne Su did learn about China, however, was how easy it was for a foreigner to be overwhelmed and helpless in the face of Chinese culture and the problems of coping with everyday life. "You can quickly become overwhelmed by a language you do not properly comprehend and by customs hemispheres from your own." In the end, Adrienne Su adjusted to Chinese life and spent a long time at Fujan University in Shanghai.[7]

The experiences of Daphne Topouzis and Adrienne Su illustrate that the world has plenty of hazards for a woman traveling alone. In Muslim countries, especially, single expatriate women are often viewed as little more than prostitutes. Indeed, practically every expatriate woman can tell her share of stories about being robbed, sexually menaced, accosted, or "felt up" while living overseas.

For years Barbara Adams lived a successful expatriate life in a large house in Kathmandu next to the Royal Palace of Nepal. Living literally on top of the world, she served as a consultant for travel agencies and film companies on location in the Himalayas. Hers was a curious route that began when she was a middle-class college girl living in Washington, D.C. Her father was an affluent stockbroker who sent her to Georgetown University and language school in the 1950s. At graduation she was supposed to join the Social Register, but Barbara opted for the life of a backpacking international beatnik and eventually found her way to Rome and a job as a magazine writer. Hers was a bohemian reaction against the smug materialist world of Eisenhower-era conservatism. Whileo in Rome she met and married an Italian photographer who took her on assignment to Kathmandu, which was just about as far away from Washington as one could get in this world. "Kathmandu then was the most beautiful place on earth," Adams said. "The Nepalese were totally innocent and in awe of everything.... It was like walking through a museum, except virtually all of these treasures were still in use." Prowling the streets of Kathmandu by foot and bicycle, Adams marveled at the strange costumes of the men and at the local women in saris, wearing bangles on their wrists and feet and jewels in pierced noses.

At the time that Adams and her husband arrived, the royal government of Nepal was beginning to make major economic and diplomatic contact with the outside world. As foreigners with press cards, Barbara and her husband were swept into the social world of embassy functions, state dinners, and audiences with the royal family. Representing King Mahendra of Nepal at this time was his brother Prince Basundhara, a suave British-educated diplomat. Although the prince had been married since the age of thirteen, he did not let these formalities get in his way and became an avid suitor of the also-married Barbara Adams. Adams's chagrined husband returned to Italy in a huff, and Barbara, to the consternation of the royal family, remained in Kathmandu as the guest of Prince Basundhara. Barbara Adams was soon installed as the prince's concubine. By Nepalese law their union had the legal status of man and wife. Soon the co-ed from Georgetown was accompanying her lover on tiger hunts in India and received the same honors as any lady of the royal house. Bored and looking for a project, Adams convinced her prince to build a tourist hotel, the Hotel Royal in Kathmandu, an idea that received the enthusiastic support of the king of Nepal. The hotel business now mixed in with Barbara Adams's life of polo tournaments and meetings with President Jimmy Carter and India's Prime Minister Nehru. It was a challenging and bewildering life compounded by the problems of the prince's chronic alcoholism. After a ten-year union, the prince succumbed both to strong drink and a heart attack, and the couple separated.

After the prince's death, Barbara Adams found herself penniless. She had to work hard against being deported on the wishes of the prince's vindictive first wife. By the 1960s, the hippies and the flower children had discovered Nepal. Their drug use and orgies gave Americans in Kathmandu a bad name, and so the king wanted the Americans removed from his country. Stereotyped with the hippies, Adams had to call on every friend that she had in high places to resist immediate deportation. Fortunately, friends came to her rescue, and she remained to start the Third Eye Travel Agency, one of the few Western travel agencies in Nepal at that time.

Barabara Adams lived in Nepal for forty years, and her life in Kathmandu was embroiled in controversy. Well into her sixties Barbara

Adams was a crusading journalist whose news dispatches criticized the royal government for its failure to protect human rights and to care for the country's poor and underprivileged. Openly critical of the Nepalese government, she fought for democratic rights in the country. From her comfortable house in Kathmandu, with its ample garden, Barbara Adams waged a one-woman war to avoid deportation. She soon began to fear for her personal safety. The Nepalease government finally forced her to leave in 2001. She reluctantly sought refuge in New York City. Meanwhile, Adams is still regularly interviewed on television for her perspective on the political and cultural development of modern Nepal.

Kathmandu is no longer the isolated romantic Shangri-la of Barbara Adams's youth. When there are no disturbances and riots, the streets are crowded with tourists and mountain trekkers from Europe and America. Kathmandu nonetheless retains the aura and mystical qualities of the Himalayas.[8]

EXPATRIATE BUSINESSWOMEN

Given the entrepreneurial climate that currently exists overseas, many American women have decided to go abroad and enter business for themselves. Lisa Frankenberg was twenty-three years old and backpacking through Europe when she arrived in Prague and saw the ferment of new business opportunities. In Prague she stumbled across some old college friends from the University of California at Santa Barbara. After writing a free English-language paper for backpacking students called *Prognosis,* she and a friend discovered that they were in the wrong market. The right market was the whole business community of the Czech Republic, which needed to be reported about in Prague and to the outside world. Virtually on a shoestring, Lisa Frankenberg started the *Prague Post,* a business-oriented newspaper that finds more readers who work for Bearing Point Consultants and Coopers and Lybrand Accountants than backpackers. Business proved to be good, and life in Prague was extremely satisfying. Today the *Prague Post* employs approximately one hundred people, boasts some forty-three thousand readers in fifty-nine countries, and is a respected and influential business voice for Central Europe. After leading the paper through six years of steady growth, Frankenberg took a leave of absence to enroll in Harvard Business School. Her experience in Prague led to a job in international sales and marketing for the *Wall Street Journal On-Line.* She retains ownership of the *Prague Post* and has been active in helping to rebuild the Jewish community of the Czech Republic.[9]

Some expatriate women build careers and businesses out of personal and professional necessity. They are usually spouses of expatriate executives. Since they cannot usually work for their husband's firm because of rules against nepotism, they are forced to branch out on their own. On some occasions it is the wife's business that saves an American expatriate family when the husband is either fired or downsized out of a job. Also, more than a few women develop business or professional skills that they can take with them wherever they go. These days the idea of a portable career is an appealing one. Elizabeth Douet has devoted much of her career to studying savvy expatriate spouses. Douet has found these women to be adaptive to the demands of change. One woman, writes Douet, was able to broaden her career into transition and self-development seminars for the expatriate community in Norway. Another American woman started her own catering business in Paris for expatriates. E-mail and telecommuting enable women with critical skills in accounting and information technology to set up businesses in whatever country they are currently living. Determination is the key measure of success for an expatriate woman. Says Douet: "Women who are not fully determined to tackle the additional stresses involved with employment will not succeed. For those who do, however, the ability to work makes all the difference between simply surviving and all out thriving." Women who can find or create jobs in the fields of teaching, writing, health and beauty, technology, secretarial work, and the arts can find employment overseas. "The ability to continue working assures greater self-esteem and confidence, allowing the trailing spouse to become an active partner in each new move."[10] Douet knows what she is talking about, for early on she carved out a successful niche for herself as an American writer living in Norway. Currently Douet lives in London and Hamburg with her French husband and two children and is the U.S. and U.K. director of Expatkit, a nonprofit organization helping families transition to living abroad.[11]

LESSONS FROM EXPATRIATE BUSINESSWOMEN

As the global operations of American corporations continue to expand, a growing number of expatriate managers are women. In turn, firms are learning about the problems and issues that expatriate women encounter. These encounters are helping change the ways companies do business overseas. Explaining the increase in American businesswomen expatriates is fairly easy. First, because in the American corporate world there has been an increase in dual career marriages, many male executives are now reluctant to leave their spouses behind for international assignments. So women are getting expatriate assignments by default. Second, women are now reaching higher levels of management in the American corporation, and there is pressure to send them abroad for much-needed international experience, just as there is with male executives. Also, when Congress passed the 1991 Civil Rights Act, writes

William Scheibal, "it specifically extended Title VII coverage to U.S. citizens working for U.S. employers overseas."[12] This act gives women legal defense against discrimination in expatriate assignments. Unfortunately, it does not take into consideration the beliefs of foreign cultures against which American women must contend overseas. In any event, women executives now have a window of international opportunity that did not exist even a decade ago.

Yet problems remain. American women executives often face difficult working environments overseas largely because they enter traditional male-centered job universes. Even though there have been some cosmetic changes in European companies, executives in overseas corporations have not been exposed to the women's rights legal revolution as have executives in the United States. Excepting in Britain and Germany, companies in Europe as well as Asia have been noticeably reluctant to promote women of their own nationality to executive positions. Also, maintaining an executive in an overseas assignment can easily cost over $300,000 a year, and companies in the past were reluctant to gamble on women executives who might not be able to adjust positively to a foreign situation.

Although there has been a rapidly increasing literature on women in international assignments, very little is known about who they are. In a recent study, "Who Are the Female Business Expatriates," Jan Selmer and Alicia Leung present some interesting findings. Female business expatriates tend to be younger than their male counterparts, frequently are unmarried, and have shorter experience with their employer. Selmer and Leung found that "gender typing" remains prevalent in international companies, which complicates the performance of expatriate women. In many instances American women are sent overseas simply because their company "has run out of male candidates." The researchers also discovered that companies sending American women abroad to work do very little to set up network and mentoring programs for them. "Hence these differences in personal attributes may require a different type of support, and possibly more support, from their companies to facilitate successful foreign assignments of female expatriates."[13]

Given the cost and legal ramifications of employing American women overseas, there has been surprisingly little research on women's job adjustment and performance abroad. Recently the *Sloan Management Review* conducted an extensive survey of expatriate women executives working in Japan, which has a particularly difficult male-centered corporate environment. The Japan data revealed that many female executives who were transferred from their American office to Japan did very well as disciplined professionals. American women working in Japan had higher access to management levels than would have normally been thought. Although some women encountered problems stemming from the conflicts they experienced when asked to perform entertainment duties outside their professional position, these problems decreased over time. According to the *Sloan* study, "The higher the position a woman occupies, however, the less she encounters this sort of role conflict." Also, the data suggest that in Japan skilled American women over age forty were much better able to overcome the doubts of Japanese businessmen about competence or authority.

Living adjustment problems for female executives tend to be just as great if not greater than they are for men. The housing market in Japan is tight, and quarters even at executive levels are not as commodious as in the United States. In addition, language and cultural stress take their toll. But the data suggest that women and men survive these problems best when they have family to support them. Being an American alone in Japan can be extremely stressful regardless of gender. Further, "single women who have dated Japanese men reported too much incompatibility in their role expectations."[14] But the major premise of the *Sloan* study is that if women can work effectively in Japan's rigorous managerial environment, then female American expatriate executives can work practically anywhere abroad. The one great advantage that American women have over men in this context is that they have more skills for building interpersonal relationships. Also, since women historically have had ample experience being excluded from traditional corporate networks, they can work well with rejection and usually overcome it. Japanese American women, however, reported having the worst work experiences as executives in Japan. Japanese men tended to see Japanese American women as "Japanese" and hence tended to see them as less competent and less accomplished.

While research suggests that women need cross-cultural training to survive abroad, training itself is not enough. Women need job support from their parent corporations. To avoid problems, women executives need clear title and job descriptions. And companies have to work harder to eliminate any ambiguity about a woman's status that would undermine her position overseas. Those women whose specific skills have brought them to the attention of an overseas company tend to do best. Those who are sent abroad by their company with the vague title of manager and poorly described responsibilities tend to fare the worst.[15]

Gender discrimination is a constant problem overseas and has been studied by management specialists Cornelius Grove and Willa Hallowell. In their interviews one female expatriate executive summed up her beliefs this way: "You can't expect to walk into a centuries-old culture with its own traditions and beliefs and change it. You've got to be flexible and able to adapt, even when things go against your values. Keep your eyes on the prize. Ask why am I here anyway? Not to make trouble!"[16] Grove and Hallowell point to three attributes that are more

likely to be a liability overseas than being female—being single, being
young, and being culturally American. Many American cultural traits,
Grove and Hallowell point out, like competitiveness and the focus on
time management, "are consciously disapproved by some cultures."[17]

Bonita Bates is a good example of this kind of pragmatic executive
who has to transcend more than gender to survive overseas. When she
was promoted to the position of product sales manager for Asia for a
U.S.-based company, it was a big move for Bates and her boss told her
to pack her bags for Japan. Her territory would be all of Asia, and she
would be traveling extensively. Bates's problems as an African American and business executive began as soon as she landed at Narita Air-
port in Japan. To her amazement, her Japanese male colleagues treated
her like a child, and she was unable to take charge of sales meetings
with her staff, though all of her questions seemed to get answered
eventually.

On a plane to Seoul, Bates shared her frustrations with another American businesswoman and was surprised to find how unsympathetic she
was to her dilemma. From the stranger's viewpoint, Bonita Bates simply
did not know much about Asia, about what people expected in terms of
leadership and hierarchy, how they used time to build relationships,
and the roles they took in meetings or with customers. The stranger's
advice to Bonita Bates as the plane was landing was simple, direct, and
extremely valuable: "Listen, observe, and try to understand the under-
lying expectations and cultural orientations and you'll be fine. Be atten-
tive, humble, and learn from your mistakes." Bonita Bates learned that
what she perceived to be racial or gender discrimination was merely
cultural difference.

In global business today companies and expatriates that pay attention
and concentrate on cultural dimensions see better results in their corporate bottom lines. In Japan, Bonita Bates experienced *kikubari,* or the
concern to protect her from surprises and to make sure that every
aspect of her stay in Japan went smoothly. Directness, as Bates learned,
does not necessarily produce results in tradition-oriented societies.
Bates tried to take control immediately instead of taking several months
gathering information about the work environment and forming relationships with customers and colleagues before actually taking charge.
Out of her Japan experience Bonita Bates came away with an increased
understanding of how cultural awareness in Asia and elsewhere can
determine the success of a woman's managerial leadership.[18]

EXPATRIATE SPOUSES

While women play many roles abroad, that of supportive expatriate
spouse of an upwardly mobile international executive continues to

figure largely. In addition to the dedicated, hard-working women in this sphere, one can also find dependent spouses who lend credence to the myth of the spoiled expatriate. Many of these women receive family allowances and enjoy corporate prerequisites like maids and cooks. In Bali, the Philippines, Hong Kong, and India, for example, American women view their domestic staff as part of the job of being a corporate wife. This kind of support enables expat families to enjoy a millionaire's lifestyle overseas, and many spouses are reluctant to leave it all behind when their husbands are transferred back to the United States. But most often for spouses the reality of life abroad is neither comfortable nor glamorous. These wives are the ones who have to deal with contentious teenagers, haggle with shopkeepers, maintain the house, entertain, and solve numerous domestic problems compounded by difficulties with language and culture.

Cherie Schorning, an expatriate wife who has lived overseas for years, notes that companies usually treat the spouses of expatriate managers as the "caboose" on a long train that gets little attention. "The caboose doesn't get much respect," she says. The expat spouse does not have much of an identity. She was here because her husband was here. All of her transitioning to her new home in Germany was done with little or no help from her husband's company, which assumed that she could work out her problems in the long run. Such assumptions are dangerous, however, especially in Germany, where gray winter skies can cast a depressing turn to life. On many occasions unhappy, alienated corporate spouses have torpedoed expensive expatriate executive assignments. Schorning found friends on Internet communities like AOL, which were a wonderful source of information and insider tips from other expats who experienced the same problems and challenges.[19]

Often female spouses suffer under the burden of misplaced intentions. Barbara Fitzgerald Turner, the wife of a career manager who lived in Indonesia, compiled a rich dossier on things that companies do to make an expatriate wife's life miserable. Companies don't give much "predeparture assistance," and they don't give much cross-cultural training, preferring to "throw dollars" at inconvenient problems. Sometimes spouses would be content with a simple apartment in a foreign country with language lessons thrown in. Also, Barbara Turner had to go to the bank constantly to exchange money, since her husband was paid in American dollars. Banks seemed to have their own rules about converting dollars.[20]

Jacquie Luce, an American married to a hotel executive, never imagined that she would end up living in Russia and enduring unbearable stresses. After living in Aruba for two years, she and her husband John were transferred to Moscow, where he became general manager of the Moscow Radisson Slavjankaya Hotel. After Aruba, moving to Russia was like moving to a frontier town of the old American West. Says Mrs. Luce: "One of our waiters handed the patron a check and the Russian patron said 'if you bring me that I will kill you.' The patron opened his coat and showed his gun. That was the end of the discussion. It's their country." In Moscow the Luces found no patent laws, no civil laws, only a general anarchy where anything could happen at any time. Thus the Luces had to explain at business meetings and social gatherings that the investment of a multimillion-dollar Radisson Hotel in Moscow was more at risk in Russia than a hotel would have been in a strife-torn Third World country.

Shortly after Mrs. Luce's arrival in 1996, a Radisson business partner, Paul Tatem, was shot and killed in Moscow. Many of his associates believed that his death was an outgrowth of business friction with the Moscow city government. Afterward, when John Luce was threatened by men with guns, he listened to his worried wife and hired a team of bodyguards. Meanwhile, although Mrs., Luce was not on the hotel pay-roll, she lived twenty-four hours a day in the hotel and worked beside her husband. Jacquie Luce summed up her experience in Moscow thus: "Americans have it pretty easy. They don't understand what it is to be dependent on others. In Russia the cowboys are running around with guns. The person who is the most clever, brave, and unstoppable, is the one benefiting."[21]

Expatriate wives, however, are a diverse community. Wallis Wilde-Menozzi writes, "One observation I hold about expats living in Italy is the ones who stop or stay encompass a variety of motives. The majority who stay are women." Italy has provided Wilde-Menozzi "a space onto which one grafts new roots."[22] Some expats, like Nadine Lichtenberger, came to Europe just to study and then decided to remain abroad indefinitely. After graduating from college at the University of California at Fullerton, Lichtenberger took the obligatory two-month trip to Europe. Her appetite whetted by foreign experiences, she enrolled in a private study-abroad program at the University of Salzburg. It was here that she met and married an Austrian. "In addition to being head over heels in love with Bernhard," she reflected, "I was fed up with California, anxious for a change of scenery, interested in carving out a new life." She soon began enjoying that new life as a spouse and teacher of English in Linz, Austria; she ultimately parlayed that assignment into a permanent job at Johannes Kepler University. She and her husband happily expanded their family with two children and settled into a comfortable life in Austria. Their children are being raised bilingual without difficulty.

Each year the possibility of Nadine Lichtenberger's return to live and work in the United Sates becomes more remote. "It's not in the stars," she reflects. Austria is beautiful and comfortable. Lichtenberger and her husband know that they would not be able to live as well socially or economically in California as they do in Austria. Also, Austria is much safer. "I'm not saying Austria is crime free, but in comparison to what goes on in the States, I feel it's a safer place to live."[23] But she recognizes that Austria is becoming more diverse with large Turkish populations. Being of Indian ancestry (her parents immigrated to the United States from Trinidad), Lichtenberger welcomes the cultural diversity that is being reflected in Vienna and other European cities.

Nadine Lichtenberger's experience highlights the fact that today the expatriate wife is often the wife of a foreign national. Her status as a "foreign wife" opens a universe of opportunities as well as problems. Erica Johnson Debeijak is married to a Slovenian national and lives in Ljubljana. When she was growing up in America, race was the flashpoint of her youth. She wonders how to explain the politics and culture of color and diversity to her young children, "brought up in Ljubljana where spotting a person of color is akin to spotting a grizzly bear in my native California."[24]

While the extent of the phenomenon is unknown, the media increasingly prints stories of American women with foreign spouses who live in their husband's country. Sometimes this makes the news when a divorce or child custody fight boils over national borders. Increasingly, American women are marrying into the Muslim cultures of Turkey and the Middle East. Their transitions in religion, culture, and general lifestyle are challenging to them, to say the least. Many American women married to Turks obtain Turkish citizenship in order to avoid the hassle of work and residency permits, but this is not advisable for male foreigners, who would become eligible for mandatory military service should they become Turkish citizens. Yet of all the transition experiences of an American spouse, the most difficult may be those endured by the American-born wife of a Japanese husband.[25]

For lack of a useful social science term, we can call it the "Jane and Akira syndrome." It works this way. Usually Akira, a hard-working young Japanese executive or "salary man" is sent by his company to the United States to attend graduate school and acquire an MBA. Far from home, the impressionable grad student is awash in new experiences and friendships. Invariably he meets Jane, an American girl who is pretty, intelligent, and self-confident and vastly different from the Japanese girls he has known. Soon Akira is smitten by Jane. The same attraction of opposites works on Jane, who likes Akira's clean-cut looks, fashionable clothes, manners, and deference. He also listens to her, something that most American men do not do on dates with women. Casual dates lead to a relationship, commitment, and finally marriage. At first the marriage seems right out of a multicultural storybook. Both Akira and Jane are deliriously happy, and the company back in Hitachi

transfers its new MBA to New York City. The couple moves to the suburbs and starts a family.

But trouble soon enters this American multicultural Garden of Eden
in the shape of Akira's transfer back to the home office in Japan. Suddenly Jane, a mother of two infants, finds herself on her way to live in a
strange land with strange customs and an almost unintelligible
language. Jane's new home is in a bedroom community far from the
cosmopolitan center of Tokyo and only one-fourth the size of her American place. Jane also must cope with Akira's parents, who often treat
her more like a servant than a daughter-in-law. She tries to learn Japanese and prepare for all the demands that the local school system will
place on her for the instruction and support of her children. Japanese
matrons in the neighborhood tend to avoid her unless they want Jane to
teach their children English. What friendships there are tend to be more
friendships of respect and obligation based on her husband's job with
the company. Meanwhile, the husband works long hours, frequently
goes out drinking with his colleagues, getting home on the 10 P.M. train.

Some wives give up in tears and return to America. Others respond
vigorously to the challenges of life in a new culture. Most, however,
seek emotional support from similar expats. In Japan, English-language
newspapers regularly carry news of "psychological support groups for
American spouses of Japanese husbands."

Corinne Tachikawa grew up in Spokane, Washington, the daughter of
Neisei Japanese (second generation) who were totally assimilated Americans and no longer spoke the old language. After attending university,
Corinne came to Tokyo on a lark and got a job teaching English at the
local YWCA. While working in Tokyo, she met a Japanese doctor and fell
in love. Nearly thirty years have passed, and Corinne now lives in the
city of Mito, where her husband practices medicine and she teaches English at a local university. Unlike many American spouses of Japanese
husbands, Corinne is often mistaken for being native Japanese. Yet,
women criticize her language skills and exclude her from intimate neighborhood gatherings. Her children bear American first names, and she is
rigorously raising them in a bilingual environment. Whatever happens in
the future, Corinne Tachikawa is preparing her children to find the best
of what Japan and the United States have to offer. In the meantime, Corinne Tachikawa has carved out a life for herself that is not quite Japanese
and not quite American. "My life is full of hard work and cultural tension. I live in Japan but I am not at home in it," she adds bitterly. "I relax
by going on shopping trips to Honolulu and Las Vegas."[26]

Debbie Wesselman moved to Japan because her husband, Koji, inher-
ited a pottery in the famous ceramic town of Kasama. The pottery had
been in the family for generations, and being the last male in the family,
he was honor-bound to return. Debbie and her husband had good

professional jobs in the United States, and Debbie could have refused to go. But "because of the love between us, we knew that we had to go to Kasama," Debbie said. It was no easy task. Although Debbie in time learned to speak fluent Japanese, she was never able to live up to the strict expectations of her mother-in-law. She always folded futons incorrectly in the morning or committed some other graceless act during the day. Impending motherhood prompted Debbie to think more and more of her old life in America. When the business improved and a cousin was capable of supervising it, Koji and Debbie returned to America.

Recently NHK Television in Tokyo produced a highly popular documentary on Western wives who married Japanese men, for today there are more American women marrying Japanese men than ever before. Those American women who have survived the Jane and Akira syndrome have profited from the sage local wisdom: "Be sure to get black eyes very soon." This means that they should learn to see Japan as the Japanese do.[27]

THE BUTTERFLY LIFE

Sometimes American women find themselves overseas, broke, alone, and desperate. For a variety of reasons stemming from pride or family problems, they are unwilling to ask for help from home. According to Dorothy Van Schoonveld, director of the Geneva-based organization, American Citizens Abroad, there are numerous cases of American women being poor and down on their luck in Europe. After all, she notes, about 17 percent of the expatriates in Europe live on an income of less that $20,000.[28] In international cities like London, Amsterdam, Hamburg, Tel Aviv, and Tokyo, a large population of American women serve as bar girls and hostesses. Their bosses and patrons help them get visas. Often they have links to criminal organizations. Lisa Louis, an American who traveled to Japan and actually lived there for a number of years, tells of the life of "butterflies," or American and Asian hostesses in Tokyo bars. When in need of some extra money, she dabbled in the night-life profession herself, working as a hostess at a bar where she poured drinks and entertained men. She was fluent in Japanese and earned a great deal of money. When her book appeared in Tokyo, she declined to appear on Japanese television, having no wish to sensationalize what is called in Japan "the pink profession."[29] In Tokyo there are numerous instances of American women who earn $700 a night giving bubble baths to Japanese salary men in local clubs. Many of these women have adapted well, speak good Japanese, and have the capital to return to the United States whenever they want. They live well as American expatriates in professions they would not have dreamed of when they first trekked abroad with their backpacks.

SUMMARY

The emergence of the American woman expatriate in recent years is testimony to the revolution in gender relations that continues to take place in the United States and abroad. Women travel more today, and they are entering occupations that only a short time ago were denied to them. As business executives and managers overseas, women have been able to prove their worth to multinational companies. As entrepreneurs and adventurers, women expatriates have developed a taste for new and demanding lifestyles that offer them challenges they do not have at home. Women abroad increasingly find themselves in the dangerous places as well as the glamorous places overseas. They are reporters and aid workers in Darfur, soldiers in Iraq, nurses in Lebanon, movie producers in India, and spa managers in Bali. Past and present, American women have added a unique angle of vision to what is called the American expatriate experience.

Chapter 7

Go East, Young Man

I am here because I am a foreigner, because I like being a foreigner. It's so reward-ing to not have to belong to things. It's really so free.

Donald Ritchie, an American writer in Japan

The stories that Americans tell one another are full of discussions of thwarted plans and frustrated experiences. Often things just don't work out, and many middle-class American frustrations have to do with bumping against glass ceilings that should not exist from a standpoint of intelligence and ability. All too often, writes social theorist Jon Elster, economic life is conditioned by social norms that do not necessarily benefit anyone.[1] They are nonetheless part of the emotional and behav-ioral propensities of individuals. Whether one uses the right fork when eating or wears a coat and tie to work may tell a good deal about the culture of a restaurant or workplace, but these behaviors reveal almost nothing of the inherent ability of a specific individual to perform a task successfully. Many careers sink, however, because of bad table habits and an unawareness of fashion.

At present many talented college-educated young people believe that many American social norms are either an unnecessary constraint or a social joke. These young adults tend to be high achievers who prefer the absolute equality of ability when it comes to rewards and dismiss office politics. Also, on given occasions, all things considered, these young people believe that short-term self-indulgence is justified and even recommended, especially if they find their own dominant culture confining and unreasonable. Ideas about self-realization are not always born of passion, but they do have a high emotional content that speaks to the actor in all of us, demanding that our inner or imagined destiny reach fruition. Perhaps the reasons for the great popularity of Asia as a place to live and work stems from the fact that its norms are so different, its value systems so at variance with our own, that it is possible for an American expatriate to carve out a totally new lifestyle and identity and enjoy himself or herself immensely in the process. Most of these young men and women are adventure-seekers with strong entrepreneurial interests that interweave with the world of play. They are less confident than other generations about the stability of jobs, earnings, and relationships. These Americans are looking beyond salaries for jobs that offer meaningful opportunity for skills acquisition and advancement. This is good news for companies in Asia that want to hire well-educated Americans at modest wages and benefits.[2]

TAKING ASIA BY STORM

Since the earliest days of our Republic there have been Americans living and working in Asia. The China trade was so uppermost on the minds of our Founding Fathers that the first ship built after the American Revolution was christened by the government as *The Empress of China*. In the nineteenth century the trans-Pacific fur trade with China linked the fortunes of Rocky Mountains beaver trappers and St. Louis's early economic and urban growth with the Orient. By the early nineteenth century, Western industrial nations like France, England, and the United States had sliced Asia into spheres of influence and colonies. To protect lives in China, the gunboats of the U.S. Navy patrolled the Yangtze River. Americans took the Philippines from the Spanish Empire in 1898 and ruled it with twenty-five thousand marines. Meanwhile, France consolidated its hold over Indochina. Germany and Japan became dominant forces in the Pacific as well.

A lot has changed over time, however; five hundred years of colonialism in Asia came to an end with the reversion of Hong Kong and Macao to China. Since 1990, business activity in Asia has exploded, and the Asians are now at the center of the world economic court. The region currently has five of the world's six largest economies and contains sixteen of the world's largest cities. For the wandering expatriate American, Asia is the place where opportunities, adventure, and excitement outstrip anything that can be found in the United States. For today's expatriate, the operative phrase is "Go east, young man." An estimated three hundred sixty thousand American citizens have taken up residence in Asia. In terms of sheer numbers, the Philippines is the leading host nation, but most Americans in the Philippines are retirees or dropouts lured there by the cheap lifestyle. For young Americans on the move, the action is in the leading host nations of China, Japan, and Taiwan. Young Americans today seem to be everywhere in Asia. They are working in Japanese schools as assistant English teachers, running businesses in Taiwan, hanging out in Hanoi in bars with names like Apocalypse Now. They are also serving burgers in Bali and extending holidays into decades on the beaches of Goa in India. Asia is both a smart career move and a cool thing to do after college. Many Americans pass through the region like social butterflies, but others stay and take root. In many areas of Asia, like Vietnam, Thailand, and India, expats with $1,500-a-month salary can afford an apartment with maid service and still have something left over for the savings account. The culture may drive them crazy, the language and ways of doing business may be different, but American expats are having fun. And fun in Asia is what it is all about.

TAIWAN: FROM STRIPPERS TO TRANSNATIONALS

Situated in the straits of the South China Sea is a political anachronism called Taiwan. It is an anachronism because it has pretensions to be independent at a time when the Chinese mainland is asserting its sovereign claims over the country. Since 1949, when the defeated nationalist army fled the Chinese communist mainland for Taiwan, it has always been a little island with big ideas. Physically just over half the size of West Virginia, modern Taiwan is very much a fast-paced nouveau-riche state where luxury and consumption patterns often startle outside visitors.[3] Unemployment is only around 2 percent, and the country is receptive to expatriates. To understand modern Taiwan and its expatriates, however, some unconventional historical background is necessary.

Part of the local bar folklore is that Courtney Love once worked as a stripper in Taiwan. Many American girls did the same in the 1970s through the 1990s, when well-endowed women from the West were all the rage for the Chinese. An American stripper with a good head for business could earn more in a summer working in the bars and strip joints of Taiwan than she could in an entire year in the United States. Also, rock groups and singers who were on the most dangerous of economic margins in Los Angeles found wealth and success in the clubs of Taiwan.

Taiwan's wealth was fueled first by military bases as Americans endeavored to protect Taiwan from the "Red Menace" of mainland China. A torrent of American dollars in military and government subsidies flowed into the island, helping finance Taiwan's emergence from a horsecart and pedicab society to a prosperous business outpost of the Cold War. From the many clubs and brothels on the island servicing

GIs, Chinese merchants took profits to open bank accounts in New York and send their sons and daughters to Columbia University. The war in Vietnam in the 1960s and 1970s brought thousands of Americans to the island. Expatriate businesspeople and backpackers followed the soldiers. Soon Taiwanese companies began to hire "utility Americans"— local American expats who helped Asians with their English and built public relations bridges with Western corporations.

College students from West Coast universities discovered Taiwan to be an inexpensive place where they could lead a good life by teaching English only ten hours a week to language-hungry Chinese businesspeople and students. Today the *Bu Xi Bans,* or private language schools, are still eager to recruit American teachers. Robert Irick, a columnist for the *Taiwan China News,* sees the current flood of Americans into Taiwan as prompted by economic and social changes in the United States. Opportunities for youth in America are not as creative as those in Taiwan. "You can't fault people who come abroad for the express purpose of earning a living." It was different in the old days, says Irick, when Americans were fleeing careers instead of acquiring them.[4] Many Americans have the computer, sales, and analytical skills that are in demand in Taiwan. Mark Heubusch didn't move to Taiwan for romance or idealism. He is a young vice president of an American bank who was transferred there. Before long he fell in love with the country and ended up marrying a Taiwanese woman. Robert Irick muses that the once-anarchistic hell-raising Americans of the bars and brothels of Taiwan have become conservative and intermarried with the population. The American Chamber of Commerce in Taipei helps American job-seekers, and the American Institute of Taiwan offers a steady flow of information for would-be expatriates.[5] In fact, with thirty-eight thousand Americans working in Taiwan, northern Taipei has come to resemble an American suburb much in the way that Victoria Peak in Hong Kong is an encapsulated British community. Americans in Taiwan have come a long way since the days of Courtney Love.

AMERICANS IN CHINA

In the past decade China has undergone enormous structural and economic changes and is becoming a modernized industrial superpower. China's industrial base thrives on technology and makes the country open to modernization and innovation from the West as long as it is of a nonpolitical nature. Once despised as "imperialist big noses who spread the vile Christian religion," Americans are now actively recruited for work in China. *Asia Times* recently reported that China's impressive economic development has prompted cities like Shanghai to embark on massive recruiting campaigns to match Asian Americans and other skilled individuals. In 2006 Shanghai officials traveled to the United States in hopes of filling two thousand job vacancies in their commercial metropolis.[6]

Business people are by far the best-treated expatriates in China. The government routinely runs interference for them in the scramble to get comfortable Western-style housing in crowded cities like Beijing and Shanghai, and it goes to great lengths to secure them some language training, employment for spouses, and English-language schools for their children. Most businesspeople also have private drivers who serve as house managers and interpreters. That is not to say that life in China is easy for American businesspeople. The Chinese bureaucracy is just beginning to deal with entrepreneurship, especially when it comes to major projects like automobile, chemical, and computer manufacturing. Visit an expatriate apartment in Beijing, and you will most likely see a number of volumes in the bookcases dealing with stress, self-development, and the problems of living in alien environments. The rewards for working in China are great, however, and engineers and information technology analysts earn three times what they would earn in the United States. They get a healthy overseas living allowance as well. For some American entrepreneurs, a five-year stint in China can lead to either being part owner of a rapidly growing business with Chinese partners or else having saved enough money in an overseas bank account to achieve financial independence.

Teachers of English, though, lead a different way of life, one that has more problems yet is freer from the confines of Chinese bureaucratic style. Many expatriate Americans end up teaching English at Chinese universities. These teachers are part of a massive modernization program in China, which includes teaching English to many of the 450 million Chinese currently studying foreign languages. Expat English teachers earn between $600 and $1,000 a month, which is three to four times what their Chinese counterparts earn. Although this is low by Western standards, it is more than adequate for a comfortable life in China, where expat teachers get free housing, free medical care, and subsidized vacations. Although housing for Western teachers is comfortable, the surroundings can often be quite spartan. Occasionally, expat teachers find themselves housed in an apartment atop a seven-storey building with no elevator! Most English teachers get two-room apartments, which are furnished and have central heating, a real boon in the land of chilling winters. Teacher turnover in China is high, however, as many of the cities and communities to which the Chinese government directs expat teachers are drab, dirty, ugly industrial centers. Pollution and traffic are common expatriate complaints. Most expats try for a teaching position at the University of Beijing or at Wuhan Technical University, a beautiful campus in central China near the gorges of the Yangtze River.

Often the teaching can be the least unpleasant part of the expatriate experience. The immense crowds in Chinese cities may spook space-conscious Americans, and the day-to-day hassles of long lines at post offices and other government agencies often wear down morale. This is where the critical difference emerges between those who are "logistically supported" and those who are not. Those American businesspeople who are "logistically supported" have a Chinese professional at beck and call to iron out every problem, from getting a work visa to securing an apartment. Those who are not thusly supported are forced to slog it out in the local culture. Furthermore, whereas teachers earn just US$600 to US$1,000, as noted, business expats earn a minimum of around US$86,000 and also get a housing allowance. Thus, in China, expat teachers live like American graduate students, whereas expat businesspeople live like kings.[7]

Expatriates and their counterparts in business work very long hours in China, an average of sixty hours a week, and complain that work plus rituals of business socializing leave them with little free time to spend with their families. But in a recent survey, American business-people reported that they were very satisfied with their experience in China. "If they had to make the decision to take the China assignment again, they would."[8]

What is missing today in China, writes Daniel Calhoun, are the proletarian masses. Only old people wear the old blue Mao costumes. Young women dress in provocative Western styles, Calhoun notes. In the old days before Mao's death, women walked and marched to a great cause. "Now they walk like sex objects." Most of the egalitarian, self-sacrificing China is now gone. In its place Calhoun sees a China more like Hong Kong, "commercialized, glitzy, and unprincipled." This new China "may take charge of the 21st century economically. But spiritually it may have died."[9]

Americans like Jenny Leal and Jim Gradoville are in China for the long haul. Leal came to China in 2001 with a master's degree in journalism. Eager to learn as much about the country as possible, she took a job as an English teacher at the Beijing Institute of Graphic Communications. Leal endured much criticism directed at her by Chinese colleagues about 9/11 and the situation in the Middle East, but she didn't have much to do with politics. Leal was in love and soon married a Chinese man from Fujian Province. The thirty-one-year-old American recently dyed her brown hair black and is intent on making herself more Chinese. Leal says that the marital bond has closely linked her with China. "Wherever we end up living, I will be bound to China for the rest of my life," she reflected.

Jim Gradoville has been living in China for five years. As Motorola's vice president of Asia-Pacific relations, Gradoville likes the fast pace of corporate change in China. Every week there are new challenges, he says. Working for the largest foreign investor in China, Gradoville is active in the local American chamber of commerce. But his consuming interest is rescuing Chinese orphans and finding homes for them either in China or in the United States. Recently, he adopted two Chinese girls and is playing an important role in getting better education and nurturing for children in Chinese orphanages. His interest in Chinese orphans "transcends any discrepancies between the two countries," he says.[10]

Meanwhile, as China seeks to emulate Hong Kong, the fabled "Pearl of the Orient" remains louder and brassier than ever. Neither reversion to communist rule nor periodic economic recessions have failed to tame Hong Kong's entrepreneurial spirit. Hong Kong is a welcome port of entry for American expatriates in Asia. Backpackers and job-seekers alike can decompress here from Asian pressures. The food is good, and expats can hang out in numerous British pubs. Hong Kong attracts American expatriates because it is a well-organized city and English is widely spoken. According to the U.S. consul, fifty-five thousand Americans reside in Hong Kong, making this expatriate community a large and influential one with a muscular chamber of commerce.[11] Jobs are fairly easy to get, and the classified section of the *South China Morning Post* carries ads that range from teaching and journalism to computer sales and banking. Although housing is very expensive, many Americans live at the "mid-levels" of Victoria Peak and have apartments with pools and tennis courts. They also have live-in Filipina maids.

If a large corporation sponsors an American in Hong Kong, that American has one of the most economically comfortable lives imaginable. The company pays the rental in a posh neighborhood, picks up the tuition costs at the Hong Kong International School, and pays a salary in the comfortable six figures. On weekends there is the private company yacht that takes expatriate employees and their families out to restaurants on the island of Lantau or on picnics and swims in private coves. When boredom sets in, one simply boards a hydrofoil for a weekend of gambling and relaxation at a hotel in nearby Macao, where Stanley Ho and his family preside over a casino empire that rivals Atlantic City.

To replace the British expatriate professional workforce that ran Hong Kong for centuries, a new breed of professionals has arrived. They are Chinese Americans whose parents and grandparents only recently immigrated to America. Bicultural and bilingual, these Chinese American expats are cashing in on their language skills and cultural knowledge to make money and enjoy benefits not to be found in jobs in the United States. Cherry Lu, a native of San Francisco and a university graduate, arrived in Hong Kong with no professional work experience whatsoever. Three months later, when in California she would still have been a novice managerial trainee, she was sent by her Hong Kong employer to serve as a project manager of a financial audit for a rocket propellant factory. "In America I was just another bright Chinese American girl with glasses," says Cherry Lu. "But here I am valued for my talent, my Berkeley education, and my American passport."

Larry Wang, another Chinese American, found opportunities in Hong Kong so lucrative that he set up his own employment agency for expats. The thirty-six-year-old engineer from Los Angeles has seen his agency grow into a major corporation with offices in Oakland and New York City. Job skills are not enough, cautions Wang. "You need Western job skills and Chinese-language skills." Having these skills really paid off for Felix Wong, who grew up in California but speaks three Chinese dialects. In his early thirties, Wong is director of new business development in Asia for Universal Studios.[12]

With China's economy growing about three times faster than that of the United States, Larry Wang, Cherry Lu, Felix Wong, and other newly arriving Chinese Americans are destined to become rich players in the region's rapidly growing economy. For them, the American dream is becoming a reality in today's Hong Kong.

GOOD MORNING, VIETNAM!

Contemporary Vietnamese society has put away memories of war and suffering and is welcoming the dawn of Western investment and economic development. Memories of the Vietnam War count for little in that country's current scramble for modernization. Today's young Vietnamese struggle to learn English, and their teachers are just as liable to be reading the *Vietnam Investment Review* as they are language instruction manuals. Vietnam's official policy is *doi moi,* or economic renovation, and the government actively recruits foreign workers, professionals, and investors who can survive in Vietnam's rough-and-tumble political economy. The United States lifted its trade embargo in 1994; the next year President Clinton established full diplomatic relations.

Vietnam can be hot, dirty, and difficult. "It is not exactly user-friendly," quips Motorola representative Patrick Aronson, "but that's the fun of it." Aronson is part of a vanguard of three thousand Americans and Vietnamese Americans who can be found in Hanoi, old Saigon, and other Vietnamese cities. Despite the government's political rhetoric, Vietnam seems wide open. Businesses as diverse as Motorola, Wild Turkey (makers of bourbon whiskey), and Caterpillar are scrambling for market shares. Living and cultural conditions are tough, and this appeals to opportunity-hungry American college graduates eager to go for it. "You can get more experience and have more responsibility in one year in Vietnam than you could ever have in five back in the States," reflects Brad Anger. There wasn't much opportunity for Anger back in his native Rhode Island when he graduated from college, so Anger set his sights overseas. Originally, he interviewed for a job in Singapore; but when the French company Pernod offered him a chance to work as a marketing manager for Wild Turkey bourbon whiskey and Jameson Irish whiskey, Anger jumped at the chance. No one looks over his shoulder in Vietnam, where results are the only thing that counts. That he should succeed as a liquor salesman in a country that has a major campaign against alcohol and other social vices is part of the irony of Vietnam. "It's the unpredictability that makes Vietnam so exciting," he says.

After little more than a year in Vietnam, Anger acquired a house, a girlfriend, a big motorcycle, and enough money for expensive holidays in Thailand's Ko Samui resort. These days Anger doesn't think much about Rhode Island, especially when his money allows him to spend languid holiday mornings under the coconut trees at Chawang Beach at Ko Samui.[13] There are plenty of young men and women like Anger working for Caterpillar tractor and for computer software businesses eager to get a toehold in Vietnam.

Other Americans burn out in Vietnam. The country is not an easy place to live in and do business. After six years there James Rockwell, one of the first American businesspeople to arrive in Vietnam after the war, closed his Hanoi office and shut down his consulting company, Vatic Inc. Rockwell was instrumental in opening up Vietnam for the Chrysler Corporation, International Harvester, and Hughes Aircraft. His Hanoi office flew a big American flag and was often mistaken for the U.S. embassy. Although he made money consulting in Vietnam and helped Chrysler establish a $192 million joint venture program in automobile production, the country's communist bureaucracy constantly hampered him. In the end, Rockwell quit, he says, because there was too much regulation, too much bribery, too much delay in negotiating business deals.[14] But the burnout did not last long. Since 2000 James Rockwell's tall, gangly frame can regularly be seen at Vietnam trade fairs, where he runs seminars on how Hanoi businesspeople can trade with their largest economic partner, the United States.

Vietnamese Americans are also returning to the land from which their parents and grandparents fled. They are often culture-shocked. "We are used to Walt Disney, pizza, and peanut butter," reflects Hien Hoang from Seattle, Washington. Hoang can speak the language, but the food and culture distract him. Hoang started out in Vietnam as a vacation backpacker. He then stayed for a while to teach English to rich Vietnamese before getting a job as marketing representative for a European power tool company. Having studied international business at the

University of Washington, Hoang knows how to get his business proposals on the desk of his Vietnamese boss. Meanwhile, Hoang has a
cultural disconnect with his ancestral fatherland. He enjoys meeting his
American friends in Saigon at the Burger Khan restaurant for cheese-
burgers and a few beers. He also shops in Saigon for a rather elusive
but cherished American commodity, peanut butter. But in a moment of
candor, Hoang recognizes that he has come a long way since his parents
reached Seattle by way of the refugee camps of Malaysia.

Americans in Hanoi like Felicity Wood have Vietnam bred in their
bones. Her parents met and married in Vietnam when her father was
there in the U.S. Foreign Service in the 1960s. Now Wood has come full
circle to enjoy the pace of Vietnam. Further, Felicity Wood knows all
about the advantages and disadvantages of doing business in Vietnam.
She was the first director of the American Chamber of Commerce in
Vietnam. Working with American corporations that were suspicious of
the intentions of the Vietnamese kept Wood busy.[15] Today she is based
in Sacramento, California, where she teaches Asian geography and
photography. But several times a year she is back in Hue and Hanoi.

There are more Americans in Vietnam now, Felicity Wood notices.
She sees them on their motor scooters putt-putting through the crowded
and humid streets of Saigon, with the city stretching before them like a
restless tide of promise. It is morning in Vietnam, and Americans are
making the most of it.

OHAYO GAIJIN! (HELLO, FOREIGNER!)

Few experiences in Asia have the intensity, the emotional joy, the
sense of accomplishment and arrival, and the sting of disappointment
as the American expatriate experience in Japan. To say that the
Westerner can be excited and overwhelmed by differences of language,
culture, and behavior in Japan is a truth that few can challenge. Japan is
racist and xenophobic, yet hospitable and generous; and most Japanese
are too busy riding the trains to work every day to dwell on their own
contradictions. Cathy Davidson, a Duke University American Studies
professor who spent a lot of time living and working in Japan as an
exchange teacher, has noted that, for all the Western expectations of
Japan being just a larger version of America, "Japan is different. Philo-
sophically and socially, it's one of the least Western countries, despite
its rampant modernization." Foreigners are usually lumped together.
"Intensity, novelty, urgency, surprise; that's what it means to me to be
a gaijin," reflects Davidson.[16]

Americans have been living and working in Japan since Commodore
Perry arrived there in the 1850s. Japan nonetheless remained relatively
unknown to Western audiences until the expatriate professor Lafcadio

Hearn explained the country and its culture in two major works, *Glimpses of an Unfamiliar Japan* (1894) and *Japan: An Essay at Interpretation* (1904). Hearn was married to Koizumi Setsuko, the daughter of a great samurai, and became a Japanese citizen.

Since Hearn's day Americans have been coming to Japan in ever-increasing numbers to teach, work, and marry. Today nearly eighty thousand Americans live in Japan. This large American community dates mostly back to the 1980s, when Japan's economic boom led to a severe labor shortage in both the working and professional classes. As Japanese corporations increasingly became dominant in global markets like automobiles, cameras, and electronics, large numbers of Americans came to Tokyo and other cities to work as translators, business analysts, and "utility Americans" to explain Western culture to occasionally befuddled Japanese business executives. Further, Japan's Immigration Control Law was revised in 1989 to permit the employment of additional professionals and teachers from abroad. Also, there was a major shift in language teaching in Japanese schools and universities from German and French to English. Today the average Japanese public school student is required to study English at least six years.

English teaching is a major industry in modern Japan. Scarcely any town in Japan is without its *juku*, or private tutoring school that employs American English teachers. Japanese public school systems employ large numbers of "Assistant English Teachers," that is, young college graduates imported directly from America to teach English to reluctant teenagers. Evening schools for adult instruction in English can usually be found near the train station of any large Japanese town or city. The AEON Corporation is one of the largest English conversation schools, with over two hundred and thirty-five branches throughout Japan. Add to this the vast array of small proprietary English schools that have recently sprung up throughout the country, and it is easy to see how American expatriates have flocked to Japan. The minimum qualification to teach English is usually a college degree from an accredited university in the United States, although recently schools have begun to emphasize TOEFL (Teaching English as a Foreign Language) credentials as well. Many teachers stay in cramped apartments called *rokujos*, miniscule dwellings the size of six beach tatami mats. Most of these modest apartments are heated with small kerosene stoves, confining expats to a lifestyle that is excruciatingly at variance with Western affluent habitats.

Modern Tokyo is an electric, fast-paced culture where many expats are willing to tolerate the inconveniences of Japanese life for the excitement and action of the big metropolis. Tokyo's trains and subways make the city easy to navigate once one has learned how to handle the immense crowds at rush hour. Expats can be found in Tokyo's Ueno and Ripongi districts, where apartments and restaurants are cheap and there are good coffeehouses and bars to hang out in. Japanese women continue to be fascinated by young American men, whose expat social life can be quite good as long as they realize that a "date" might mean four or five people going out together to a noodle shop for *soba*. Americans also have problems with the Japanese style of communication. Americans usually come straight to the point. The Japanese, on the other hand, value ambiguity and tact. They emphasize what someone wants to hear rather than what is most direct or honest. The difference between what Japanese say (*tatemae*) and what they really think (*hone*) is a great source of expatriate frustration. Expat Mark Hancock began his overseas career as an English language teacher in Japan. Currently, Hancock lives well as a business consultant in Tokyo.

A similar though somewhat less intense social pace prevails for expatriates out in the prefectures. On weekends the Drunken Duck Tavern in Katsuda, a suburb of Hitachi in Ibaraki Prefecture, is a roaring, smoke-filled joint crowded with expats from nearly a dozen countries. American food is plentiful, from fried chicken to burgers and pizzas. Prices are not cheap, and so it is easy to drop $100 in the course of an evening. One of the Drunken Duck's regulars is Duane Isham from Oregon. Twenty years ago he quit a dead-end job as a copy machine mechanic and answered an ad in the *San Francisco Examiner* for an English teacher for the AEON system in Tokyo. A failed marriage and a string of bad financial experiences left him with little to look forward to on the West Coast, so he jumped at the chance to head East. In the years that Isham has been in Japan, he has moved on to a better job as an English instructor at a prefectural university and has a Japanese girlfriend whose business acumen keeps him out of financial difficulties. "Japan has been the best thing that ever happened to me, bar none," says Isham as he quaffs a pint of Kirin beer. "I was going nowhere back in the States. I awoke one morning, and all I had was an apartment with the rent due, some change on the dresser, and a box of dirty clothes. Japan really helped me get straightened out." Recently, Isham earned a master's degree in teaching English as a foreign language (TOEFL) at the Tokyo Center of Temple University, and the lanky instructor has not lacked employment since he got off the plane in Tokyo. Isham's prefecture lifestyle is vastly cheaper than living in Tokyo, and he gets around the city of Mito on a bicycle.[17]

While Japan attracts motivated Americans, it also attracts expats who are on the borderline of social stability and the law. In Tokyo the bars of Rappongi have more than their share of fast-buck artists who will take the expat's last yen with business deals like being a representative for Amway soap or buying a vitamin distributorship. Some expats conjure up new identities on their business cards and attempt to pass themselves off to elegant Japanese women as movie producers or modeling agents from big companies back in America. Sometimes this kind of guile works. Sometimes it results in a visit from the local police.

Inasmuch as Japan is so different from the United States and has few publishing outlets in English, it is not a place where Western writers tend to gravitate. Yet a small but growing community of artists and writers there do use their vantage point in Japan to focus on themes that demonstrate the human condition both in Japan and elsewhere. During the last fifty years Donald Ritchie has been the most elegant American voice in Japan, seeking to understand Japan through a foreigner's eyes. Ritchie is a recognized worldwide authority on Japan, and his nearly forty books speak with the authority of a writer skilled in understanding the nuances of culture. His book *The Inland Sea* was Ritchie's autobiographical travel epic tracing his classic journey from Kobe to Miyajama. It was made into an award-winning documentary film. In his books Ritchie has served as a medium between two cultures. Ritchie considers himself primarily an observer, and his books on politics, labor, and cultural transformation have provided Westerners with an elegant window on what Japan was and what Japan has become. For Ritchie, the English language has been the bridge that has connected him with America. Physical distance has been irrelevant. Highly regarded in Japanese cultural and political circles, Ritchie is amiable and down-to-earth rather than intellectually aloof. From his perch as a culture columnist for the *Japan Times,* Ritchie encourages expatriate writers to explore their muse, and many a young reporter and nonfiction writer has moved ahead with Ritchie's gentle encouragement.

Today Ritchie is not a lone American writing in Japan. There is a small but growing community of writers like Phyllis Birnbaum and Alan Brown, who use their vantage point in Japan to hone a sharp angle of vision on modern times. Birnbaum is best noted for her stories about modern life in Japan. Her short story "A Roasted Potato at Dusk," the story of a doomed marriage between a Jewish American woman and a Japanese man from Tokyo, has been anthologized in the West. Her stories have appeared in the *New Yorker,* and most recently her book *Modern Girls, Shining Stars, the Skies of Tokyo: Five Japanese Women* has received wide critical acclaim in Canada, Japan, and the United States. The book brings to life five women in Japan from other times and shows how they went beyond the confines of their culture to establish messy careers filled with accomplishment and sorrow. The lives of these girls stretch over a century and a half of cultural and political explosions in Japan. Birnbaum shows how five Japanese women, whose careers ranged from novelist to actress to cultural revolutionary to feminist, laid the groundwork for the emancipation of modern women in Japan. Birnbaum notes that until she came to Japan, she had not learned to look at things in a close, almost microscopic manner. To understand the Japanese, she says, you must be aware that "the Japanese see things very close up in a detailed way."

Alan Brown wrote his first critically acclaimed novel, *Audrey Hepburn's Neck,* while living in Tokyo. The novel detailed an obsession of a Japanese cartoonist with the slim necklines and figures of American women. Concerned about sex as an obsession and the erotics of cultural differences, Brown not only conjures up a humorous tale of the coming of age of a Japanese cartoonist, but he also gives a sense of expatriate revelries that range from homosexual parties to the cultural meanings the Japanese ascribe to a Häagen Dazs ice cream parlor.

Both Birnbaum and Brown assert that values are cultural and grow out of the political and social environment and the needs of the country. Currently Japan offers American writers a place to reflect, to see things differently, and to test their inner beliefs and strengths. For Birnbaum and Brown, the expatriate writer's life in Japan has been difficult because it takes time to settle in and understand a new culture and then begin comparing it to your own. But in Phyllis Birnbaum's view, the greatest gift she has received is "the Japanese ways of seeing things."[18]

SUMMARY

Americans working and living in Asia have certainly become part of what social scientists had long predicted as "the Pacific Century." While presidents and policy makers in Washington cope with the economic renaissance of Asia, American men and women are heading East in growing numbers. Many are retiring, for example, in friendly social climates like Thailand's Pattaya. Thailand has at least five hundred Vietnam War veterans living in Pattaya and elsewhere.[19] Recently, computer companies in India, like Infosys Technology, are recruiting young Americans to participate in the economic boom on the subcontinent. Although only a handful of Americans had been recruited by the end of 2006, the *New York Times* reported that American college graduates of non-Indian ancestry are sampling the fruits of India's high-tech expansion.[20]

Expatriates recognize the depth of change taking place in Asia because they are part of that change. They are living through a transition so beguilingly fresh and so fraught with opportunity that the experiences they are having in Asia may never be experienced elsewhere. In the words of Pico Iyer, himself a well-known expatriate writer, the Asia of the expatriate American "is definitely postcolonial. It is dynamic, urban and highly mobile."[21] If and when these expatriates return to their native shore, America could do well to tap their talents.

Chapter 8

Gringo Gulch: Retired Expatriates and Sojourners in Latin America

People here are either running away or trying to find something or don't know what they want, but didn't want what they had in the States.

Betsy Parish, San Miguel de Allende

CASHING IN ON THE AMERICAN DREAM

Today's American retirees who settle abroad provide an illuminating perspective on the mobility and sociology of aging in America. In the United States, social life, mobility, self-realization, and the aging process have become remarkably conflated. The American dream of the good life has always been one of the sustaining forces in the culture, and retirement has become that moment of dream fulfillment. Until now, the Sun Belt, that broad band or retirement geography that stretches from San Diego to Miami, has been the focal point of this dream fulfillment.

For with the aged, the time to enjoy life is now. There is no tomorrow because life at the point of retirement has become, in a psychological sense, terrifyingly finite. Also, notes sociologist Helmut Loiskandl, "the public culture of America caters essentially to teenagers," and so it is difficult for the aged to hold onto their place in the American social and psychological landscape when they are being marginalized by youth-oriented revolutions in entertainment, lifestyles, and consumption. Retirees can easily conclude that America is not a fit place for old people. All they have to do is watch American television to detect the noticeable absence of the retirees in particular and the aged in general from media programming.[1] Thus it should come as no surprise that the retired are emigrating, albeit for slightly different reasons.

It is ironic that the aged, once one of the most rooted of American social groups, should now become transnationally mobile. Like immigrants everywhere, they are being pushed by economic necessities and by their own cultural marginalization. The vision of a good life in a safe and temperate climate pulls them onward.

Retirement abroad is not a new social phenomenon. In the past it was a byproduct of the end of European imperial systems after World War II, when large numbers of civil servants and soldiers decided to stay on in the former colonies after their retirement. The British retirees in India and the French in Algeria comprised for a time large population centers of expatriates. The British, in fact, have always had a love of life abroad, and in the 1960s and 1970s they began to retire in large numbers to Marbella and other places along the southern coast of Spain and along the Algarve in Portugal. Stretching a pension farther in a low-cost country while lazing in the sun did not seem such a bad idea. More recently, the Germans have followed their fellow European retirees overseas to beaches and warm climates like Tunisia and Thailand.

The trend toward retirement abroad has been accelerated in the present era by the portability of pensions and medical insurance, allowing greater freedom of relocation. Also, in an age of entitlement, when citizens of Western nations are entitled to good pensions, good benefits, good health care, and stable currencies, a life of retirement abroad no longer seems like a dream. From a sociological standpoint, one can also point to the growing respectability of migration itself as a modern intellectual construct. Everywhere in the world today traditional lives are being uprooted and populations are in motion; relocation of people to new countries is no longer unusual. Finally, the end of the Cold War has ushered in a kind of global peace that has removed ideological considerations from the notion of expatriate retirement, especially to countries under former dictatorial regimes or communist control.

Not all nations make it easy for their citizens to retire overseas, however. Many countries have national health systems that are geared for "home use" only. Canada, for example, has an annual statute of limitations on days spent abroad before the Canadian retiree is ineligible for medical coverage in the national health system. As the six-month deadline nears, thousands of Canadians begin their annual trek northward from places in Florida and the Caribbean. Likewise, Scandinavian health systems are not that favorably disposed toward extending medical insurance to their retired citizens who have fled to sunnier environments.

In the past, most of the elderly Americans who retired abroad were returning to the homeland from which they had emigrated while young. After a long and prosperous work life in the United States, they returned to Poland, Italy, Germany, or Ireland, among other countries of origin, where the cost of living was lower than in the United States and the language and culture were comfortable. Thus today over one hundred thousand Social Security checks are mailed each month to countries ranging from Canada to Panama. In Eastern Europe especially, a Social Security income goes much farther than it currently does in the United States.

"GO SOUTH, OLD MAN"

Today's retirement generation, however, is not merely going back to the old country. It is more adventuresome than the generation that came before. Senior citizens are more used to travel, and the media have made the world part of their American village. Instead of living in America on diminished incomes, they retire abroad and enjoy a life more luxurious than the one they had when they worked for a living. Many Americans retire to Latin America and elsewhere, says Shirley Waldron, senior program specialist with the thirty-million-member AARP, for one simple reason: "The pace of life is slower."[2]

According to a recent study by the *U.S. News and World Report*, more than four times as many Americans are retiring abroad than the number that did so thirty years ago. Currently there are about 130,000 Americans living overseas who have retired in the last ten years and have their pension checks mailed overseas. At least that many people are also having their pension checks deposited in American banks and simply drawing on them.[3] Those who retire successfully abroad usually have some connection with their new host country. Either they have lived there before or vacationed there. Panama is a case in point. Thousands of Americans worked in the Canal Zone or served there in the military when the canal was an American property. Many of these Americans retired there, and so Panama now tops the list of countries to which the U.S. government sends civil service annuity checks.

Increased interest in immigration to Latin America has come at the same time that more and more Americans are taking retirement while they are still young enough and physically vigorous enough to adapt to the challenges of expatriate life south of the border. Paul Terhorst was a pioneer in this regard. In 1988 Terhorst published a book entitled *Cashing In on the American Dream: How to Retire at 35*, which became an overnight bestseller and went through several editions and an audiocassette version. Terhorst practiced what he preached and retired from the rat race of a high-pressure CPA firm in California at the age of thirty-five. Cashing in all their assets, Terhorst and his wife assembled a nest egg of $400,000 and said goodbye to the corporate world. Terhorst knew he would not be able to live as he wanted on a company pension or on Social Security, and so he invested his money in high-interest-bearing bonds and blue chip stocks. After traveling around the United States and sampling retirement spots in the American South, the Terhorsts packed their bags and headed for Argentina. They bought a beachfront condo in a resort near Buenos Aires, learned Spanish, and settled into the good life. Currently they live half a year in Argentina and travel the other half. The difference of seasons between the Northern Hemisphere and the Southern Hemisphere allows them to live an endless summer.[4]

Cashing in on the American dream is hardly an idea that originated with the Terhorsts. What is new, however, is the combination of age and location that proves so seductively attractive to many discontented, middle-aged American couples. Latin America is financially affordable for those who dare to cash in. Writers like Peter Dickinson, John Howells, and others have capitalized on the idea by writing guidebooks to "Retirement Edens" abroad.[5]

In the resort areas and cities of Latin America you can usually find a place called "Gringo Gulch." It is a suburb or hillside overlooking the sea, or a verdant valley dotted with comfortable villas and located a short distance from fashionable restaurants and shopping malls. Most of the residents are prosperous retirees or middle-aged sojourners who have fled both the weather and the uncertain social climate of "el Norte." Here you can also find an important small section of business-people who have become engaged in local real estate and the commercial life of their host countries. Today, for example, retired Americans are finding their Edens in places like Antigua, Guatemala, with its cobblestone streets, ornately decorated public buildings, and purple bougainvilleas—everywhere. The city Antigua, Guatemala, at five thousand feet above sea level, has a fantastic climate and sits in the shadow of a spectacular ten-thousand-foot volcano. Every day is sunny and dry. Likewise, Antigua is the expatriate retiree's dream comes true. Others find their Eden at a beachfront condominium development like "Paradise Village," a short trip north of Puerto Vallarta, Mexico, with its health spa and exercise clinic and easy access to well-maintained golf courses.

For the moment, American retirees are the vanguard of a growing retirement diaspora that will play an increasingly important role in the economies of Latin American countries and elsewhere because they, together with American investors, are pumping significant amounts of capital into once-ailing economies. Retired American expatriates can be engines of social transformation, both good and bad, in the countries in which they locate. Currently Argentina is the focus of expat attention. Apartments in Buenos Aires are cheap compared to New York. For $30,000 an American can buy a condo in the heart of this vibrant cosmopolitan city. Rents average $250 a month, which is attracting droves of backpackers.[6]

At Lake Chapala, a pleasant Mexican resort just outside Guadalajara, live nearly twenty thousand retired expatriate Americans. So pervasive are they that English has become the second local language, and a huge Wal-Mart and other franchise stores ring the Guadalajara suburbs. Guadalajara has modern hospitals and an enticing climate, nearly seventy degrees year round. The social climate is peaceful. Guadalajara has three English-language newspapers and some 80 organizations for American expatriates, who enjoy everything from golf to bridge, from cooking to line dancing. And out in the countryside, the mountains and banana plantations give testimony to the very real scenic beauty of Mexico. When Malcolm Lowry wrote about the intense blinding beauty of Mexico in his novel *Under the Volcano,* he knew what he was talking about.

The main issue, of course, is money, and retired expatriates can really stretch their pensions and investment income in Latin America. An apartment that rents for $1,250 a month in Sarasota, Florida, can be enjoyed in the suburbs of San José, Costa Rica, for $750 a month or in Mexico at Lake Chapala for $315 a month.[7] Most of these expats who retire in Latin America have their pension checks deposited in banks in the United States and simply draw on them.

Relocation and personnel companies have now entered the "retirement abroad" market. Gerald Celente, director of the Trends Institute in Rhinebeck, New York, sees Central America as an increasingly popular retirement venue because its currencies are relatively stable and it is relatively close to the United States. Celente also predicts that Cuba will be a "retirement suburb" of the United States as soon as politics permits. Currently the Trends Institute believes that the Pacific coast of Nicaragua, with beachfront property only one-hundredth the cost of California land, will be the next retirement hot spot for Americans.[8] Furthermore, Latin America is popular with American retirees because many former Edens in the Caribbean have become economically or socially unstable. Famous retirement havens like Spain's Costa del Sol are either overly crowded or priced out of reach, or they are just too far away from family members. According to Jane Parker, a travel and relocation consultant who is head of Retirement Explorations Inc. out of Modesto, California, most Americans are retiring overseas and to Latin America because they want to live in a peaceful and relaxed social environment and believe that such an environment is getting increasingly more difficult to find in the United States. Also, many of these retirees believe that in their homeland they are more preyed upon than respected. Retirement Explorations takes groups of Americans on personal evaluation tours of foreign countries as retirement havens.[9] The popularity of retirement relocation firms like Jane Parker's shows that in the United States many retired Americans are looking overseas for the American dream.

Potential middle-aged expatriates who want to work tend to dismiss Latin America as a difficult place to find employment. Thus they are often surprised to learn that it is easy to start businesses in tourist areas abroad as long as one has a business partner who is a citizen of the host country. Also, American and English-language schools in Mexico and Latin America generally face an unprecedented shortage of qualified teachers. According to Forest A. Broman, president of International Educators Institute, a nonprofit corporation headquartered in Cape Cod, Massachusetts, there are excellent opportunities for American teachers in interesting places in Latin America. Currently there have been major expansions of American schools in Mexico, Brazil, Venezuela, and Nicaragua. "A teacher with a few years' experience with really good recommendations can get a job," says Broman. And "there are no prejudices against older teachers. Lots of professional Americans over age fifty are being hired as teachers or administrators in these schools," he claims.[10] Teachers are provided living accommodations, small classes, and a working environment that has fewer restrictions for teachers than in the United States. Savvy teachers, though, strive to be paid in U.S. dollars to avoid the perils of inflation in local currencies. Sometimes this is possible, sometimes not.

BYE BYE, AMERICAN PIE

A stone's throw from the rat race of modern American life are the quaint and peaceful fishing villages of Mexico. Towns on the Caribbean and Pacific coasts, like Zihuatanejo-Ixtapa, are filled with American expatriates, especially in winter. Some of these Americans fit the stereotype of aged cane-wielding retirees, but many look like tanned and mellow clones of Jimmy Buffet minus the hard drinking and the tattoos. Zihuatanejo keeps most of its tourists confined to the resorts of Ixtapa, a short distance outside of town. The permanent American residents like it that way. Zihuatanejo, located in the state of Guerrero along the Pacific coast, used to be a tiny fishing village. But its population exploded from twenty-five hundred in 1968 to nearly eighty thousand in 1998 because of the American expatriate and tourist influx. This invasion has not been big enough, however, to crush the spirit of the place. Zihuatanejo still retains its small-town flavor. There is no McDonald's and no UPS service, notes American resident Dennis Cass, "just the psychic quiet of the village." Expatriates lounge on their balconies at the Hotel Ima that sits on a hill overlooking La Playa Madera, one of the town's four beaches, and the bay ringed with sharp hills beyond. Beer and tequila are inexpensive, and for ten pesos or one U.S. dollar Americans can catch a taxi to the beach for a late afternoon swim. After sunset the Americans repair to the Perla Beach Club at La Playa Ropa for fresh seafood and an entertaining evening. With the waves crashing softly on the beach and the sound of guitar music in the air, American retirees have a difficult time thinking of the lifestyle they have left behind in the United States.[11]

Despite the recent escalation of real estate prices, Mexico remains a bargain compared to California and the East Coast. A newly retired couple can easily set up housekeeping in a rented apartment or house in Zihuatanejo or Cancún or Taxco and live well on a budget of $1,500 a month. A really nice house with stateside amenities can sell for about $100,000; but since most sellers demand cash, it is easier to rent. A variety of locations appeal to American retirees: colonial San Miguel de Allende, the rugged port of La Paz on the Baja peninsula, or something quaint like Zihuatanejo. Not by coincidence, the places where most retired American expatriates are to be found are in altitudes high enough to enjoy "eternal spring," or they are on the Pacific coast, where temperatures are higher but tempered by continual ocean breezes. The U.S. State Department reported in 2004 that 385,000 Americans lived year round in Mexico. That number is almost certainly higher today. Americans are building homes at Mexican beach resorts at a record pace, getting a waterfront hacienda for a third of what it would cost in the United States. According to a CNN media report, "Creature comforts of American life are becoming more available south of the border. Satellite and cable television brings news and entertainment right into the expat's living room, the Internet keeps them in touch with hometown newspapers, and American food brands are available in the supermarket."[12] Americans are flocking to the waterfront corridors of Cabo San Lucas, Puerto Vallarta, Amarillo, and the Tulum area of Cancún. Their oral histories and published interviews constitute a compelling expatriate vision.

Several years ago, Polly Vicars retired to Puerto Vallarta on the Pacific coast with her husband and became a permanent resident of the town's "Gringo Gulch." In Puerto Vallarta, most Americans live in villas high in the hills and gulches overlooking Puerto Vallarta. Their well-appointed homes command stunning views of Banderas Bay and the Pacific Ocean beyond. Gringo Gulch is an American residential community of long standing, and more than a few expatriate Americans can trace their background in Puerto Vallarta back to the days when Elizabeth Taylor and Richard Burton carried on an explosive romance in their hillside villa in the 1960s after a hard day on the set of filming *The Night of the Iguana*. The old American community is a bit stuffy and insular; and more recent expatriates have located in the oceanside villages to the south and north of town. But what unites old-timers like Polly Vicars and newly relocated retirees is their love of the town with its old church and the lovely broad walk along the beach called the

Malecon.[13] The town is preoccupied with the safety of its foreign residents, and "tourist police" snappily dressed in white are everywhere to be seen in town to protect carousing tourists from themselves and to protect foreign residents from the criminal elements. Expatriates in Puerto Vallarta seem to fall into several distinct groups and have relatively little to do with one another. The homosexuals frequent the beachfront bars and condos in the old section of town; the respectable old guard relax on the hillsides overlooking the town, and the young retirees inhabit the pool and golf resorts outside town while the tourists drink tequila shooters in the cantinas and party on the beach. But Puerto Vallarta is not unique. Similar "Mediterranean" social scenes can be found in Mexico at Cancún, Rosario Beach, and Ensenada on the Mexican Baja.

The big expatriate center of Mexico, as we have seen, is Guadalajara's Lake Chapala. Bob and Maile Bowles were attracted to Chapala after he retired as an insurance broker in 1989. He and his wife built a four-bedroom house with a swimming pool and a fishpond for $170,000 and settled into the good life. Their living costs are about $18,000 a year, which includes a maid, a gardener, flights home, and membership in the local golf club. Now at an advanced age, Bob Bowles and his wife give scant thought to returning home to Danville, California. "In the States, retiring with even a semblance of our previous lifestyle would have been impossible," they argue. "Here we've actually improved on it."[14]

Guadalajara is similarly attractive. A bustling metropolis of five million people, the city has somehow managed to retain the colonial charm of its 450-year-old heritage. American retirees can be found in the historic downtown area with its seventeenth-century cathedral and sweeping plaza because they like the cultural opportunities of Guadalajara. The Degollado Theater hosts the national philharmonic orchestra, the opera, local dance groups, and the folkloric ballet. Art exhibits of all types are abundant, and American movies are in local theaters one month after their release in the United States. Americans who love to shop can choose from megastores to traditional markets, and the craft-producing towns with their *artesania* at Tonala and Tlaquepaque are a short drive away by car or bus. Finally, Guadalajara and Lake Chapala offer expatriate residents the kind of banking services they are used to in the United States, including ATMs, which are conveniently located. Americans are good spenders in Mexico, and the business community endeavors to keep them happy shoppers. When the travel writer John Howells was compiling information for his book on retiring in Mexico, he sent a questionnaire to retired Americans living in Mexico. One of the questions he asked was, "What do you like best about Mexico?" To his surprise and delight, the answer most frequently on the top of the list was "the people." American expatriates like the easy friendliness of the Mexicans and their willingness to come to the assistance of someone in need, either a neighbor or a foreigner.[15]

In Guadalajara you can also find more than a few retired expatriates who flaunt the immigration rules. "Robert A.," for example, lives permanently in Guadalajara and has no intention of going back to his native Texas. Once in Mexico he quickly tired of the hassle of having to leave Mexico every six months to obtain a new tourist visa. So he just disappeared into Guadalajara. Robert is secure in his knowledge that if he is caught, his punishment will be to leave Mexico in forty-eight hours. But Mexican authorities are not anxious to deport gringo illegals because of the dollars that they pump into the local economy. Mexican authorities estimate that there may be as many as one hundred thousand Americans breaking the immigration laws in Mexico. Immigration laws in Mexico are easy for Americans to circumvent because the terms "legal" and "illegal" are increasingly intertwined in this country. Robert's income is $700 a month, primarily from Social Security. He was a well-paid graphic designer in Houston, but when he retired he found himself dipping frequently into his diminished savings account just to meet expenses. In Mexico his Social Security pension covers all his expenses and he can actually save a bit. His income is well below the US$1,200 a month minimum required by Mexican law for expatriates. But Robert A. is not as poor as he would be if he lived in the United States. He lives modestly in a furnished room in the historic part of the city, which costs $165 a month and shares a kitchen with his landlord. "I don't have a TV," he laughs. "I don't have a car. I am certainly experiencing Mexico." He takes local buses to get around. In the two years that he has lived in Mexico, he has avoided the expatriate community and become fluent in Spanish. The one thing that does bother Robert is that Mexico is currently portrayed as a low-cost expatriate dream. He believes that most of the books on retirement in Mexico are simply scams. Americans who don't know how to hold onto money will lose it just as quickly in Mexico as elsewhere. And real estate, despite the hype, tends to be expensive, reflects Robert A.

Robert A. likes his standard of living in Mexico and is "hooked on the Mexican people and local culture." He spends most of his time sitting at plazas or else painting or reading. Occasionally he frequents cantinas with friends. "I have never been frightened here," Robert says. "I see young women walking home at 3:00 a.m. It is safe." When will Robert A. return to the United States? Never, he hopes. Only failing health could prompt him to return to Houston. "I really like it here. It is just beautiful and the people are great."[16]

Kenneth Tucker, a Vietnam veteran from Massachusetts, found love, marriage, and happiness in the dusty town of San Luis de Cordero in the state of Durango. He built an inexpensive home complete with satellite dish and jacuzzi and heavy screens to keep out the flies. Every six months he drives up to El Paso, shops, and renews his tourist visa at the Mexican consulate. The drive up is a bit of a bother, but it gives him a chance to go to an American bank and load up on creature comforts and food at the Wal-Mart.[17] Tucker is part of the "every-six-month exodus" of gringos who drive north to the border to renew their visa. Essentially, Americans receive a ninety-day tourist visa that they can renew for another ninety days in any Mexican municipality. But after that, it is the long drive north to the border. American expatriates are by law not supposed to be using tourist visas to stay in Mexico indefinitely; but as long as they leave the country every six months and return with a new visa and fresh wads of cash, no questions are asked.

One of the lesser-known American expatriate enclaves is the Anglo-Mormon colony in Chihuahua. These members of the Church of Latter-Day Saints are descendants of several hundred polygamous Mormons who fled Utah to practice their faith south of the border after 1880. Except for American Mormon women imported into the colony from the United States, most of the people of Colonia Dublán and Colonia Juárez are direct descendants of these Mormon pioneers. The Mormons keep themselves aloof from the Mexicans, and in over a century there has been very little Mormon assimilation into the local culture and society. Mormon men take Mexican citizenship to protect assets while their wives retain their American citizenship. According to one study, these Mormon farmers and businesspeople have maintained the American way of life in Mexico. Even their community looks like an imprint of an American suburb transplanted onto the dusty roads and plains of Chihuahua. Behind their manicured lawns and gated communities, the Mormons have a Utah-centered colony. The deep emotional ties that transcend distance and link people to their homeland are what distinguish the Mormons from being just another ethnic enclave in Mexico, report geographers Jeffrey S. Smith and Benjamin N. White.[18]

"THE CARMEL OF THE SOUTH"

Five thousand Americans live in the beautiful colonial city of San Miguel de Allende, Mexico's premier art colony. Here in the central state of Guanajuato they have come to eat, party, and sleep in the sun. In San Miguel de Allende the sybaritic lifestyle is easily maintained because of the festive nature of the place, the local language and art institutes, and the persistent entertaining of affluent Americans. "All these old goats need is a beach and it would be South Miami," complained fellow American Richard Pelham, eighty-three, a former museum curator in America. But as long as Americans don't meddle in local politics, they are generally embraced as friends in San Miguel de Allende.

To Mexicans, San Miguel de Allende is the birthplace of Mexican independence. This is where the first uprising for independence, led by the priest Father Miguel Hidalgo, took place in 1810 in the town's main plaza. But for American expatriate retirees and sojourners, San Miguel de Allende is one of the most comfortable and enjoyable towns in Mexico. About 250 kilometers south of Mexico City, San Miguel is one of the old colonial cities of the silver trade. San Miguel de Allende is known throughout Mexico for its freedom from neon, fast food, and traffic lights. The entire town has been declared a national historic site by the government, and it has been spared the sprawling overdevelopment of most Mexican cities. American artists discovered San Miguel de Allende in the 1930s and 1940s. The GI Bill students enrolled in Mexico's best art college, Instituto Allende, in the 1950s; the hippies and backpackers came in the 1960s and 1970s. Today the town is under invasion again, this time from American and Canadian retirees. Since the 1980s many middle-aged American men and women have begun to arrive in San Miguel de Allende as well.

San Miguel de Allende is the one town in Mexico where visitors will run across large numbers of accomplished professional American women. Single, educated women feel safe here, where there is a sense of community that has attracted independent-minded women from the States. Mostly these "gringas" are fleeing the stress of modern American life. Rita Torlen, for example, left New York City and a successful career at CBS television because she finally got fed up with the sounds of gunshots and police sirens at night. Says Torlen: "My friends said I needed to see a psychiatrist because Mexico was so dangerous. And I was in New York. Give me a break!" In San Miguel de Allende, Torlen does not have to worry about police sirens or late-night violence. The worst noise comes from chugging buses and braying donkeys.

San Miguel attracts American women usually in the thirty to fifty age range who are seeking a deeper meaning to life. Here the tolling of church bells mark the time; the months are defined by fiestas, the seasons by flowers and food. Susan Porter Smith left New York for Mexico after winning a landmark sexual discrimination suit against *Reader's Digest*, where she worked as a scientific research editor. She fell in love with San Miguel de Allende and headed the local Audubon Society. She doubted that she would ever return to New York. She had to make a choice between a career and her sanity and chose the latter. But her friends in Manhattan said she was a fool to give up a career and move to Mexico. "They thought I wasn't using my talents, that I wasn't going to get ahead in life," she reflected.[19] Smith loved Mexico's natural environment. Only death by cancer could take her away from San Miguel.

Of the five thousand expatriates in San Miguel de Allende, there are four single American women to every unmarried American man, says local businesswoman Joane Barcal. Most of these women know that in coming down to Mexico, they may never marry. "A single woman after age twenty-three is an old maid here," says Kris Rudolph, a twenty-nine-year-old owner of El Buen Café, a successful restaurant and cooking school near San Miguel's main square. "The Mexican women feel sorry for me because no one will marry me." Rudolph works long hours at her coffeehouse, especially during the high seasons of winter, August, and Easter. But she has more problems in obtaining supplies, cutting through bureaucratic red tape, and coping with water shortages and undependable electricity than she has as just being a woman in Mexico. Most women in San Miguel de Allende are feminists; they are free spirits who comprise a tossed salad of political and social viewpoints. Some come to retire, some to set up a business, study art or Spanish, write a novel, or escape an abusive relationship. Some come to find healing refuge from a bitter and protracted divorce. Some of the women are tough hard-drinkers who come to pursue a cowgirl's dream and raise hell in the cantinas and find a Mexican lover. But most of the gringas don't hang out in bars. Theirs is a more sedate life marked by eating dessert with friends in the local coffeehouse or enjoying margaritas with the girls at La Fragua Bar. "In San Miguel," notes Joanne Barcal, "an American woman can find out what she can be." The potential for everything from artist to businesswoman, to therapist and spiritual teacher, is there. The bottom line for Americans in San Miguel is that there is a concentrated and accessible community of like-minded American women of all ages and backgrounds who have discovered what is truly important about themselves in particular and life in general.

Most of the year in San Miguel de Allende there is plenty of time to relax. The rat race that most American men and women knew back in Manhattan or Los Angeles does not seem to prevail here. Even when the pace of life gets hectic during high tourist season in winter, expatriates can reflect on the simple fact that it is incredibly beautiful in San Miguel de Allende. Consolation comes in the form of two-hour lunches in the gardens graced with fragrant bougainvillea. As well, by Mexican standards even the poorest American woman or man is middle class. Whereas phones are expensive and unreliable, food is cheap and $20 can buy almost a week's groceries. Clothing is inexpensive and can be purchased in open markets in the town. For some unexplainable reason, San Miguel de Allende has become the expatriate home of a number of psychological therapists and spiritual healers. Some were drawn to the town because of the mineral waters of nearby Escondido Hot Springs. Others came because they learned of the close-knit living-room culture of the expatriate community. Says April Wolf, one of San Miguel's therapists: "The community here is family. What do you want to choose? America or this community and the bells of La Parroquia

Church?" For reasons that the expatriates can't quite explain, the town seems to be a medium of healing and growth. The only scary times, expatriates admit, are when illness strikes.

Usually after breakfast the more elderly American expatriates of San Miguel de Allende gather at the main plaza to sit and chat with their wives and friends and to check the American stock market reports and sports pages of the English-language *Mexico City News*. As the expats bask in the sunlight, the morning gradually slips away until it is time for lunch and drinks and a siesta. Locals call these Americans "*los momios*," like the Egyptian mummys that have been preserved in old age.

Charles Leining and his wife, Joel, both in their sixties, retired from Los Angeles to San Miguel de Allende. To them the town is the "Carmel of the South" and a cultural vortex for expatriates. Leining retired from a job as an administrator at Redlands University and found a furnished apartment with beamed ceilings for $300 a month. He serves as a volunteer English teacher at a nearby Mexican elementary school and writes for the local English-language paper. In the afternoons he plays cribbage with fellow expats or attends meetings of the local Rotary. Leining notes that not all expatriates are happy in San Miguel. The haven has a fair number of "brooding elderly." Yet many retired American expatriates have lived in San Miguel for ten or twenty years. According to Leining, "They left their native land because they had become disillusioned."[20]

Nothing serious takes place in San Miguel de Allende. No one is here to advance a career. Betsy Parrish summed it up recently over black bean soup and coffee: "People here are either running away or trying to find something or don't know what they want, but didn't want what they had in the States."[21]

As the cost of living in major cultural centers like New York, Chicago, and San Francisco has escalated, artists and writers have sought and found an alternative life in the cities and cultural centers south of the border. Cities like Oaxaca and San Miguel de Allende have become arts centers where aspiring American writers can be seen in the coffee shops and cafes along the public squares.

Stan Gotlieb likes to think of himself as an honest man in Mexico. A freelance writer who is married to a gringa and living in Oaxaca, Gotlieb has experienced all the problems and pitfalls of being an expatriate in Latin America. He knows the envy and annoyance of friends back in California who were critical about his moving south of the border. From his own experience he is also aware that not all American expatriates are rich. Some expatriates live in Oaxaca on threadbare budgets. Gotlieb chose Oaxaca because of its indigenous art and culture and "strong support for contemporary arts from the state government." It is "an exciting

place to be, safe, dignified," he says. So far his freelance writing career
has cost him more in computer and Internet time than it has made. But
he has hopes. "If the writing (and some other schemes I have set in
motion) doesn't pay off in the next couple of years, I will be in deep doo-
doo. But I feel positive and committed." Nonetheless, for Gotlieb, Oaxaca
is better than Los Angeles. He sold his house in California with absolutely
no fear about what would happen when this money ran out. The best that
any expatriate in Mexico can hope for is to learn to deal with the normal
expatriate angst. Looking back home at his friends in the urban malaise
of Los Angeles, Gotlieb claims, "I am one of the lucky ones."[22]

While Americans retiring abroad is part of a worldwide phenomenon
involving affluent Westerners, the American demographic penetration
of Mexico is having benefits for Mexico that were largely unforeseen.
Americans prefer to retire in the smaller towns of Mexico. As they settle
and purchase property, they help to create the necessary infrastructure
for community economic development. This gives local entrepreneurs a
chance to build businesses and services that help local citizens as well
as retirees.[23]

FARTHER SOUTH OF THE BORDER

Costa Rica

Robert August left Los Angeles at the age of fifty-seven to find an
endless summer on the beaches of Costa Rica. A surfboard manufac-
turer from Huntington Beach who years ago starred in the surfer film
Endless Summer, August is part of a small group of California exiles at
Tamarindo Beach on the Pacific side of Costa Rica. With his partners
Joey Vogan, a discontented electrician, and Rick Karren, a Huntington
Beach artist, August came to enjoy the beach life. August first visited
Costa Rica in 1991 to participate in a surfing contest organized by the
legendary surfer Greg Noll. One trip was enough to convince August to
cash out his assets and leave America. Within a year after his first visit
to Costa Rica, August purchased a lot on Tamarindo Beach and built a
house with a sweeping vista of Tamarindo's Crescent Bay, with its
sandy beaches and mangroves. Since August's arrival, Tamarindo
Beach has grown from a "few oxcarts" to a thriving community of
retired expatriates and disenchanted nonconformists.

August and his fellow surfers spearheaded Costa Rica's six-hundred-
thousand-tourists-a-year boom that brings in wealthy and middle-class
Americans searching for something they lost in California or elsewhere
in the United States. Robert August likes "the laid-back atmosphere and
the warmth of the Ticos." Besides, says August, where else would a
surfer retire? Mexico is "too Americanized," Hawaii, "get real!", and
the "fantastic waves" of South African beaches are too far from home.

August and his friends arrived just before the boom took off in Costa Rican beach real estate and so were able to purchase land for $10,000 an acre. Today that same land sells for $80,000 an acre. August used his savings to construct a house for $150,000 that is only a two-minute walk from the beach.

For expatriate Russell E. Weinrich, the popular interest in Costa Rica has resulted in a tourist surge of surfers and ecology buffs. Currently Weinrich runs a hotel for surfers on Tamarindo Bay, where he and his wife have lived for thirty years. He is developing his land into an American-style resort. "You need patience and perseverance" to survive in Costa Rica, Weinrich reflects. The main problem is that although foreigners can own land, they can only get three-month visas. America expatriates have to go to Panama or Nicaragua for twenty-four hours every three months to renew their visas.

Meanwhile, the expatriates continue to flock to San José, the capital, which boasts two English-language newspapers, the weekly *Tico Times* and *Costa Rica Today*. Despite some complaints from expatriates, the Costa Rican government sees itself as quite progressive in dealing with foreigners. It gives expatriate businesspeople preferential loans through its national banking system, and many Americans doing business in Costa Rica receive partial exemption from municipal taxes.

Stephen Pingree came to Costa Rica as a tourist and never left because he fell in love with the climate, the high literacy rate, and the inexpensive cost of living. By investing $50,000 in a government-approved Reforestation Project, Pingree was able to get a Permanent Residency Permit in Costa Rica (similar to a U.S. Green Card). Another American, Joe Davis, finally got tired of traveling after his thirteenth trip from the United States to Costa Rica and bought a bar and hotel in the western province of Guanacaste. A short distance from the village of Nosara and the beaches of the Pacific coast, he plays host on the weekends to crowds of happy natives and expatriates. Many Americans stay at his hotel, *The Gilded Iguana*, to try out expatriate life in Costa Rica.[24]

For artist Barry Biesanz, Costa Rica has been a dream come true. Biesanz is an extraordinarily gifted woodcarver whose works have been exhibited in the major art galleries of the United States. In his studio at Bello Horizonte in the mountains of Costa Rica, Biesanz and his wife, Sara, have found an area that is ecologically stable while providing him the wood to craft his bowls and furniture into works of art. Biesanz came with his parents to Costa Rica while a teenager. After his artistic training and some world travel, Biesanz returned to Costa Rica to carve art and a life out of Costa Rica's exotic woods. Today his bowls and boxes can be found in the collections of three U.S. presidents and assorted European royalty. A favorite story at Bello Horizonte is that

Queen Sofia of Spain skipped an official luncheon while in Costa Rica to go on a shopping trip in pursuit of a Biesanz wooden box. Also, being in Costa Rica gives Biesanz and his wife the chance not only to craft fine wooden objects but to work for forest conservation as well. Currently Biesanz employs over twenty Costa Rican workers at his studio and likes to think of himself as the kind of expatriate businessman-artist who can help Costa Rica maintain itself as a beautiful and livable country.[25]

Belize

Recently, a small but significant stream of expatriate retirees has found its way to Belize, the one English-speaking country in Latin America. For retired Americans who have difficulties with foreign languages, this is a tremendous plus. Belize used to be a British colony, so all the signs are in English, the schools teach in English, and the government is patterned on British institutions. The only drawback is that the pace of life in Belize is decidedly laid-back and no one is in a hurry to do anything. Sometimes people interpret the unhurried pace as pure laziness on the part of natives, and they get frustrated and nervous in dealing with locals. But some retirees find, says local businessman Bill Gray, "that they, for possibly the first time in their lives, can completely unwind and enjoy life. Isn't that what retirement is all about?" There is little industry in Belize; this means that the environment is remarkably clean. Also, notes Bill Gray's wife, Claire, the cost of living is surprisingly low if you don't try to buy American status comforts or products that have to be imported from the United States. Washing machines are expensive to buy, but servants to wash your clothes by hand are cheap and reliable. A maid costs $15 a day, buses are cheap, and Americans can enroll their children in private school for $800 a year, a fantastic bargain when compared with the United States and other foreign locales. The Grays retired to Belize and began a tourist and expatriate advisory service in Belize five years ago. They centered on Belize when they discovered that it was only a two-hour flight out of New Orleans and that the weather is an average balmy seventy-nine degrees with no winter and no snow. The beaches, say the Grays, are gorgeous, and the waters of Belize are a fisherman's paradise. Bill and Claire Gray are eager to welcome newcomers. "Belize remains untouched," they claim. "Think of Belize as a kind of Central American Switzerland, politically speaking."[26] Relocation specialists like Lan Sludder believe that Belize, Costa Rica, and Guatemala could be part of a big new Sun-Belt retirement surge in Central America. After all, says Sludder, seventy-eight million Americans will begin to retire in the next decade, and they will choose from a variety of places to live besides Florida. Sludder is editor and publisher of *Belize First* magazine and a long-time expatriate in Central America. What he calls the "New Sun Belt" is rich in beauty, mild in climate, and possessed of almost limitless recreational opportunities.

Most expatriates shun Belize City, with its reputation for sleaziness and crime, and opt instead for the island community of Ambergris Caye, a casual, barefoot kind of place popular with retired Americans as well as tourists. Currently condominium development is transforming Ambergris Caye into an island American community. On Ambergris Caye, the town of San Pedro seems carved out of an earlier place and time when the area was a whaling center and people prospered from selling the innards of sperm whales for wax and perfume. Similar expatriate hot spots at Hopkins Point in Belize are transforming small village communities into American resort areas.

Argentina

Once a country marked by tragedy and turmoil, Argentina is now attracting a growing number of American retirees and expatriate businesspeople. Since the leadership of President Carlos Menem, the former hyperinflated Argentine peso has been stabilized and foreign countries are investing in the country at a rate of $33 billion a year. Inflation, which decimated Argentina's economy at the rate of 500 percent, has been reduced to less than 5 percent. The future looks bright in Argentina, a land of enormously beautiful landscapes, and many American multinational companies are sending their top managers there. Although Buenos Aires is a teeming city of ten million (more than a third of all Argentineans live there), the northern suburbs are attractive and tranquil, and there a nice home with a swimming pool can be purchased for $150,000. Private schools are good, and there is a large expatriate community of British and Americans. Retired expatriates prefer to live in smaller cities like the architectural treasure of Córdoba or at one of Argentina's many beach resorts at the Mar del Plata. Lately, retirees have been settling in Argentina's wine-producing areas. But for the moment, given the distances involved and the problems of resettlement, Argentina appeals more to the sojourner than the retiree looking for a permanent residence abroad.

Uruguay

At first glance the Republic of Uruguay is a country far distant from American life. Nor is it as accessible by train, plane, and automobile as are border countries like Mexico. Yet, expatriates have found Uruguay to be an incredibly comfortable place in which to retire on $2,000 a month for food, lodging, and all the other amenities of retirement. The population of Uruguay is a mixture of Spanish, Italian, and German; and the country retains a decidedly European ambiance. Montevideo is a beautiful modern city with good air service to nearby Buenos Aires and capital cities to the north. Especially attractive to retired expatriates are the high quality of Uruguay's medical care, inexpensive hospital costs (standard rate of $100 a day), high literacy rates, and low crime. "The truth," says Walter Vela, a retired economist from Michigan who lives in Montevideo, "is that my pension would be insufficient in the United States for my wife and me to maintain an acceptable standard of living such as we enjoy in Uruguay." Vela, a Phi Beta Kappa graduate of Swarthmore, worked for many years in Latin America as an economist for General Motors. He advised General Motors on sales campaigns and plant-site acquisitions. The pay was good and he was treated well. But when it came time for retirement "General Motors was not Generous Motors," he said. For the past ten years Walter Vela and his wife have lived the good life in the suburbs of Punta del Este. "We can walk in the parks or in the woods at night without any worries." Recently, the cost of living has increased in Montevideo, and $1,000-a-month rentals for condominium apartments in the best sections of Montevideo are now common. Still, food and medical care remain cheap, and the Velas have no trouble living on $20,000 in pension and dividends. Uruguay's one drawback, however, is that the American community is small; and it is difficult to survive in local life without a good grasp of the Spanish language.[27]

PROBLEMS OF LATIN LIFE

Latin American countries like Mexico and Costa Rica, with their Wal-Marts and fast-food chains that remind expats of home, are nonetheless foreign countries; often even there, expatriate retirees from the United States feel a sense of alienation and being out of sync with their surroundings. The biggest obstacle that the retiree or sojourner encounters in Latin America is "the bureaucracy." Whether in government, business, or banking, expatriates have to run the gauntlet of getting signatures and stamps from many different people, and this process tends to be very frustrating to direct-speaking, results-oriented Americans. Also, Americans are not used to the pervasive Latin American system of petty bribery, called *la mordida*, or "bite," to resolve problems in public and private life. Despite the increase of English-speaking populations in Latin America, Spanish remains the language of the majority of the people. Thus Americans need to speak Spanish moderately well in order to accomplish even routine daily tasks. Last, expatriates in search of the simple leisurely life are surprised by the noise and congestion of Latin American cities.

Just as in all major cities of the world, many Latin American urban areas have crime problems. Retirees who have chosen to live "south of the border" are often surprised to find themselves living behind large walls in well-fortified houses with security patrols. Mexico, for example, is less safe than it once was. In Mexico City, according to María del Pilar Hiroishi, Secretary of Tourism for the Mexico City government, on average twenty foreigners are attacked in the city every day. American tourists have experienced an escalation of highway robberies in Mexico reminiscent of the Old West, and some Americans even complain that the bandits are members of the Mexican Judicial Police. Their stories are being recounted in the Los Angeles media and circulated widely in the United States.[28] Because Americans are the most frequent visitors to Mexico, they are the hardest hit. Of ten foreigners killed in Mexico City in 1998, eight were Americans. Recently, the most publicized murder of an American in Mexico was that of artist Carol Schlosberg in April 1998. Schlosberg traveled by motorcycle from her home in Vermont to the sleepy Pacific coast beach town of Puerto Escondido. While walking on the beach she was attacked, raped, and drowned. Shortly thereafter the U.S. State Department issued a travel advisory warning Americans about dangerous conditions in Mexico. But Mexico is hardly Colombia; and given the over nine hundred thousand U.S. citizens who reside in Mexico and the thousands of others visiting there, the number of killings is relatively small. Mexican officials point out that New York, Paris, and Madrid also have their problems with attacks on foreigners.

Currently the Mexican Secretariat of Foreign Affairs has launched an extensive public relations campaign directed at the United States to get Americans to spend time in or relocate to Mexico. The coveted dollar-spending American from el Norte, says the government, will be well looked after. As a means of attracting more American retirees and tourists, Mexico has facilitated the process of getting a tourist visa. Now Americans must show a valid passport and photo identification.

Americans generally have an easier time bringing themselves into Mexico than transporting their automobiles. Cars are expensive in Latin America and a black-market staple. Mexico, for example, controls automobile imports in order to protect its local car industry. Expatriates who wish to bring their cars with them have to obtain a special automobile permit from the government, buy Mexican insurance, and have the car title and registration in their possession. Finally, expatriates must use their credit cards to purchase a surety bond for the car they are driving into Mexico. If they sell the car in Mexico, they lose the bond. To avoid the hassle, many Americans simply buy old Volkswagens or Chevrolets in Mexico and drive them around as transport of convenience. Most expatriates know that, in Mexico, Chevrolets and Volkswagens do not have a life—they have a half-life—and are kept roadworthy by industrious Mexican mechanics long after they have disappeared from American highways. Automobile laws of a similar nature are also in force in Turkey and many underdeveloped countries. Often customs officials are more concerned about the status of the automobile than the owner's visa.

In Costa Rica, American farmers and ranchers like Donald Hayes, who has an ecology school on six hundred acres of rainforest, have problems with the government bureaucracy and with squatters. Hayes uses armed guards to patrol his land to keep the squatters out. A favorite tactic of unscrupulous Costa Rican businesspeople is to allow Americans to spend their capital to develop a parcel of land and then, once the business is successfully launched, to send in professional squatters to get the land cheap. Thus it is much easier simply to retire in one of the fashionable suburbs of San José, take a few courses at the local national university, and enjoy a comfortable life. But whether a retiree, a farmer, or a developer, everyone admits that for good or ill, Costa Rica is "a different place."[29]

Even in sleepy Belize there are downsides for potential expatriates to consider. If you can't live without your classical music station, your trendy bookstore, and your gourmet delicatessen, then Central America is not for you, says Lan Sludder. Belize, especially, concludes Sludder, can be "exasperating." The rules are different in Belize. Writes Sludder: "The people who make and enforce the rules are different. Sometimes there are no rules. Sometimes there is a set of rules for you, and a different one for everyone else."[30] Lin Sutherland, a freelance writer, found life in Belize to be akin to what one might have experienced decades earlier in old Key West. But he liked it for only a year. If you are involved in the affairs of the world and need more than an occasional shot of culture, Belize can be maddening, Sutherland notes. There is only so much beach, sand, blue sky, and solitude that a progress-addled American can endure.[31]

SUMMARY

It is easy to satirize expatriate retirees in Latin America. Whether they are dozing in the plaza of a Mexican resort or complaining about the shiftless and irresponsible Latinos, endlessly discoursing on the stock market or prowling the markets and chatting in "Dick and Jane" Spanish, they seem more a parody than a reflection of America. They dress too well in their "Tilley Endurables," they talk too loudly, and they drink too much. Also, it is easy to be critical of the way retirees and their money can overnight turn lovely Latin American hideaways into affluent citadels of privilege much as they have reshaped Chapel Hill, North Carolina; Santa Fe, New Mexico; and Monterey, California.

Yet, is this not how the American dream is supposed to work out? Isn't it the tale of endless movement onward or westward in search of new opportunities or experiences? Criticism aside, one can make a point that the retirement generation of expatriates have come to towns and cities abroad with great climates and gorgeous scenery as community seekers. And in their own fashion they are building small-town America abroad much like their younger "Latte Generation" compatriots. The impact of this American community building abroad may have overtones of cultural imperialism, but at the moment it is not necessarily clear what real harm is being done. Retired expats are finding good places abroad in which to live, and soon many other Americans will follow in their path.

Expatriates bring powerful economic resources with them when they retire abroad. Although most are not rich, they are certainly rich by Latin American standards. The hairdresser in Puerto Vallarta who earns $5 a day knows that her American matron is mistress of the financial universe. The impact of this economic power varies from place to place. At present it is most visible in Mexico, Costa Rica, and Panama; the local economies of these countries get plenty of bounce from the expatriate dollar.

Even a preliminary overview of the retired expatriate in Latin America such as this makes abundantly clear that Americans today, of whatever age, are more mobile than they ever have been. Ours is an age of global culture that is fed by travel, mass media, and the commodification of the exotic. The retired American lives in an age of migration that has already changed the world and is contributing in his or her own way to the growing cultural diversity of countries. How rich and poor, retiree and worker, white and nonwhite intermix in this new global culture remains to be seen. Social analyst Stanley Kurtz of the Hoover Institution suggests that retirees may be forced to leave the United States for foreign climes as intergenerational demographic stresses continue to mount with the birth declines and the rise of public resentment over tax support of disproportionate numbers of elderly citizens.[32] At the first signs of stress, will the retired expatriates take flight like a flock of snow geese to return to the native habitat? Probably not. Today our ever-moving populations have displaced the sedentary economies of towns and cities. To survive, Americans have been prompted to pursue livelihoods and maintain social ties over vast expanses of geography.

"Nomadism may well be the hallmark of our post-industrial future," notes social observer Cullen Murphy. Twenty-five million Americans now live out of their cars in an "affluent peripatetic" state for part of the year, and a herd of nine million recreation vehicles roams the American range.[33]

The aged have become modern bedouins just like the younger expatriates. They know that, despite their search for stability, the old ties to America don't have much meaning. What's left in America is consumption without community and a society as fascinating and rootless as beautiful cut flowers in a Japanese ikebana.

Nomadism becomes a kind of sensibility that affects all avenues of culture. The "RV" is just one part of the nomadic *geist*. It can be seen in the clothes we buy and the books on leisure and travel that we read, as well as in our way of looking at the world as one big tourist resort. Americans have access to global satellite networks, so retirees in Lake Chapala or Buenos Aires can check the Dow Jones industrial averages or converse with their families by cell phone. The world is easily accessible, and the American dream is lightweight and packs well. Like their computers and cell phones, the culture of Americans has become another form of "maximum legal carry-on luggage."

Chapter 9

The Return of the Native

Ah, one doesn't give up one's country any more than one gives up one's grand-mother. They're both antecedent to choice.

Henry James, *Portrait of a Lady*

So I came home. To stuff in storage I can't identify and friends who can scarcely identify me.

Lois Gould

HOME AS FOUND

American expatriate intellectuals ranging from James Fennimore Cooper to Henry James, Thomas Wolfe, and James Baldwin have grappled with the problem of dealing with the homeland, with that core that makes the American what he or she is. The problem becomes particularly acute when the expatriate returns. Americans who have stayed abroad a long time often notice upon their return that the American language and thought processes as well as cultural clues to behavior have changed dramatically. Like some modern-day Rip Van Winkle fresh from a twenty-year nap on a mountain, they find a new, changed America upon their return. Home as found seems to be a country that has gotten far ahead of the returning expat. Often returning expatriates have a reverse culture shock from America that is as surprising and debilitating as anything experienced overseas. Home as found is not always a welcome home.

James Fennimore Cooper departed for Europe in 1826 at the height of his fame as author of *The Last of the Mohicans*. What ostensibly was to be a one- or two-year stint as the American consul in Lyon, France, became a six-year tenure.[1] Cooper found America much changed for the worse upon his return. What bothered Cooper the most was that he found an America where the materialistic values of getting ahead and "money grubbing" took precedence over the loftier moral principles of American republicanism. Cooper's literary characters reveal much about his views as a returned expatriate. "Steadfast Dodge" in *Homeward Bound*, for example, is the kind of American who thinks one person's opinion is as good as another's and who believes that everything in life should be operated through "manipulation." Steadfast Dodge, true to his name, is a man without principle—a man on the make—and exemplifies what Cooper found wrong with the country when he returned. Cooper rendered a final critical judgment of his country in his novel *Home as Found*, where he described an America that had become contemptuous of restraints on individualism and a nation that little realized that the maintenance of order was the first step toward the preservation of freedom. Cooper used his characters to portray American types, most of whom are social-climbing braggarts and vulgar gossips who try to pull everyone down to their own level. The expatriate years moderated Cooper's republicanism, which had been so evident in his earlier Leatherstocking novels like *The Last of the Mohicans* and *The Spy*. Cooper's buoyant political optimism ultimately gave way to tempered conservatism and troubled concern for the well-being of the country.[2]

In the Gilded Age of late-nineteenth-century America, immense fortunes were being obtained by men whose ideas of themselves and of their relationship to society required a costly medieval style of architecture and pretensions of landed nobility. Henry James was repelled by this parvenu society and gave it withering criticism in his novels. Emigrating to Europe, James found a sense of tradition and the leisured life that gave him an alternative to Americans' absorption in making money. Although James's novels, like *Roderick Hudson*, are set in Europe, for the most part they are critiques of the American dedication to business, America's hostility to leisure, and the pretensions of nouveau riche Americans to the aristocratic life. These Americans, James wrote in *Portrait of a Lady*, had grown up to be "rank Tories and bigots."[3]

Early in the twentieth century, Randolph Bourne, the writer and social critic, noted that the realities of the American homeland tended to mock the very ideals that it instilled in its youth. Bourne and many of his pre–World War I generation believed that ideals were important, but those ideals were being ground under by America's advancing material and technological wealth. During his first trip to Europe in 1913, Bourne found that it was time for what he called "the hot chaos of America," its love of freedom and its creative energy, to spill over the world before it was extinguished in his native land. He called this new cosmopolitan approach "Transnational America." Bourne believed that America could be a "home" only in the sense that the democratic ideology could be applied both in America and abroad to enhance society and control "the money power."[4]

Sometimes expatriates find that the cultural, emotional, or historical roots that once anchored them have frayed or atrophied and have set them adrift. Thomas Wolfe, author of the splendidly incisive *You Can't Go Home Again*, found the roots of his alienation from America in his hometown. Wolfe grew up in his mother's crowded boarding house in Asheville, North Carolina, in the 1920s. The boarders were transients, the furniture nondescript, the meals uneventful, the house boring but secure. The whole feeling of the place was one of rootlessness and emotional sterility. Today, the Wolfe boarding house is the Thomas Wolfe Museum; and a casual stroll through the place as a tourist is enough to see why Wolfe escaped the home place as soon as he was physically and intellectually able. For the expatriate, America is much like that boarding house. It is safe and secure, but transient and sterile.

From the 1920s until the 1970s, a significant amount of expatriate criticism focused on the limitations of American political culture. Black expatriates especially, like Ollie Harrington, Richard Wright, and James Baldwin, showed how residence abroad gave them a sense of critical perspective to attack the segregated society they had fled. Also, the several thousand Americans who went into exile in Canada and Sweden as draft resisters during the Vietnam War testify to the enduring significance of expatriates as political dissenters. Both blacks and draft resisters abroad were spied on by the FBI and other American intelligence organizations during the Cold War and the Vietnam conflict. Expatriate criticism of American life was muted in the late twentieth century because of the end of the Cold War. Recently, however, the expatriate view has become increasingly strident and ideological owing to the Iraq war and escalating American social and environmental problems.

TOWARD A NEW AMERICAN MIGRATION NARRATIVE

In the process of self-discovery many American expatriates have to deal with their belief in America as a Promised Land. As citizens they internalized the story of the American dream, the search and discovery of a newfound land of inventiveness, individualism, and freedom. Two oceans, the Pacific and the Atlantic, served as a protective moat, a barrier that allowed Americans to grow and prosper while shielded from foreign despotism and cultural and religious oppression. This in time came to be part of the immigrant narrative of life in the New World, a narrative that told of vast rolling prairies, teeming cities, and limitless opportunities—a place where the migrant could shed his debilitating Old-World identity and start anew. Americans get used to looking at their country from certain angles, and surely the immigrant narrative has profoundly conditioned how we think about our country, even when immigrants have at times been unwelcome, and foreigners, then and now, have seen the welcoming torch of the Statue of Liberty to be a disheartening mirage.

There is another countervailing narrative, however, to the American story. It is the narrative of Americans who have left their native land to pursue their great and ennobling dreams elsewhere. This narrative extends outward and connects the American with the vast periphery of the globe.[5] In effect, it internationalizes the American. Thus the immigration narrative and the expatriate narrative become as one in the story of the making of the American. For lack of a better term, one can call this the development of a double-sided American experience. Perhaps this explanation is not as secure as earlier "Virgin Land" myths of America, but nothing in life is simply the safe passage from one place to another. All migration has consequences. Like Ulysses, the migrant knows that the passage to Ithaca is difficult, dangerous, and sometimes rewarding, sometimes not.

American creativeness, which has always added a contagious vitality to world affairs, is now moving overseas at an increased rate to stimulate thought and action in Europe, Asia, and other parts of the world. Whether this constitutes a brain drain is debatable. The American expatriate looks beyond the shores of his or her native land and sees a world devoid of national boundaries. He or she sees a global reality that goes beyond cultural boundaries and transcends the old notion that only in America's geographic space is something exceptional to be found. Today American men and women of a variety of races and ages, an immutably mixed and hybrid lot, transcend the national unit. Like modern corporations, expatriates are creating networks that bypass the nation-state framework, and what we now have is an archipelago of talented Americans strung out across international zones or borders.

Our modern nomads live in communities of their own temporary construction. These expats are world citizens, yet they have none of the obligations that citizenship normally implies.[6] This is the dark side of cosmopolitanism. For without the strong attachments of national loyalty that extend beyond family ties, it may be difficult for expatriates to develop habits and attitudes of social responsibility. Eventually the locus of American expatriate activity will most likely be found in two areas:

"National Geographic scenes"—areas of immense physical beauty, lush exoticism, and physical comfort—and "brain scenes"—intellectual and commercial centers like Singapore, Hong Kong, Geneva, and London. It is doubtful that expatriates will be attracted to rogue nations like Iraq or Libya or impoverished countries like Haiti and North Korea.

For expatriates, the center and the periphery, or the metropole and the colony, are not as important binaries of world identity as they used to be. From a cultural standpoint there is much more fluidity to our perceptions of home, hearth, and country than there used to be. Some expatriates become nomads like the writer Paul Theroux, equally at home in London or Africa, riding the trains of Asia, or exploring Micronesia by kayak. Home is "nowhere"—the word that Thomas Moore delineated as "utopia." Further, today the expatriate is one who indigenizes much that is foreign to suit his or her own uses.

WHY THEY LEFT

"Live, live all you can; it is a mistake not to," Henry James writes in his novel *The Ambassadors*. In this novel James relates the story of how a man goes to Europe to rescue his widowed girlfriend's son from the fleshpots of Paris. The irony of the story is that the rescuer discovers that the son is living a life of freedom and creativity in Paris that most people only dream of. The novel ends sadly when the son, responding to duty, returns to America to run the family factory, "which at unbelievable expense produces unnamable objects." Today not so many expatriates will act like the dutiful son in *The Ambassadors* and return. The expatriate has the sanction to become his or her own self; and to do this he or she must become a wanderer from the American shore. Expatriates do not wish to be condemned to the "unbelievable expense" of living in a country that may not really have a place for them. Expatriates also fear that to return to the United States is to risk what Doris Lessing once called "the atrophy of imagination."

People leave a country when they conclude that their society and its leaders are incapable of dealing with their own problems. Interviewed for this book were numerous people who have chosen to remain abroad because of what they called "America's unwillingness to be America"—in short, to solve the problems that a democratic society should be solving. In one important respect America has faltered because its leadership has ignored its key job: to build and maintain a stable and livable political economy. When, for example, we see the ladder of social mobility dissolving for both blue collar and middle class alike, when we witness the flight of corporations to low-wage countries of the Third World, what future can the American anticipate? This book has dealt with dozens of case studies of Americans who have gone elsewhere to find what had been promised them in the land of their nativity. In other times expatriates went overseas to "have a life." New expatriates today journey abroad to "have a life" and an income to support it. Thus we now have an inversion of the American dream. Americans are discovering that the new frontier lies in the lands that their parents and grandparents abandoned. By moving overseas a new generation is finding room to profitably reinvent itself.

Finally, many of the expatriates studied or interviewed for this book admitted that their concern about the fate of their children had much to do with their leaving America. Simply put, they did not want to bring up their children in a society where widespread sociopathic behavior jeopardizes their upbringing. Further, each year, owing to divorce, the decline of the two-parent family, and the decreasing availability of safe, supportive neighborhoods, fewer children in America are experiencing the essentials of a good, well-nurtured childhood.[7] Safe societies like those of Canada, New Zealand, Singapore, Belize, Holland, and Sweden are very high on the emigration lists of expatriate parents. Despite their lives overseas, expatriate Americans remain remarkably informed about developments taking place in their home country. Usually these developments or trends confirm their convictions that leaving the country was the right thing to do. Most of the news that comes abroad out of America is bad. Newspapers carry disturbing accounts of violence, culture wars, and the exhaustion of commonality in the United States.[8]

America has never been betrayed by its own success. What has betrayed America is that its leadership has ceased believing in success for all. We now have an increasingly two-tiered society, with the concentration of wealth in the top 10 percent of American families, a level reminiscent of the economic dystopia of America during the Gilded Age of the late nineteenth century. The selfishness and the pursuit of privilege that are so rampant in America today have rendered many Americans the hapless victims of forces beyond their control. An image comes to mind: in a sleek, white "stretch" limousine, affluent passengers sip champagne en route to an elegant party as their vehicle comfortably cruises through the city's mean streets, littered with the refuse of an uncaring society. We behave in our civic and political life as though anything goes, so long as our side wins. And we are surprised when our compatriots reveal themselves to be graceless winners, self-centered jerks, and occasional killers. Were James Fennimore Cooper and Randolph Bourne to return today, they would discover that many Americans are the willing collaborators of their own oppression and find surcease of their problems in the soporific effects of mindless consumption, television, or drugs.

One of the ironies of American expatriate life is that citizens who have internalized the Jeffersonian prejudice against cities in their own nation flock to urban areas abroad. Thus, people who would be shocked to entertain thoughts of living in Chicago, New York, or Los Angeles will readily migrate to Rome, Tel Aviv, or Tokyo and endure many discomforts there. There is a simple reason for this: American cities are for the most part unpleasant. Boston lacks the ambience of Paris; and Chicago has not a quarter of the architecture and beauty of a city like Florence. Further, in America the word "city" has been color coded to mean black and Hispanic communities that are potentially as violent as any group in Bosnia or Baghdad. Meanwhile, older industrial American cities decline and public sector employment for the poor evaporates. In some respects the prospects for American cities today are more dismal than they were during the Great Depression of the 1930s; and the gentrification of urban areas like Washington, D.C., Seattle, or Charleston will do relatively little to attract the multiclass populations that make cities livable entities. Today, when urban experts point to models of "livable cities," they point to cities in Canada, Britain, France, and Australia before they look to American examples. The late Jane Jacobs, the city planner who long ago in her book *The Life and Death of Great American Cities* issued a warning that American urban areas were in trouble, emigrated with her family to Canada.[9] Expatriates settle in cities like Paris and Tokyo because they are safe, diverse, interesting, attractive, and a lot of fun. In addition, cities like Prague and Budapest are rich in heritage and lively ambiance and are a most pleasant alternative to the new spatial apartheid of edge cities on the suburban fringes of metropolitan America. In the United States the middle class has fled to the suburbs, where it is concerned about education and taxes, not human welfare and economic development.

Crime rates have always been high in America, and since 1960 6.6 million Americans have become victims of murder, rape, assault, or robbery each year. A murder occurs every twenty-two minutes, a rape every five minutes, an aggravated assault every twenty-eight seconds! Even suburban security, once the keystone of the American dream, is no longer a given. Now suburbs are filled with "gated communities" with chain-link fences and floodlights reminiscent of the balkanized and tribalized Third World societies.[10] Although most expatriates have had little real contact with violence in American cities, they nonetheless stress in interviews how "safe" they feel in their city of choice overseas.[11]

Ultimately, as we have seen in this book, expatriates leave America because it has become difficult for them to earn a living in their homeland. To keep today's American in a lifestyle currently identified as a middle-class way of life, says economist Lester Thurow, will require in the future housing, education, and infrastructure in excess of $240,000 per individual. This is what it takes to be a "self-sufficient, average citizen worker-consumer." But using simple multiplication, Thurow says, even if the United States were to have a 4 percent economic growth rate, more than 40 percent of the country's gross national product would have to be devoted to providing for these Americans.[12] This can come about only through a major redistribution of wealth, which is unlikely. Despite all the media noise about economic growth in America, nearly 14 percent of all Americans live below the government poverty level ($20,650 for a family of four). And the high-paying, high-tech jobs in our country account for only 4 percent of total job growth. Whether we like to admit it or not, America is becoming the land of the minimum wage dead-end job. According to a recent study of the Bureau of Labor Statistics, almost half of all new jobs created in America in the future will be positions that require the least training and the smallest salary. The Bureau reports that the profession with the most growth will be that of cashier.[13]

What looms ahead is a century of rather mediocre economic performance matched by rapid population growth. The standard of living will decrease significantly, Thurow predicts, and the United States will become a much more contentious nation, especially since it has lost control of its borders and is now experiencing historic levels of immigration, both legal and illegal.[14]

America today is in the midst of an assimilation crisis because of the confusion between what we should demand of the throngs of immigrants on our shores and what we should expect of them. Although immigrants need to become a part of American society rather than sojourners in it, "Americanization programs" have been largely abandoned as a prerequisite for residence and citizenship. Writes veteran social observer and journalist Georgie Anne Geyer, "There is a real possibility that the idea and practice of citizenship in America may for all intents and purposes die in our lifetime."[15] Certainly a truly multiracial society will undoubtedly prove much harder to govern, and many Americans may be unwilling to face the future of a balkanized America rife with enormous unrest and violence.

One of history's clear lessons is that it is difficult for a nation to become rich. It is also difficult for a nation to stay rich, for its assets can be squandered by wars and reckless development; its citizens may become burdened by excessive taxation or even by environmental despoliation; and its society may founder in ethnic chauvinism and uncontrolled immigration. The current war in Iraq, according to the Congressional Budget Office, is costing the U.S. Treasury $9 billion per month on top of the initial troop deployment costs of $13 billion. The economic and social stresses that arise out of these developments will perhaps lead to increasing emigration; as a result, overseas Americans may soon become as common as their British counterparts were in the days of nineteenth-century empire.

THE TRIBAL DIASPORA

Americans do not think of themselves as members of a particular tribe. They are nonetheless a singular breed. They think differently and act differently from the members of other tribes. Americans are, for example, a very self-reliant people and believe they have personal responsibility for making their own way in the world. Americans can be generous in helping the needy, but they resist collective guarantees of security. They also prefer to accord respect based on achievement rather than on social standing or position. Finally, most Americans place strong emphasis on immediate achievement, an attitude not characteristic of cultures with a longer view of time and a greater acceptance of the cycles of life.

Regardless of problems at home, most Americans have difficulty getting America out of their heads. Even when they are residents of long standing in foreign countries, expats are constantly reminded of their American identity in countless ways. Jon Reed, who teaches American Studies at a small university near Kyoto, Japan, suggests that it is this immutable tribalism that marks the American when abroad. "I was given the charge of developing ideas for an advertising campaign to recruit American students to our American Studies program here in Japan," he said. "When the recruitment committee members, who were all Japanese, read the promotional literature I had written, they severely criticized me for making the material *so American*."[16] Further, these tribal traits manifest themselves in other forms. Take Israel on America's national holiday, for example. What could be more American than hot dogs and fireworks on the Fourth of July? And in Tel Aviv the "Fourth" is taken as a serious event by natives and expats alike, with plenty of hot dogs and fireworks. Usually on the Fourth, the Israeli government sponsors an American concert for the Israeli philharmonic to be led by an American conductor like the talented transnational Zubin Mehta. Many neighborhoods hold street fairs; children light sparklers, and adults wear T-shirts with the American flag and other symbols of the United States. Most celebrants are happily ignorant of the incongruity of the event. Throughout the world the proliferation of American Clubs and Americans Abroad Inc. organizations illustrates the ways in which Americans find group identity in the expatriate diaspora.

Such aspects of the tribal diaspora reveal that there is no such thing as a man (or woman) without a country. All individuals, no matter how wretched their past or how pleasant their exile, have the contours and heart of their country permanently etched in their minds. The country of their nativity comes to each of them in the countless reflections and experiences of daily life—from the smell of a particular food to laughter on a street corner to memories of old school days. When home drops below the horizon, wrote James Baldwin, "it rises in one's breast and acquires the overwhelming power of menaced love."[17]

Since James Fennimore Cooper's time, Americans have discovered through their experiences of life abroad the way in which American culture has shaped their minds and impressed upon them the power of the American dream. The experience of expatriation has enabled them, says critic Harold T. McCarthy, "to delve deeper into the truth of what it means to be an American and to bear witness against those divisive influences that act to pervert that meaning."[18] Thus, home can be found in the American imagination as well as in the national heartland. Ultimately, the expatriate experience sharpens or crystallizes certain ideas or contexts and makes them more understandable. Henry James and James Baldwin came to a better understanding of America when they were able to view it from afar. This experience is not unique to Americans. Isaac Bashevis Singer wrote of Jewish peasant life in Eastern Europe before World War II from the confines of his comfortable Manhattan apartment. And James Joyce wrote of nights in Dublin pubs while living with his wife in a cramped apartment in Trieste, Italy.

Americans who live abroad tend to be more critical of their country than are their homeland counterparts. Essentially, this is because expatriates are usually better educated than the American man or woman on the street and are comfortable with a critical attitude. Also, the domestic preoccupations and emotional buffers of everyday American life are nonexistent for the expatriate, who thus tends to focus on America intellectually rather than in terms of simple, nonreflective, workday experience.

To be an American expatriate is a complex fate, Henry James noted long ago. The American expatriate learns quickly that what often passes for an American identity is nothing more than a series of myths about one's heroic ancestors; and that these ancestors were as susceptible to greed, violence, and rapaciousness as any other people in the world. Ultimately, the expatriate finds that heritage, skin color, language, or manners are rather superficial cultural instruments. A person's freedom can be judged not by the home country but only by the individual's flexibility, by his or her openness toward life. Thus it is not a specific situation that makes individuals free, but the individuals themselves.

Although Americans often move to new countries to live and work, they are well known for their reluctance to acquire citizenship in their new homelands. Studies have shown numerous examples of these "quiet expatriates" who have moved on. Most Americans abroad continue to feel strong cultural ties to their country, and ideological considerations do not loom large in their decision to remain abroad or return home. Says one emigration researcher who has examined the matter at length, "Indeed, we found few who totally disavowed their American heritage or who felt politically alienated from the United States."[19] Also, Americans' motives for moving abroad often differ from the motives that they cite for remaining abroad. In many cases expatriates express surprise that they have been abroad sometimes as long as thirty years when they meant to stay away only for a short time. Whatever the expatriate's notions of living outside the United States, the notion of *permanence* is clearly not what the expat originally had in mind.[20]

Ultimately, the main difference between the expatriate and the native is that the expat is there by choice, whereas the native is there largely by circumstance. Natives are mired in the diurnal problems of survival, whereas expatriates, because of their education and their passports, have a kind of diplomatic immunity against the social and economic realities of foreign life. Also, expatriates cannot escape their origins, the marks of which they carry everywhere. Paul Fussel, in his provocative work *Abroad,* suggests that the expatriate, though part of a diaspora, comes to his or her new land as both a lover and a conqueror.[21]

THE COUNTRY BEHIND US AND THE COUNTRY AHEAD

Why people emigrate is indeed a complicated question. To answer it, this study has attempted to provide a number of explanations of the contemporary expatriate experience. Further, this study tends to corroborate findings in the scholarly literature that posit emigration as a normal repercussion of immigration.[22] It should not be surprising that the phenomenon of leaving America arises during a period when rapid and highly volatile immigration waves crash on the American shores. Last, in explaining recent American expatriate trends we have seen how what sociologists call "self-expressive factors": the search for adventure, the quest for fulfillment or religious identity, and the desire for economic advancement are important aspects of the decision to leave America. Still for some, says writer Lois Gould, who returned to America after living several years abroad, "the urge to flee remains a constant. Nomads, gypsies, writers and artists may be born with a 'gottago' gene."[23]

Long after concluding the research for this book, I began to have fitful stirrings late at night. In the dream currents of a writer's mind there emerged faces and voices that mixed together like streams joining a river, until I could see them as a sum of the whole restless American migratory experience:

American women, like Corinne Tachikawa, married to Japanese men, trying to cross cultures, raise families, and retain at least a semblance of their own identities in an Asian country.

African Americans like Patricia Collins and Mal Waldron, feeling more comfortable and more American while resident in Paris and Belgium than they ever could in Atlanta or New York.

Middle-class pioneers like Susan Rogers and her husband, who have journeyed to the shores of New Zealand in search of a better life for their children and themselves. Or Barbara Duvoisin, who left America to work for a multinational company in Russia, married a Russian, and is raising a family in Moscow.

Artists like Barry Biesanz, who have found careers in Costa Rica and other countries "south of the border," where the living is cheap and easy. And expatriates like Bill and Claire Gray, who have found retirement in Belize to be one of the best social and economic decisions that they have ever made.

These are the new wanderers who make up the whole of the American expatriate experience today. This book is about their dreams and migrations. The lives of these people mirror the expatriate tradition in American culture. The expatriate experience is a story of passages. And if there is any reliable passage to life, it is in the idea that we are connected to these wanderers because they are putting into practice the dreams we all have of going to Xanadu.

The cost of expatriate life is not as great as it used to be. Nor does the expatriate life require the personal sacrifices that it did in former days. Airlines offer expatriates a cheap and reliable mode of exit. And as we have seen, a laptop computer and modem can connect even a remotely situated expatriate to the global communications network of the Internet. Furthermore, the foreign experience is not so foreign anymore. When expatriates settled in Paris after World War II, they were shocked to find a world without Coca-Cola, doughnuts, milkshakes, or dry martinis. Now, one can eat Ben and Jerry's ice cream in Tel Aviv, feast on McDonald's burgers in Paris, and watch American television programs like *CSI Miami* and *Oprah* in Tokyo.

Finally, the expatriate story reveals how much we are all in it together as Americans. The country that we thought we knew presents us with disturbing news and feelings of anxiety. The country ahead of us, though a mystery, fuels our optimism. Today the American wanders anew, and it remains to be seen if the journey will lead to the glowing dawn of the American dream or into the heart of darkness.

THE PRICE OF THE TICKET

Whether expatriates will return home to the United States in the future will ultimately be determined by what the writer James Baldwin called "the price of the ticket," or the personal and psychic costs of being an American.[24] While the vision of home can be idealized in the expatriate memory, there are realities to consider like employment, ease of readjustment, and the ability of a spouse or children reared abroad to adjust to the myriad challenges of contemporary American culture.

James Joyce called these visions epiphanies: flashes of insight when the haze clears and meaning crystallizes. At the very heart of the expatriate experience are epiphanies of patriotism, quality of life, and personal freedom that make the decision to leave America or to return both simple and complex. How it will all end and where our "American" home will be in the future is an extremely complicated question in this age of international economic transformation and global population shifts.

Canaries with their fragile respiratory systems were once used by coal miners to warn of increasing levels of toxicity in the air. What this book suggests is that expatriates are America's canaries. They warn us about economic and political toxicity in the social atmosphere. And when many of our best and brightest Americans of all ages are leaving the country for foreign shores, we ought to take notice. We ought to worry about what this tells us about our nation and how it will affect the great American dream for ourselves and our posterity. These days the expatriate road to Xanadu is becoming increasingly crowded with Americans, and the old homeland ties are fraying.

Regardless of the boom-and-bust cycles of the global economy, most expatriates with skill, money, and determination will adapt and survive in any problematic locale. And if not Russia, China, or Costa Rica, there are always other lands that beckon. For ultimately the American expatriate is a pioneer who creates new forms of inventiveness and expression that may be the beginning of a new culture or civilization. Seen in this perspective, what remains of what Randolph Bourne called the "hot chaos of America" for the expatriate is the *America as a creative idea* that continues to resonate with power long after the facts and forms of the country have lost their reality.

Perhaps at the end of the day, when we are far from our native land, we can find solace in the insight of Pico Iyer, a thoughtful expatriate writer of our era, who reminds us that "home has nothing to do with hearth and everything to do with a state of mind; that one man's home may be his compatriot's exile, that home is finally not the physical place, but the role and the self we choose to occupy."[25]

Appendix A: American Citizens Living Abroad by Country

(STATISTICS AS OF 1999, AS REPORTED BY THE U.S. BUREAU OF CONSULAR AFFAIRS, U.S. DEPARTMENT OF STATE)

The census data for Americans abroad in 1999–2000 may be the last official attempt to fully count Americans overseas. After a brief testing period in 2004, the U.S. Government Accounting Office issued a report stating that any count of overseas Americans for the upcoming census of 2010 "would not be cost effective." The U.S. Census Bureau, however, will continue to count members of overseas military, federal employees, and their dependents.

American Citizens Abroad (ACA), an expatriate citizens' lobby, has argued that failure to count Americans abroad is a profound constitutional wrong. Gloria Otto of ACA summed up the matter succinctly: "How can Americans abroad be recognized as a valuable asset (economic, political, and cultural) when it is not even known how many there are? How can the U.S. government address specific concerns of these Americans when certain statistics are not available."[1] Further, an accurate count of American citizens abroad could be applied toward a more equitable reapportionment of representatives in the U.S. Congress.

Overseas Americans living in the area of consulates and embassies are encouraged to register, which simply means they fill out a form to let the embassy or consulate know they are there. This helps in

[1]Gloria Otto, "ACA's Position on the Census Issue," April 1997, http://www.aca.ch; U.S. Accountability Office, "2010 Census: Counting Americans Overseas as Part of the Decennial Census Would Not Be Cost Effective" (2004).

situations like natural disasters and political upheavals. Many do not register, however, which means that in theory the number of Americans abroad could be far higher than estimated. Current estimates of the number of Americans vary from four to seven million. But this information is mostly anecdotal. Although this list is from 1999, and somewhat dated, it still gives an indication of where Americans are.

Country: Number of Resident Americans
(This list excludes members of the military, U.S. government employees, and dependents abroad.)

ALBANIA Tirana 646
ALGERIA Algiers 793
ANGOLA Luanda 845
ARGENTINA Buenos Aires 27,600
ARMENIA Yerevan 229
AUSTRALIA Canberra 2,500
    Melbourne 38,000
    Sydney 55,500
    Perth 6,800
AUSTRIA Vienna 14,000
AZERBAIJAN Baku 600
BAHAMAS Nassau 7,050
BAHRAIN Manama 1,800
BANGLADESH Dhaka 1,320
BARBADOS Bridgetown 12,000
BELARUS Minsk 190
BELGIUM Brussels 35,328
BELIZE Belize City 2,700
BENIN Cotonou 250
BERMUDA Hamilton 4,300
BOLIVIA La Paz 3,000
BOSNIA-HERZEGOVINA Sarajevo 1,600
BOTSWANA Gaborone 800
BRAZIL Brasilia 7,200
    Rio de Janeiro 14,460
    São Paolo 16,480
    Recife 2,500
BRUNEI Bandar Seri Begawan 248
BULGARIA Sofia 400
BURKINA FASO Ouagadougou 329
BURMA Rangoon 332
BURUNDI Bujumbura 46
CAMBODIA Phnom Penh 1,200

CAMEROON Yaounde 1,161
CANADA Ottawa 24,300
    Calgary 105,000
    Halifax 40,000
    Montreal 65,000
    Quebec 3,400
    Toronto 250,000
    Vancouver 200,000
CAPE VERDE Praia 1,000
CENTRAL AFRICAN REPUBLIC Bangui 91
CHAD N'Djamena 162
CHILE Santiago 11,790
CHINA Beijing 10,000
    Guangzhou 3,200
    Hong Kong 48,220
    Shanghai 2,382
    Shenyang 555
    Chengdu 800
COLOMBIA Bogota 30,680
CONGO (Democratic Republic of) Kinshasa 440
CONGO (Republic of) Brazzaville 233
COSTA RICA San José 19,800
COTE D'IVOIRE Abidjan 2,100
CROATIA Zagreb 1,921
CUBA Havana 2,000
CYPRUS Nicosia 4,175
CZECH REPUBLIC Prague 10,000
DENMARK Copenhagen 9,380
DJIBOUTI Djibouti 50
DOMINICAN REPUBLIC Santo Domingo 82,000
ECUADOR Quito 7,950
    Guayquil 5,874
EGYPT Cairo 10,892
EL SALVADOR San Salvador 10,000
EQUATORIAL GUINEA Malabo 30
ERITREA Asmara 356
ESTONIA Tallinn 1,000
ETHIOPIA Addis Ababa 2,190
FIJI Suva 5,288
FINLAND Helsinki 4,700
FRANCE Paris 75,000
    Marseille 23,700
    Strasbourg 3,050
GABON Libreville 298

GAMBIA Banjul 546
GEORGIA Tbilisi 303
GERMANY Bonn 692
        Berlin 14,619
        Frankfurt am Main 138,815
        Hamburg 11,754
        Munich 45,000
GHANA Accra 3,780
GREECE Athens 65,000
        Thessaloniki 7,500
GRENADA St. George's 2,000
GUATEMALA Guatemala City 10,000
GUINEA Conakry 660
GUINEA-BISSAU Bissau 25
GUYANA Georgetown 1,500
HAITI Port-Au-Prince 11,000
HONDURAS Tegucigalpa 10,500
HUNGARY Budapest 15,000
ICELAND Reykjavik 1,730
INDIA New Delhi 1,397
        Mumbai 9,400
        Calcutta 672
        Madras 3,900
INDONESIA Jakarta 6,818
        Surabaya 2,240
IRELAND Dublin 46,984
ISRAEL Tel Aviv 18,000
        Jerusalem 76,195
ITALY Rome 40,000
        Milan 20,000
        Naples 72,000
        Florence 36,967
JAMAICA Kingston 7,500
JAPAN Tokyo 45,000
        Naha, Okinawa 3,415
        Osaka-Kobe 13,484
        Sapporo 2,756
        Fukuoka 5,695
JORDAN Amman 8,000
KAZAKHSTAN Almaty 3,600
KENYA Nairobi 4,237
KOREA Seoul 30,000
KUWAIT Kuwait 7,710
KYRGYZSTAN Bishkek 150

LAOS Vientiane 293
LATVIA Riga 2,084
LEBANON Beirut 10,000
LESOTHO Maseru 190
LIBERIA Monrovia 220
LITHUANIA Vilnius 1,500
LUXEMBOURG Luxembourg 1,527
MACEDONIA Skopje 800
MADAGASCAR Antananarivo 372
MALAWI Lilongwe 863
MALAYSIA Kuala Lumpur 6,639
MALI Bamako 460
MALTA Valletta 700
MARSHALL ISLANDS Majuro 580
MAURITANIA Nouakchott 100
MAURITIUS Port Louis 320
MEXICO Mexico City 441,680
      Ciudad Juárez 63,480
      Guadalajara 111,100
      Monterrey 29,900
      Tijuana 196,000
      Hermosillo 80,600
      Matamoros 60,960
      Mérida 49,000
      Nuevo Laredo 3,580
MICRONESIA Kolonia 760
MOLDOVA Chisinau 125
MONGOLIA Ulaanbaatar 450
MOROCCO Rabat 1,401
MOZAMBIQUE Maputo 641
NAMIBIA Windhoek 350
NEPAL Kathmandu 1,600
NETHERLANDS Amsterdam 23,707
NETHERLANDS ANTILLES Curacao 6,075
NEW ZEALAND Auckland 14,540
NICARAGUA Managua 5,000
NIGER Niamey 335
NIGERIA Lagos 10,000
NORWAY Oslo 15,000
OMAN Muscat 1,444
PAKISTAN Islamabad 506
    Karachi 2,100
    Lahore 1,250
    Peshawar 375

PALAU Koror 300
PANAMA Panama City 19,700
PAPUA NEW GUINEA Port Moresby 2,468
PARAGUAY Asunción 2,368
PERU Lima 14,143
PHILIPPINES Manila 105,000
POLAND Warsaw 21,300
     Krakow 18,000
PORTUGAL Lisbon 1,072
     Ponta Delgada 1,100
QATAR Doha 3,775
ROMANIA Bucharest 13,152
RUSSIA Moscow 8,000
     St. Petersburg 900
     Vladivostok 348
     Yekaterinburg 200
RWANDA Kigali 165
SAUDI ARABIA Riyadh 11,506
     Dhahran 13,600
     Jeddah 10,883
SENEGAL Dakar 791
SERBIA-MONTENEGRO Belgrade 4,514
SIERRA LEONE Freetown 130
SINGAPORE Singapore 15,000
SLOVAK REPUBLIC Bratislava 850
SLOVENIA Ljubljana 650
SOMALIA Mogadishu 12
SOUTH AFRICA Pretoria 8,100
     Cape Town 2,647
     Durban 720
SPAIN Madrid 75,596
     Barcelona 18,917
SRI LANKA Colombo 658
SUDAN Khartoum 1,479
SURINAME Paramaribo 425
SWAZILAND Mbabane 352
SWEDEN Stockholm 18,000
SWITZERLAND Bern 12,113
SYRIA Damascus 3,856
TAIWAN Taipei 38,000
TAJIKISTAN Dushanbe 117
TANZANIA Dar Es Salaam 1,186
THAILAND Bangkok 16,500
     Chiang Mai 1,600

TOGO Lome 329
TRINIDAD & TOBAGO Port-of-Spain 3,200
TUNISIA Tunis 700
TURKEY Ankara 2,010
    Istanbul 4,800
    Adana 266
TURKMENISTAN Ashgabat 107
UGANDA Kampala 1,350
UKRAINE Kiev 3,000
UNITED ARAB EMIRATES
    Abu Dhabi 7,500
    Dubai 9,000
UNITED KINGDOM London, England 200,000
    Belfast, Ireland 4,000
    Edinburgh, Scotland 20,000
URUGUAY Montevideo 3,500
UZBEKISTAN Tashkent 590
VENEZUELA Caracas 25,000
VIETNAM Hanoi 3,000
WESTERN SAMOA Apia 495
YEMEN Sanaa 15,300
ZAMBIA Lusaka 980
ZIMBABWE Harare 2,125

GRAND TOTAL 3,784,693

Appendix B: Top Ten Countries Where Most Expatriate Americans Live, 2006

1. Mexico – 1,036,300
2. Canada – 687,700
3. United Kingdom – 224,000
4. Germany – 210,880
5. Israel – 184,195
6. Italy – 168,967
7. Philippines – 105,000
8. Australia – 102,800
9. France – 101,750
10. Spain – 94,513

Source: Association of Americans Resident Overseas (AARO), 2006, http://www.aaro.org

Appendix C: Ten Most Popular Expatriate Meccas

BASED ON LIFESTYLE, EMPLOYMENT OPPORTUNITIES, POLITICAL CLIMATE, AND SOCIAL RECEPTIVITY TO AMERICANS

1. Toronto, Canada
2. Tokyo, Japan
3. Wellington, New Zealand
4. Ambergris Quay, Belize
5. San Miguel de Allende, Mexico
6. London, England
7. Tel Aviv, Israel
8. Cancún, Mexico
9. United Arab Emirates
10. Buenos Aires, Argentina

Source: Network for Living Abroad, http://www.liveabroad.com; http://escapeartist.com; American Citizens Abroad, http://www .aca.ch (accessed 2006).

Appendix D: Compendium of English Online International Newspapers

Afghanistan
Afghanistan Daily, http://www.afghandaily.com

Africa
Accra Mail, http://www.accra-mail.com

Algeria
Algeria Press Service, http://www.aps.dz

Angola
Angola Press, http://www.Angolapress-angop.ao

Arab World
Arab News, http://www.arabnews.com

Argentina
Buenos Aires Herald, http://www.buenosairesherald.com

Asia
Channel News, http://www.channelnewsasia.com

Australia
ABC News, http://www.abc.com.au

Azerbaijan
Azerbaijan News, http://www.azernews.net

Bahamas
The Nassau Guardian, http://www.thenassauguardian.com

Bahrain
Bahrain Tribune, http://www.bahraintribune.com

Brazil
Information-Brazil, http://www.infobrazil.com

Brunei
Borneo Bulletin, http://www.Brunei-online.com

Chile
Santiago News, http://www.tcgnews.com

China
English People Daily, http://www.englishpeopledaily.com

Czech Republic
Prague Post, http://www.praguepost.com

Egypt
Al Ahram, http://www.ahram.org.eg

Ethiopia
Ethiopia Commentator, http://www.ethiopiancommentator.com

France
French Press Agency, http://www.afp.com/english

Hong Kong
South China Morning Post, http://www.scmp.com

India
India Express, http://www.India-express.com

Indonesia
Jakarta Post, http://www.thejakartapost.com

Israel
Jerusalem Post, http://www.jpost.com

Italy
Rome Post, http://www.romepost.com

Japan
Japan Times, http://www.japantimes.co.jp

Kenya
Daily Nation, http://www.nationalmedia.com

Korea
Korea Times, http://www.koreatimes.co.kr

Kuwait
Kuwait Times, http://www.kuwaittimes.net

Lebanon
The Daily Star, http://www.dailystar.com

Mexico
Gringo Gazette, http://www.gringogazette.com

Mongolia
Mongolia Today, http://www.mongoliatoday.com

Nepal
Himalayan Times, http://www.himalayantimes.com

New Zealand
New Zealand Herald, http://www.nzherald.co.nz

Nicaragua
Nicaragua News, http://www.nicaraguanews.com

Panama
Panama News, http://www.panamanews.com

Singapore
Straits Times, http://www.straitstimes.com

Thailand
Bangkok Post, http://www.bangkokpost.com

Turkey
Turkish Daily News, http://www.turkishdailynews.com

United Kingdom
International Herald Tribune, http://www.iht.com

Zimbabwe
The Independent, http://www.theindependent.co.zw

Appendix E: Online Expatriate Networks

The following Web sites contain helpful information. Excluded are the many so-called Web sites for expatriates that merely sell real estate, offer relocation services, or tout doubtful entrepreneurial activities. Most online networks have come into existence since 2004 and may not have a long tenure. They should be used with some degree of caution. Although the URLs were accurate at press time, they may have changed since then.

Africa and Asia General
http://www.expatfocus.com

American Association of Singapore
http://www.aasingapore.com

Argentina
http://www.expat-argentina.blogspot.com

Canada
http://www.relocatecanada.com

Central Intelligence Agency World Fact Book
http://www.cia.gov.cia/publications/factbook

Federation of American Women's Clubs Overseas
http://www.fawco.org

France
http://www.expatica.com

General Interest
http://www.expatexchange.com (Expat Exchange—A World of Friends Abroad)

http://www.aca.ch (American Citizens Abroad, one of the oldest expat online sites)

http://www.expat.network.com

http://www.expatinterviews.com

http://www.expatfocus.com

http://www.escapeartist.com (large general interest Web site for those who wish to "escape from America." This site also maintains several e-zines.)

Germany
http://www.german-way.com

Great Britain
http://www.americanexpats.co.uk

Hong Kong
http://www.geoexpat.com

Spain
http://www.spainexpat.com

Notes

CHAPTER 1. EXPLAINING EXPATRIATE MOTIVATION

1. A. W. Finifter and B. M. Finifter, "American Emigration," *Society* 13 (July/August 1976): 30–36.

2. Stacey A. Teicher, "White Collar Jobs Moving Abroad," *Christian Science Monitor*, July 29, 2003.

3. See Edward Everett Hale, *The Man Without a Country*, 2nd ed. (New York: Ticknor & Fields, 1897). For an insight on the power American nationalism, see William Preston, *Aliens and Dissenters: Federal Suppression of Radicals, 1903–1933* (Cambridge: Harvard University Press, 1963), 480–490.

4. *Money*, July 1994; U.S. Population Abroad by Country, *Statistical Abstract of the United States, 1994* (Washington, D.C.: U.S. Department of Commerce), 849.

5. Donald Green Lees, "International Schools Grapple with Staggering Demand," *International Herald Tribune*, September 3–October 1, 2006; "Private Citizens Residing Abroad" (Bureau of Consular Affairs, United States Department of State, April 1998).

6. Stephen Castles and Mark J. Miller, *The Age of Migration: International Population Movements in the Modern World.* (London: Macmillan Press, 1998), 8–9.

7. Brent Bratsberg and Dick Terrel, "Where Do Americans Live Abroad," *International Migration Review* 30 (Fall 1996): 788 et passim.

8. Arnold Dashevsky et al., *Americans Abroad: A Comparative Study of Emigrants from the United States* (New York: Plenum Press, 1992), 151.

9. Ibid., 13.

10. Douglas R. Casey, *The New International Man* (Alexandria, Va.: Alexandria House Books, 1978), 3.

11. For an overview, see Alan Ehrenhalt, "Looking for the Latte Life," *National Times*, May 1, 1996.

12. Todd Gitlin, *The Twilight of Common Dreams: Why America Is Wracked by Culture Wars* (New York: Holt, 1995), 154–155.

13. See especially William Julius Wilson, *When Work Disappears: The World of the New Urban Poor* (New York: Knopf, 1996); and Sheldon H. Danziger and Peter Gottschalk, *Uneven Tide: Rising Inequality in America* (New York: Russell Sage Foundation, 1993).

14. Daniel Bell, *The Cultural Contradictions of Capitalism* (New York: Basic Books, 1976), 281.

15. G. S. Fields, "Americans Abroad," *Comparative Study of Emigrants from the United States* (New York: Plenum Press, 1992).

16. "The Top Takes Off," Editorial, *Washington Post*, May 7, 2006.

17. "Social Immobility, Land of the Less Free," Commentary, *Virginian-Pilot*, Sunday, October 29, 1995.

18. Will Hutton, "The American Prosperity Myth," *Nation*, September 1, 2003.

19. See Paul Krugman's review of Robert J. Samuelson's book *The Good Life and Its Discontents: The American Dream in the Age of Entitlement, 1945–1995*, in *Washington Monthly*, January 1, 1996.

20. Robert Heilbroner, "Lifting the Silent Depression," *New York Review of Books*, October 24, 1991.

21. Peter Schrag, *Paradise Lost: California's Experience, America's Future* (New York: New Press, 1998), 116–117.

22. See Krugman on the "wonderful life" in America, *Washington Monthly*, January 1, 1996.

23. Jack Beatty, "The Year of Talking Dangerously," *Atlantic Monthly*, June 1996, 20.

24. William Pfaff, "Job Security Is Disappearing around the World," *International Herald Tribune*, July 8, 1996.

25. T. R. Reid, "Confucious Says: Go East, Young Man," *National Times*, April 1, 1996.

26. For perspective see Lewis H. Lapham, *Money and Class in America: Notes on the Civil Religion* (London: Picador Books, 1988); Donald L. Bartlett and James B. Steele, *America: What Went Wrong* (Kansas City: Universal Press Syndicate, 1992); Jack Beatty, "The Year of Talking Radically," *Atlantic Monthly*, June 1996, 20; Liesl Schillinger, "Who's Afraid of the Year 2000?" *National Times*, October/November 1995.

27. Steve Rubenstein, "Inquiries Up from Anti-Bush Americans Seeking to Leave U.S.," *San Francisco Chronicle*, November 4, 2004.

28. "Social Immobility: Land of the Less Free," Editorial, *Virginian-Pilot*, Sunday, October 29, 1995.

29. Gretchen Lang, "When Roots Translate into a Second Passport," *International Herald Tribune*, September 30–October 1, 2006.

30. Jennifer Fulkerson and Diane Caspell, "Americans in Paris and Elsewhere," *American Demographics* 19 (March 1997): 48.

31. R. Warren and J. Peck, "The Elusive Exodus: Emigration from the United States," *Population Trends and Public Policy* 8 (1985): 1–17.

32. Edward Krickel, "The Study of Expatriates," *South Atlantic Bulletin* 35 (May 1970): 29.

CHAPTER 2. THE EXPATRIATE ARCHIPELAGO

1. *Americans Abroad Digest: The Newsletter for Americans Living Abroad*, http://www.overseasdigest.com.

2. Gary Belsky, "Escape from America," *Money*, July 1994.

3. Quoted in Anora Sutherland, "Are You a Global Nomad?" 1998, http://www.globalnomads.com.

4. Ada Louise Huxtable, *The Unreal America: Architecture and Illusion* (New York: New Press, 1997), 75.

5. See Richard Florida, *The Flight of the Creative Class: The New Global Competition for Talent* (New York: HarperCollins, 2005).

6. Bill Breen, "Where Are You on the Talent Map?" *Fast Company*, January 2001, 102.

7. Richard Florida, "Creative Class War," *Washington Monthly*, January/February 2004.

8. "Expatriate Assignments on the Rise," *Relocation Journal*, June 1997.

9. *Private American Citizens Residing Abroad* (U.S. Bureau of Consular Affairs, Department of State, April 1998).

10. Valerie Belz, "Continental Drift: Why Young Americans Are Flocking Abroad," *Munich Found*, January 1998.

11. Ed Henry, "Americans In Poland," *Kiplinger Personal Finance*, August 1995, 112.

12. "Making Real Dough in Eastern Europe," *Money*, July 1994.

13. Jane Roe, "Going Hungary!" *Overseas Job Express*, January 15, 1998, http://www.OverseasJobs.com.

14. Marthe Haubert, "You Can Get There from Here—Relocating to the Former Soviet Union," *Relocation Journal and Real Estate News*, June 1998.

15. Peter Ford et al., "Many Seek American Dream—Outside America," *Christian Science Monitor*, March 19, 1997.

16. Nahal Toosi, "Americans Build Comfortable Lives in Cairo," *Milwaukee Sentinel*, February 27, 2005.

17. Michael Field, "Interview with Jonathan Carroll," *Publishers Weekly*, January 27, 1972.

18. For background on the Peace Corps, see Elizabeth Cobbs Hoffman, *All You Need Is Love: The Peace Corps and the Spirit of the 1960s* (Cambridge, Mass.: Harvard University Press, 1998).

19. Brian Knowlton, "Americans Take a Worldly View," *International Herald Tribune*, June 19, 1998.

20. Barbara Crosette, "Worldwide Tourist Industry Takes Off," *International Herald Tribune*, April 13, 1998.

21. Robert D. Hershey, "Americans Learn Studies Abroad Can Be a Bargain," *New York Times*, March 1, 1998; "Studying Overseas," *Washington Post*, November 16, 2006.

22. See "Websters Look East," *International Herald Tribune*, June 24, 1998.

23. Gary Belsky, "Escape from America," *Money*, July 1994.

24. Suzanne Daley, "A Piece of America in Malongo," *International Herald Tribune*, June 26, 1998.

25. Richard Sennett, "Address to the Conference on Post-Modern Democracy," University of Virginia, April 1998.

CHAPTER 3. DISSENTERS, TAX FUGITIVES, AND UTOPIANS

1. Kevin P. Kelly, "The White Loyalists of Williamsburg," *Colonial Williamsburg Interpreter* 17 (Summer 1996): 1–15.

2. See Mary Beth Norton, *The British Americans: The Loyalist Exiles in England, 1774–1789* (London: Constable, 1974).

3. William Hesseltine and Hazel C. Wolf, *Blue and Gray on the Nile* (Chicago: University of Chicago Press, 1961).

4. Eugene C. Harter, *The Lost Colony of the Confederacy* (Texas: A&M Press, 2000), 3–11, 71–86.

5. For background see Eugene C. Harter, *The Lost Colony of the Confederacy* (Oxford: University Press of Mississippi, 1985). Harter is a descendant of the exiles who settled in Brazil.

6. Quoted in Emmett Tyrell, "La Boeheme," *American Spectator* 26, June 1993.

7. Laura Carlson, "Americans Abroad, George W. Bush: Persona Non Grata," *Counterpunch,* February 27, 2004.

8. Richard Boudreaux, "Americans Abroad Are Itching to Get Their Hands on Ballots," *Los Angeles Times,* October 20, 2004.

9. Craig McInnes, "Election Raises the Dilemma Confronting an American Expatriate," *Vancouver Sun,* September 23, 2004.

10. Michael Woods, "Campaigns Target Voters Living Abroad," *Pittsburgh Post Gazette,* September 28, 2004.

11. Kathy M. Kristof, "Tax Breaks Lure More American Workers to Foreign Shores," *Detroit News,* July 26, 1995.

12. See U.S. Federal Code, sec. 349 p. 5, Immigration and Nationality Act, 1994.

13. Robert Lenzer and Phillipe Mao, "The New Refugees: Americans Who Gave Up Citizenship to Save on Taxes," *Forbes,* November 21, 1994.

14. See *American Citizens Abroad (ACA) Newsletter,* March 2006, http://www.aca.ch.

15. Gloria Otto, "Summary of ACA's Position on the Census Issue," *ACA Newsletter,* April 1997, http://www.aca.ch.

16. GAO Report to the Subcommittee on Technology, Information Policy, Intergovernmental Relations and the Census, Committee on Government Reform, House of Representatives, "2110 Census, Counting Americans Overseas as Part of the Decennial Census Would Not Be Cost Effective" (Washington, D.C., August 2004).

17. Quoted in Rick Smith, "Finding the Uncounted, U.S. States See Gold in Overseas Voters," *International Herald Tribune,* February 16, 2002. See U.S. Government Accounting Office Report, "Overseas Enumeration Test Raises Need for Clear Policy Direction," May, 2004. See also GAO Report, "2010 Census Cost and Design Issues Need to Be Addressed Soon," January 2004.

18. *Utah v. Evans,* 534 U.S. 1038 (2001).

19. Immigration and Nationality Act Update, 1996, 8 U.S. Code 1401.

20. Nora Jacobson, Viewpoint, "Canada Rife with Not-So-Subtle Anti-Americanism," *Orlando Sentinel*, December 5, 2004, G-1.

21. Barbara Rosen, "Frightening Nights of the Expat Life," *International Herald Tribune*, April 7, 1998.

22. Alfred Borcover, "One Way Ticket to Jail," *Chicago Tribune*, May 12, 1996.

23. "American Expatriates Start Utopian Communities Overseas," August 27, 2000, http://www.CNN.com.

24. Erwin S. Strauss, *How to Start Your Own Country* (Port Townsend, Wash.: Breakout Press, 1999), 2.

25. "New Utopia News," Principality of New Utopia, http://www.carbonfusion. com/utopia.

26. Oceania—The Atlantis Project, http://www.oceania.org.

27. James H. Lee, "Castles in the Sea: A Survey of Artificial Islands and Floating Utopias," April 20, 2003, http://www.seasteading.org.

28. See "Seasteading: The Market," November 2005, http://www. seasteading.org.

29. Lee, "Castles in the Sea."

CHAPTER 4. THE EXPATRIATE COUNTRIES: CANADA, ISRAEL, AUSTRALIA, AND NEW ZEALAND

1. See Gary L. Segal, *Immigrating to Canada* (Vancouver, British Columbia: Self-Counsel Press, 1996), 48.

2. Mark Clayton et al., "Many Seek American Dream—Outside America," *Christian Science Monitor*, March 19, 1997.

3. "Israel," *Private American Citizens Residing Abroad* (U.S. Bureau of Consular Affairs, April 1998).

4. Israel Central Bureau of Statistics, 1967–1985 (Jerusalem, Israel Bureau of Statistics).

5. Arnold Dashefsky et al., *Americans Abroad: A Comparative Study of Emigrants from the United States* (New York: Plenum Press, 1992), 47.

6. Ibid., 52.

7. Ibid., 67.

8. Quoted in ibid., 78.

9. Elmer J. Winter, "Israel Hangs Out a Help Wanted Sign," *Jewish Post of New York*, September 1995.

10. Mike Clayton et al., "Many Seek American Dream—Outside America," *Christian Science Monitor*, March 19, 1997.

11. Dinah Shiloh, "Israeli Entrepreneurs Strike It Rich on Internet," *International Herald Tribune*, July 16, 1998.

12. Harry Gordon, "Americans Are Emigrating to Australia: In Search of the USA More and More," *New York Times Sunday Magazine*, May 17, 1970.

13. Interview with Matthew Wennersten, February 15, 1998.

14. "Kiwi Crisis as Migration Slumps," Overseas Jobs Issue, June 15, 1998, http://www.OverseasJobs.com.

15. Gary Belsky, "Escape from America," *Money*, July 1994.

CHAPTER 5. BLACK EXILES AND SOJOURNERS

1. Orlando Patterson, "Why Whites and Blacks Seem So Divided: The Paradox of Integration," *New Republic*, November 6, 1995.

2. Ibid.

3. Sean Wilentz, "Echoes of Marcus Garvey: Backward March," *New Republic*, November 6, 1995.

4. Carl T. Rowan, *The Coming Race War in America: A Wake-up Call* (New York: Little Brown, 1996), 22.

5. Harold T. McCarthy, *The Expatriate Perspective: American Novelists and the Idea of America* (Rutherford, N.J.: Fairleigh Dickinson University Press, 1974), 18.

6. Ursula Broschke Davis, *Paris without Regret: James Baldwin, Kenny Clarke, Chester Himes, and Donald Byrd* (Iowa City: University of Iowa Press, 1986), xiii.

7. Tyler Stovall, *Paris Noir: African Americans in the City of Light* (New York: Houghton Mifflin, 1997).

8. McCarthy, *The Expatriate Perspective*, 175–195.

9. For a good overview of Wright's career, see ibid., 175–196.

10. See Oliver W. Harrington, "The Mysterious Death of Richard Wright," in *Why I Left America and Other Essays* (Jackson: University Press of Mississippi, 1993), 20–25.

11. LeRoy S. Hodges, Jr., *Portrait of an Expatriate: William Gardner Smith, Writer* (Westport, Conn.: Greenwood Press, 1985), 53.

12. Ibid., 52–55.

13. James Baldwin, "The Negro at Home and Abroad," in *Collected Essays* (New York: New American Library, 601–605. In the 1950s and 1960s Baldwin wrote a number of important essays on black expatriates that give an important perspective on Afro-American emigrant thinking in the twentieth century.

14. James Baldwin, "A Stranger in the Village," in *Collected Essays*, 117–129.

15. James Baldwin, "A Talk to Teachers," in *Collected Essays*, 683.

16. James Baldwin, "The New Lost Generation," in *Collected Essays*, 667–668.

17. Baldwin, "A Stranger in the Village," 118.

18. Baldwin, "The Negro at Home and Abroad," 602.

19. Baldwin, "The New Lost Generation," 663.

20. James Baldwin, "Color," in *Collected Essays*, 666.

21. For perspective on contemporary Afro-American expatriate life in Paris, see, Fern Gillespie, "April in Paris: African-Americans Visit Expatriates' Haunts in the City of Light," *About Time Magazine*, June 1996.

22. Michel Marriott, "Multiracial Americans Defy Limbo," *International Herald Tribune*, July 22, 1996.

23. Ernest Dunbar, ed., *The Black Expatriates: A Study of Negroes in Exile* (New York: Dutton, 1968), 50.

24. Suzanne Daley, "American Blacks Find a Chill in South Africa," *International Herald Tribune*, April 9, 1998.

25. Bill Moody, *The Jazz Exiles: American Musicians Abroad* (Reno: University of Nevada Press, 1993), 5–9.

26. Ibid., 154.

27. Mike Zwerin, "Mal Waldron: Looking for Musical Surprises," *International Herald Tribune*, January 22, 1998.

28. "K. B.," "An American Who Happens to Be Black" (Web Site Newsgroup, University of Pennsylvania, July 15, 1996).

29. See Ernest Dunbar, ed., "Mattiwilda Dobbs" and "Diane Gray," in *The Black Expatriates: A Study of Negroes in Exile* (New York: Dutton, 1968), 214, 231.

30. Viki Radden, "Whose Side Do You Think I'm On," in *Women Travel: The Real Guides* (New York: Prentice Hall, 1990), 339.

31. Ellis Cose, "Leaving America for Good," *Essence*, February 2004, 114.

32. Randall Robinson, *Quitting America: The Departure of a Black Man from His Native Land* (New York: Dutton, 2004), 152–244.

33. Dunbar, *The Black Expatriates.*

CHAPTER 6. WOMEN EXPATRIATES

1. See Geoff Payne and Pamela Abbott, eds., *The Social Mobility of Women: Beyond Male Mobility Models* (New York: Falmer Press, 1990), 1–73; Ronald Inglehart and Pippa Norris, *Rising Tide: Gender Equality and Cultural Change around the World* (New York: Cambridge University Press, 2003). In chapter 7 the authors assert that the social mobility of women is closely linked to three forces: economic change, changes in cultural norms, and "demographic processes of generational turnover."

2. Janet McDonald, "X-Patriate," *Literary Review* 47, Fall 2003.

3. For background see Jane Hunter, *The Gospel of Gentility: American Women Missionaries in Turn-of-the-century China* (New Haven, Conn.: Yale University Press, 1989).

4. Martha Gellhorn, *Travels with Myself and Another: A Memoir* (New York: Putnam, 1978); Caroline Moorehead, *Gellhorn: A Twentieth-Century Life* (New York: Holt, 2003); "Remembering Martha Gellhorn," *Atlantic Monthly*, March 11, 1998.

5. See Winnie Smith, *American Daughter Gone to War: On the Front Lines with American Army Nurses in Vietnam* (New York: Pocket Books, 1994).

6. Daphne Topouzis, "Life with the Diops," in Miranda Davies and Natania Jansz, eds., *Women Travel* (New York: Prentice Hall, 1990), 418.

7. Adrienne Su, "An Eastern Westerner in China," *Women's Travel,* 108–110.

8. See essay on Barbara Adams in Harold Stephens, *At Home in Asia: Expatriates in Southeast Asia and Their Stories* (Miranda, Calif.: Wolfden Press, 1995), 173–186.

9. Featured in Gary Belsky, "Escape from America," *Money,* July 1994; "Lisa Frankenberg: Making News," *Harvard Business School Bulletin,* June 1998; *New York Times,* September 9, 2001.

10. Elizabeth Douet, "Careers to Go," *Relocation News and Real Estate Journal,* February 1997.

11. Joanna Parfitt, "Careers in Your Suitcase: Believe in Blue Sky," *Escape from America,* May 2002.

12. William Scheibal, "When Cultures Clash: Applying Title VII Abroad," *Business Horizons,* September–October 1995.

13. Jan Selmer and Alicia S. Leung, "Who Are the Female Business Expatriates?" *Business Research Center Papers on Cross-cultural Management* (Hong Kong Baptist University, 2002), no. 99. 17–25.

14. Sully Taylor and Nancy Napier, "Working in Japan: Lessons from Women Expatriates," *Sloan Management Review,* Spring 1996, 78.

15. R. Tung, *The New Expatriates: Managing Human Resources Abroad* (New York: Bollinger, 1988).

16. Cornelius Grove and Willa Hallowell, "Guidelines for Women Expatriates" (Brooklyn, N.Y.: Cornelius Grove & Associates, 1998), http://www.bcsolutions.com/women.

17. C. Grove and W. Hallowell, "Dispelling Two Myths about Female Expatriates," *Overseas Digest,* May 2006.

18. Jacquie Luce, "The Cultural Journey of Bonita Bates," *Relocation News and Real Estate Journal,* April 1997. Since returning to the United States, Bates has been a successful consultant and lecturer at St. John Fisher College in Rochester, New York.

19. "Expat Interview: An American Abroad Living in Germany," in Hyde Flippo, *When in Germany,* http://www.german-way.com.

20. Barbara Fitzgerald Turner, "Myths of Expatriate Life," *Human Resources,* June 1997.

21. Jacquie Luce, "Moscow in 1998: The Challenge of Change," *The Art of International Living,* In-depth interview, March 1998, http://www.artofliving.org.

22. Wallis Wilde-Menozzi, "Grafting on Italian Roots," *Literary Review* 47, Fall 2003.

23. "A California Girl in Austria," German-way interview, June 27, 1998, http://www.german-way.com.

24. Erica Johnson Debeljak, "The World's Skin," *Literary Review* 47, Fall 2003.

25. Although some may argue that American women marrying Muslim men in the Middle East have a difficult time, the author has yet to see advertisements for psychological support groups for these spouses in Middle Eastern newspapers. The Japanese papers regularly carry such announcements.

26. Interview with Corinne Tachikawa, Mito, Japan, May 25, 1999.

27. Jean Pearce, "Living History," *Japan Times,* July 17, 1996; Debbie Lee Wesselmen, "Stone Daughter," *Literary Review,* April 1, 1996. See also Wesselman's collection of stories based on her experiences in Japan, *The Earth and the Sky* (Dallas: Southern Methodist University Press, 1997).

28. Quoted in Helen Bachman, "Hidden Group: US Citizens Living Overseas in Poverty," *USA Today,* January 13, 1995.

29. Lisa Louis, *Butterflies of the Night: Mama-Sans, Geisha, Strippers, and the Japanese Men They Serve* (New York: Tengu Books, 2004).

CHAPTER 7. GO EAST, YOUNG MAN

1. Jon Elster, "Social Norms and Economic Theory," *Journal of Economic Perspectives* 3 (1989): 99–117.

2. Andrew Lam, "Generation S in East Asia: Reinventing the Self and Redefining the Frontier," *Pacific News Service,* November 2, 1995.

3. For background on modern Taiwan, see Thomas B. Gold, *State and Society in the Taiwan Miracle* (New York: Sharpe, 1997).

4. "Interview with Robert Irick," *New Expatriate,* no. 7, 1995.

5. American Institute of Taiwan, http://www.AIT.org.

6. Brian Schwarz, "Shanghai Searches for US Talent," *Asia Times,* September 14, 2006.

7. "New Survey Reveals Pollution and Traffic Top Gripes of Expatriates in China," China CSR, Corporate Social Responsibility in China, January 9, 2006, http://www.ChinaCSR.com.

8. William R. Riley, Maria Yester, and Randy Elkin, "The Expatriate Experience in China: A Survey," *Relocation Journal,* December 2000.

9. Daniel Calhoun, "China Notes," *Recreation and Travel,* September 20, 1996.

10. "A Tie Transcending Discrepancies—Americans in China," Xinhua News Agency, December 9, 2003.

11. Remarks of James R. Keith, U.S. Consul General, Hong Kong, January 2005, http://www.hongkong.usconsulate.gov.

12. Michael Dorgan, "Americans Poised to Strike It Rich," *Santa Clara (Calif.) Mercury News,* June 28, 1997; "Young Chinese Americans Are Thriving in Hong Kong," *Wang-Li Asia Resources,* 2006, http://www.wang-li.com.

13. Cameron W. Barr, "Vietnam Lures Many to a Career of Expatriate," *Christian Science Monitor,* September 18, 1997.

14. Kevin Bubel, "An Investor Burns Out in Vietnam," *International Herald Tribune,* May 30–31, 1998.

15. Bonnie Rochman, "Twentysomethings Land in Vietnam," Fortune, June 24, 1996.

16. Cathy N. Davidson, *Thirty-six Views of Mt. Fuji: On Finding Myself in Japan* (New York: Dutton, 1993), 19, 22.

17. Interviews with Duane Isham, November 2, 2004, and November 13, 1997.

18. Karen Ma, "Expatriate Writers Bridge Cultures," *Japan Times,* May 21, 1998. The best introduction to Donald Ritchie is Arturo Silva, ed., *The Donald Ritchie Reader: Fifty Years of Writing on Japan* (New York: Stonebridge Press, 1999); and Donald Ritchie, *The Inland Sea* (New York: Kodansha, 1993). See also Phyllis Birnbaum, *Modern Girls, Shining Stars, The Skies of Tokyo: Five Japanese Women* (New York: Columbia University Press, 2000); and Alan Brown, *Audrey Hepburn's Neck: A Novel* (New York: Pocket Books, 2000).

19. Carrie Ching, "Thailand: The Vet Who Didn't Come Home," *Frontline/ World,* August 10, 2004.

20. Somini Sengupta, "In a Twist, Americans Appear in the Ranks of Indian Firms," *New York Times,* October 17, 2006.

21. Pico Iyer, *Video Night in Kathmandu* (New York: Vintage Press, 1989), 358.

CHAPTER 8. GRINGO GULCH: RETIRED EXPATRIATES AND SOJOURNERS IN LATIN AMERICA

1. Conversations with Dr. Helmut Loiskandl, Tokiwa University Faculty Seminar, Mito, Japan, October 29, 1998.

2. David Larsen, "For Better or Worse, Many Retirees Say Bye Bye, American Pie," *Los Angeles Times,* June 23, 1989.

3. "Retired Americans Flood to Mexico," *The Economist,* November 24, 2005.

4. Paul Terhorst, *Cashing In on the American Dream: How to Retire at 35* (New York: Bantam Books, 1988); Ruth Halcomb, "Retire Abroad—Live Well for Less," 2005, http://www.liveabroad.com.

5. Peter A. Dickinson, *Travel and Retirement Edens Abroad* (New York: Dutton, 1989); John Howells, *Choose Spain* (San Francisco: Gateway Books, 1990).

6. Allan Salkin, "Expatriate Games," *Washington Post*, Travel Section, April 23, 2006.

7. Justin Martin, "Or, If You'd Rather Retire Abroad," *Fortune*, July 24, 1995; "The Quest for Escape and Affordable Retirement," 2006, http://www.boomersabroad.com.

8. Dianna Marder, "Finding Their Place in the Sun," *Philadelphia Inquirer*, May 11, 1998.

9. David Larsen, "Americans Retirees Say Bye Bye, American Pie," *Los Angeles Times*, June 23, 1989.

10. Marie Franklin, "International Shortage of Teachers Opens Jobs for Americans Abroad," *Boston Globe*, May 31, 1998; "International Schools Grapple with Staggering Demand," *International Herald Tribune*, September 29, 2006.

11. Dennis Cass, "A Twist on Margaritaville," *Minneapolis–St. Paul Magazine*, January 1998, 28.

12. Les Christie, "Retire in Style South of the Border," February 14, 2006, http://www.CNNMoney.com.

13. See Polly G. Vicars, *Tales of Retirement in Paradise: Life in Puerto Vallarta, Mexico* (Puerto Vallarta: America-Mexica Foundation, 1995).

14. Justin Martin, "Retire Abroad," *Fortune*, July 24, 1995.

15. John Howells, "Three Good Reasons and One Bad Reason for Choosing Mexico," http://www.discoverypress.com.

16. Ignacio Lobes, "Guadalajara—Life without the Proper Papers—Gringo Style," *Seattle Times*, September 25, 1994.

17. Alfredo Corchado, "Gringos in Mexico," *Orange County (Calif.) Register*, March 19, 1998.

18. Jeffrey S. Smith and Benjamin N. White, "Detached from Their Homeland: The Latter-Day Saints of Chihuahua, Mexico," *Journal of Cultural Geography*, Spring-Summer 2004.

19. Jeff Spurier, "The Gringas of San Miguel de Allende," *Los Angeles Times*, July 31, 1994; Christina Nelson, "Mexico Notes: San Miguel Allende," 2004, http://www.mexicoconnect.com.

20. David Larsen, "American Retirees Say Bye Bye, American Pie," *Los Angeles Times*, June 23, 1989.

21. Jeff Spurier, "The Gringas of San Miguel de Allende," *Los Angeles Times*, July 31, 1994.

22. Interview with Stan Gotlieb, July 1, 1996.

23. Lorena Melton Young Ortero, "U.S. Retired Persons in Mexico," *American Behavioral Scientist* 40 (June-July 1997): 914–919.

24. "Expat Chat, Costa Rica Message Board," May 11, 1997, http://www.expatforum.com.

25. Anne Newton,"Biesanz Woodworks," *Guide*, Summer 1998.

26. Bill Gray and Claire Gray, "Choose Belize for Retirement," *Belize First*, Summer 1998; "Retirement Report," *Belize First*, 2004, http://www.Belizefirst.com.

27. David Larsen, "American Retirees Say Bye Bye, American Pie," *Los Angeles Times*, June 23, 1989.

28. Javier Rodriguez, "Mexico's 'Safe Trip' Promise Rings Hollow to Mexican Americans," January 28, 1996, http://www.latino.com.

29. David Reyes, "He's Found His Endless Summer," *Los Angeles Times,* May 1, 1997.

30. Lan Sludder, Special Report, "Living, Retiring and Investing in Belize," *Belize First,* Summer 1998.

31. Lin Sutherland, "From Whale Vomit to Lobsters to Tourists," *Belize First,* Summer 1996.

32. Stanley Kurtz, "Demographics and the Culture War," *Policy Review,* February-March 2005.

33. Cullen Murphy, "The Oasis of Memory," *Atlantic Monthly,* May 1998, 24–26.

CHAPTER 9. THE RETURN OF THE NATIVE

1. For an analysis of Cooper's evaluation of European and American traits, see Donald A. Range, *James Fennimore Cooper* (Boston: Hall, 1988), 124–130.

2. For an overview of Cooper's personal and political views see Stephen Railton, *Fennimore Cooper: A Study of His Life and Imagination* (Princeton, N.J.: Princeton University Press, 1978); *Cooper: Home as Found* (Philadelphia: Lea and Blanchard, 1838).

3. Quoted in Harold T. McCarthy, *The Expatriate Perspective: American Novelists and the Idea of America* (Rutherford, N.J.: Fairleigh Dickinson University Press, 1974), 81–93.

4. Randolph Bourne, *Youth and Life* (Boston: Houghton Mifflin, 1913), 343–346; See also Edward Abrahams, *The Lyrical Left: Randolph Bourne, Alfred Stieglitz and the Origins of Cultural Radicalism in America* (Charlottesville: University Press of Virginia, 1986), 23–92; Randolph Bourne, "Transnational America," *Atlantic Monthly,* July 1916, 90.

5. For thoughts on a countervailing narrative I am indebted to Professor Gary Y. Okihiro, *"Towards a Pacific Civilization,"* Annual Meeting of the Japan Association for American Studies, Chiba University, Japan, June 6–7, 1998.

6. For a discussion of the dark side of cosmopolitanism, see Christopher Lasch, *The Revolt of the Elites and the Betrayal of Democracy* (New York: Norton, 1995).

7. David Popenoe, "Scholars Should Worry about the Disintegration of the American Family," *Chronicle of Higher Education,* April 14, 1993.

8. Todd Gitlin, *The Twilight of Common Dreams: Why America Is Wracked by Culture Wars* (New York: Holt, 1995), 39–84.

9. Jane Jacobs, *The Life and Death of Great American Cities* (New York: Vintage Books, 1967).

10. Federal Bureau of Investigation, *Crime in the United States,* Uniform Crime Reports in the United States (Washington, D.C.: Department of Justice, 1992), 4.

11. This information is compiled from a database of sixty-five interviews with American expatriates on "why they left" America during the period 1984–1998.

12. Lester Thurow, *Head to Head: The Coming Economic Battle between Japan, Europe and America* (New York: William Morrow, 1992), 175, 206–207.

13. *New York Times Magazine,* June 7, 1998, 75.

14. John J. Miller, "America's Assimilation Crisis," *International Herald Tribune,* May 27, 1998.

15. Georgie Anne Geyer, *Americans No More: The Death of Citizenship* (New York: Atlantic Monthly Press, 1996), 55.

16. Interview with Jon Reed, Annual Meeting of Japan Association for American Studies, Chiba University, Japan, June 6, 1998.

17. James Baldwin, "Every Goodbye Ain't Gone," *Collected Essays* (New York: Library of America, 1998), 778.

18. McCarthy. *Expatriate Perspective,* 198.

19. Arnold Dashefsky et al., *Americans Abroad: A Comparative Study of Emigrants from the United States* (New York: Plenum Press, 1992), 134.

20. A. W. Finifter and B. M. Finifter, "American Emigration," *Society* 13 (July/August, 1976): 30–36.

21. See Fussell's comments on how travel corrupts host societies in *Abroad: British Literary Travelling between the Wars* (New York: Oxford University Press, 1980).

22. Dashefsky et al., *Americans Abroad,* 134.

23. Lois Gould, "Disappearing Acts," *New York Times Sunday Magazine,* June 30, 1996.

24. James Baldwin, "The Price of the Ticket," *Collected Essays,* 835–842.

25. Pico Iyer, *Video Night in Kathmandu* (New York: Vintage, 1989), 9.

Select Bibliography

Backhurst, Paul. *Alternatives to the Peace Corps.* Oakland, CA: Food First Books, 2006.

Bell, Lilian Lida. *The Expatriates: A Novel.* New York: Harper & Brothers, 1900.

Belsky, Gary. "Escape from America." *Money,* July 1994.

Bratsberg, Brent, and Dick Terrel. "Where Do Americans Live Abroad?" *International Migration Review* 30, Fall 1996.

Castles, Stephen, and Mark Miller. *The Age of Migration: International Population Movements in the Modern World.* London: Macmillan Books, 1998.

Collins, Joseph, and Stefan De Zerega. *How to Live Your Dream of Volunteering Overseas.* New York: Penguin Books, 2002.

Danziger, Sheldon, and Peter Gottschalk. *Uneven Tide: Rising Inequality in America.* New York: Russell Sage Foundation, 1993.

Dashevsky, Arnold, et al. *Americans Abroad: A Comparative Study of Emigrants from the United States.* New York: Plenum Press, 1996.

Davidson, Cathy N. *Thirty-six Views of Mt. Fuji: On Finding Myself in Japan.* New York: Dutton, 1993.

Dickinson, Peter A. *Retirement Edens Abroad.* New York: Dutton, 1989.

Dunbar, Ernest. *The Black Expatriates: A Story of Negroes in Exile.* New York: Dutton, 1968.

Ehrman, Mark. *Getting Out: Your Guide to Leaving America.* Los Angeles: Process Media, 2006.

Finifter, A. W., and B. M. Finifter. "American Emigration." *Society* 13, July/August 1976.

Florida, Richard. *The Flight of the Creative Class: The New Global Competition for Talent.* New York: HarperCollins, 2005.

Fulkerson, Jennifer, and Diane Caspell. "Americans in Paris and Elsewhere." *American Demographics* 19, March 1997.

Geyer, Georgie Anne. *Americans No More: The Death of Citizenship.* New York: Atlantic Monthly Press, 1996.

Gitlin, Todd. *The Twilight of Common Dreams: Why America Is Wracked with Culture Wars.* New York: Holt, 1995.

Gould, Lois. "Disappearing Acts." *New York Times Sunday Magazine,* June 30, 1996.

Harter, Eugene. *The Lost Colony of the Confederacy.* College Station: Texas A&M Press, 2000.

Heseltine, William. *The Blue and the Gray on the Nile.* Chicago: University of Chicago Press, 1961.

Inglehart, Philip, and Pippa Norris. *Rising Tide: Gender Equality and Cultural Change around the World.* New York: Cambridge University Press, 2003.

Iyer, Pico. *Video Night in Kathmandu.* New York: Vintage, 1989.

Kohls, Robert. *Survival Kit for Overseas Living.* Yarmouth, Maine: Intercultural Press, 2001.

Lasch, Christopher. *The Revolt of the Elites and the Betrayal of Democracy.* New York: Norton, 1995.

Lenzer, Robert, and Philip Mao. "The New Refugees: Americans Who Gave Up Their Citizenship to Save on Taxes." *Forbes,* November 21, 1994.

Louis, Lisa. *Butterflies of the Night: Mama-Sans, Geisha, Strippers, and the Japanese Men They Serve.* New York: Tengu Books, 2004.

Malewski, Margaret. *GenXpat: A Professional's Guide to Making a Successful Life Abroad.* Yarmouth, Maine: Intercultural Press, 2005.

McCarthy, Harold. *The Expatriate Perspective: American Novelists and the Idea of America.* Rutherford, NJ: Fairleigh Dickinson Press, 1974.

Moody, Bill. *Jazz Exiles: American Musicians Abroad.* Reno: University of Nevada Press, 1993.

Moorehead, Caroline. *Gellhorn: A Twentieth-Century Life.* New York: Holt, 2003.

Ritchie, Donald. *The Inland Sea.* New York: Kodansha, 1993.

Robinson, Randall. *Quitting America: The Departure of a Black American from His Native Land.* New York: Dutton, 2004.

Selmer, Jan, and Alicia S. Leung. "Who Are the Female Business Expatriates?" *Business Research Center Papers on Cross-cultural Management.* Hong Kong Baptist University, 2002.

Stovall, Tyler. *Paris Noir: African Americans in the City of Light.* New York: Houghton Mifflin, 1997.

Taylor, Sully, and Nancy Napier. "Working in Japan: Lessons from Women Expatriates." *Sloan Management Review,* Spring 1996.

Terhorst, Paul. *Cashing In on the American Dream: How to Retire at 35.* New York: Bantam Books, 1985.

Tung, R. *The New Expatriates: Managing Human Resources Abroad.* New York: Bollinger, 1998.

Vicars, Polly G. *Tales of Retirement in Paradise: Life in Puerto Vallarta, Mexico.* Puerto Vallarta: America-Mexico Foundation, 1995.

Warren, R., and J. Peck. "The Elusive Exodus: Emigration from the United States." *Population Trends and Public Policy* 8, 1985.

Wilentz, Sean. "Echoes of Marcus Garvey: Backward March." *New Republic,* November 6, 1995.

Wiser, William. *The Great Good Place: American Expatriate Women in Paris.* New York: Norton, 1991.

Index

Adams, Barbara, on Americans in Nepal, 88–90
AEON Corporation, English schools in Japan, 111
African Americans abroad, 34; Ghana, 69; Japan, 75–78; New Zealand, 80; Paris, 65–77, passport problems, 68; South Africa, 75
Afroyim v. Rusk, 42
Americans Abroad Inc., 26, 41, 99, 145
American Colonization Society, 63
American Revolution and Tory exiles, 33–34
Americans Abroad Digest, 19
Americans in Egypt, 34
Anger, Brad, 109
Angola, 31; Chevron oil, 31
Argentina, 131
Aronson, Patrick, 108
Asia, American expatriates in, 101–114
Association of Americans and Canadians in Israel, 55
August, Robert, on Americans in Costa Rica, 128
Australia, Americans in, 56–58
Avigdor, Lisa, 55

Baker, Josephine, 65
Baldwin, James: *Another Country*, 70–73, 79, 146, 148; *Giovanni's Room*, 71
Bates, Bonita, on Americans in Japan, 94
Beach, Sylvia, 85
Belize, 130
Belz, Valerie, 21
Biesanz, Barry, on Americans in Costa Rica, 129
Birnbaum, Phyllis, American writer in Japan, 113
Bourne, Randolph, 138–139, 149
Broman, Forest A., International Educators Institute, 120
Brown, Alan, 114
Brown, Whitney, CEO, Affordable Luxuries, Prague, 24
Buchwald, Art, *International Herald Tribune*, 36
Buck, Pearl S., 85
Budapest, New York Bagel Store, 22
Butterfly Life, American hostesses in Japan, 99

Canada: African Americans in, 52; Americans in, 43–44, 51–53
Carmichael, Stokley, 75

About the Author

JOHN R. WENNERSTEN has lived a total of eleven years abroad in Europe, Hong Kong, Singapore, and Japan. He was recently a Senior Fellow at the National Museum of American History at the Smithsonian Institution. Currently he is a writer-lecturer for the Maryland Humanities Commission. He is Professor Emeritus of American Studies at the University of Maryland, Eastern Shore, and held a tenured professorship at Tokiwa University in Japan.